Under the Tree of Talking:
leadership for change in Africa

Edited and with an introduction by Onyekachi Wambu
Foreword by John Githongo

Counterpoint

Born in Nigeria in 1960, Onyekachi Wambu arrived in the UK after the Biafran war. Educated in London and at the universities of Essex and Cambridge, he has worked as a journalist since 1983, and edited the leading black newspaper, *The Voice*, at the end of the 1980s. He is also a television producer and director, and has made documentaries for the BBC, Channel 4 and PBS. His publications include *Empire Windrush: Fifty years of writing about black Britain* (ed.). He is currently the Information Officer for the African Foundation for Development, a charity established to expand and enhance the contributions Africans in the diaspora make to Africa's development.

First published in Great Britain in 2007
by Counterpoint: the cultural relations think-tank of the British Council
10 Spring Gardens
London SW1A 2BN

counterpoint@britishcouncil.org
www.counterpoint-online.org
www.britishcouncil.org

Designed by Design Department
Cover design HGV

Printed and bound in Great Britain by Galloways

A CIP catalogue record for this book is available from the British Library.

ISBN 0-86355-586-1

ISBN 978-0-86355-586-2

'A must-read for all those, global Africans and others, who care about the continent's future. Wambu has assembled a great heavyweight cast to shed light – from deep past to present, from north to south, from top downwards and bottom upwards – on a matter that probably more than any other has affected Africa's fortunes these last fifty years: leadership.'

DIRAN ADEBAYO, NOVELIST AND AUTHOR OF
MY ONCE UPON A TIME AND *SOME KIND OF BLACK*

'Can a book about leadership produce better leaders in a continent whose presidents, prime ministers, generals, chiefs are considered to have singularly failed their people in the fifty years since Ghana first raised her Black Star of Independence? An ambitious goal which has so far eluded the prior efforts of some of our most brilliant minds. But this is the brave aim of Onyekachi Wambu's work: a collection of remarkable essays by some of Africa's most notable writers and academics, including Chinua Achebe and Professor Ali Mazrui – fearless scholars who are brutally honest in their analysis of where things have gone wrong, but still refuse to indulge in Afro-pessimism. This book should be a must-read for those who would seek to lead their people, and those who allow themselves to be led.'

HENRY BONSU, AWARD-WINNING BROADCASTER AND JOURNALIST

Contents

For my mother, Mgbafo,
and grandmother, Erekamma,
the best leaders I know.

Monica, a golden radiance
Osun, sweet water

Acknowledgements

Meg Dosunmu, Josephine Osikena, madeleine kennedy-macfoy, for their support. I am grateful to the British Council – particularly Nick Wadham-Smith, Sue Wason and the team at Counterpoint for unstinting dedication; Eva Kiiru, David Higgs and the rest of the East and West Africa team for organising the powerful InterAction Programme on Cultures, Leadership and Development, held at Naivasha, Kenya in February 2007, and for understanding the need for a book.

Foreword

John Githongo

Chinua Achebe's famous *Things fall apart* summed up most of the challenges that Africa faced in the last half of the 20th century and which continue to dog post-colonial Africa today. It is therefore refreshing to see him address the question of leadership anew, by revisiting his essay *The Trouble with Nigeria* alongside other established as well as emergent voices. This is a timely, wide-ranging book whose resonance will further tease out the central contemporary debate about the location of the modern African and the African nation state in a globalised world.

The volume is also timely as it comes when the world is reflecting on the successes and failures of independence as Ghana, the first country to gain independence, celebrates its 50th anniversary, and when many, including Africans themselves, have been wondering whether there is any hope for Africa. It is important to remember that the whole colonial project came to an end only ten years ago with the abolition of apartheid and the emergence of today's South Africa.

Africa is also just beginning to emerge as an entity itself, with initiatives such as the African Union, comprised of entirely 'independent' states for the first time. Today, the non-interference in the internal affairs of neighbours that was one of the tenets of the Organization of African Unity is history, as African troops positively 'intervene' in Darfur and Somalia. One hopes that the other odious inheritance – the inviolability of our colonial borders – will be robustly challenged this century as we Africans define our own history.

This question of location in relation to leadership ties in aptly with the concerns of the spatial–time conundrum as it addresses tradition, modernity, transnationalism, time itself, culture, language, identity, values, geography, history and the wider political and socio-economic issues which have an impact on Africa, Africans and the world in general. Most significantly, it addresses their underlying issues of suffering and freedom from suffering for the majority of Africans.

Two common strands emerge through these essays: the question of self-determination through action driven by individual and collective effort, and the question of moral accountability, whether on the continent or in the diaspora. The convergence of ideas from the disparate locations, disciplines and across gender, generation and their concurrence in transitional Africa make this discussion on the location of leadership even more critical.

The complexities of religion, ideology, heterogeneity, identity, social and cultural practice, expectation, desire, will and migration invite us to evaluate anew what the values of social justice, democracy and equality mean or can mean.

My own work has been in ethics and governance and therefore, like those whose voices are reflected in this book, my life has been dedicated to engaging with and devising systems for what can be termed universal ethical values of good governance, good social practice and a good society. This has led me to believe that what is considered to be good private practice is closely tied to the public domain and I am pleased to see that people are increasingly calling their leaders (or those purporting to make decisions on their behalf) to account in unprecedented ways. The uphill struggle to bring to book culprits of sophisticated corruption scams involving local, national and international players has graphically demonstrated the challenges as well as the possibilities of good leadership. The greater task is turning these challenges into reality for the majority of Africans who continue to receive a raw deal unnecessarily because of, greed, selfishness and an absence of vision.

Many of the essays make much of the past and present through relying on the lessons learnt from history and from elsewhere. They remind you that all societies have to continually grapple with issues of leadership and governance by envisioning themselves as better places. The question of the means and ends is one which has always provided challenges. Their boldness is in their singular quest for a transformational visionary practice and this is particularly satisfying. The essays therefore make a convincing case for the merits of sustained dialogue, of exploration, of learning lessons, but most significantly, of implementation.

John Githongo
St Antony's College, Oxford

Introduction

Onyekachi Wambu

What is a book about leadership for and what might it do in response to the very serious issues facing Africa? One ambitious answer is that it is intended simply to produce better leaders, so they can be better managers of their society in order to:

- bring peace and security
- create fair and transparent rules and systems that are considered legitimate, endorsed by their people, and which perpetuate themselves without conflict
- improve the health and quality of life of those they are leading
- make people valued, while nurturing and drawing out their creative potential
- facilitate partnerships to solve existing problems and face new challenges looming on the horizon
- and having achieved all the above, perhaps simply to be respected, appreciated and loved by their people.

In other words, at the most basic level, a book about leadership is about people – how they are given security, governed, nurtured, empowered and treated with respect and dignity. In large parts of Africa, even as we celebrate 50 years of Ghana's independence, it could be argued that our leadership, at all levels, has manifestly failed in almost all the areas identified above. In many African states, people are now worse off than at independence.

We can write huge academic volumes about the complex reasons for this situation, which we know has been shaped by culture, religion, ethnicity and neo-colonialism. Yet when all is said and done, most of those who lead us simply do not trust us, nor respect what we think. Nor do they derive their legitimacy or authority from us. (Why else would they rig elections?)

Together, leader and led, it seems that we are unable to accept a set of rules that we would all follow and which are monitored and enforced impartially and fairly. (Why else all the racial, ethnic and religious politics?)

In too many instances we seem unable to accept a workable system of conflict resolution, overseen by fair and impartial arbiters whose decision is final and respected. (Why else all the violence and wars?)

We refuse truly to invest in the potential of our future, the potential of our own currencies, or our own economies. (Why else are most of our savings and capital abroad?)

We openly steal from each other and from our common patrimony. (Why else all the corruption?)

One could go on and on, citing one problematic area after another. Sometimes even the sense that as Africans we have the will, capacity or resources to solve our own problems is missing. Many of our young people are escaping from the lack of jobs, the hopelessness of our societies, by walking across the scorching desert, then getting on rickety boats to get to a future that offers hope, dignity and self-respect. Listen to this anguished voice, posted on a BBC blog:

> 'We are right here in Europe and America after our poor countries have spent so much on educating us. Conditions are such that any young educated mind will want to leave – at least I can say that for Ghana. About 90 per cent of my mates I graduated with are out here trying to make life a bit better for themselves and the family who managed to see them through their education. One day if things change we will go back but until then we are staying put.'
>
> AHMED, LONDON

So a book specifically about African leadership is also about providing a space where some of these issues can be discussed, where experience and insights can be shared, and where, hopefully, as Africans, we can understand and mobilise our own resources, and find answers to the problems and challenges that are facing us.

Beyond this, the contributors I brought 'under the tree' to discuss and exchange ideas, have their own interests and aspirations as Africans. What they think about their continent, their diverse and complex relationship to it, and the issues they believe are critical for moving it forward have shaped the narrative. Many of the contributors have lived through extraordinary times – genocide, civil wars, exile – and here they share their experiences and reflect on the important and wider leadership lessons drawn from their various engagements and interventions. Their insights are frequently controversial, but they are courageous people of action, observers/participants, who have stared at the realities of Africa, and responded with the four 'Ss': *suggestions, strategies, solutions* and *service*.

So many people now speak on behalf of Africa and Africans that it is important to hear what Africans themselves have to say about their own issues. By locating many of the essays within this personal perspective, I hope also to locate the personal within a specific culture that acts as the backdrop for action and change. The twists and turns, people's dreams and solutions, unfold against the background of real history and real conditions.

The discussions that developed 'under the tree' reflect the broad diversity of Africa, but also, paradoxically, the incredible, underlying similarity. The title of this book is a quotation from a speech delivered at the height of an epic struggle in 1990 to peacefully overthrow Mathieu Kérékou, the military dictator of Benin Republic, by means of a Sovereign National Conference. As the battle heated up, Kérékou's military supporters threatened violence. Martin Dohou Azonhiho, Benin's interior minister and one of Kérékou's staunchest supporters, later laid out his objections to the democrats, wanting peaceful change:

> 'We are in Africa, under the Tree of Talking…And when you are under that tree, there is a chief. You are invited to come and eat. You come in, you are a guest, and you take the pot! What does that mean? We told them, "No!" I was among those who said, "No." If the Conference is Sovereign, you would kick out of the door both the revolutionaries and the chiefs. And if you do this, you will lead the country to civil war.'

As an Igbo from neighbouring Nigeria, I was puzzled when I first read Azonhiho's warnings to the conference. Wangui wa Goro captures this feeling in a later chapter – perhaps I was suffering a 'translation moment'. Benin's interior minister meant a lot of things when he accused the conference of ignoring the required 'etiquette' that governed proper behaviour 'under the tree of talking'. Implied in his understanding of that 'etiquette' is the sense of the 'ownership' of the very space and political processes taking place there by the 'chiefs' and 'revolutionaries'. There is also the idea of the mass of the people coming as humble petitioners, grateful for whatever scraps they were being thrown by the 'chiefs'.

Most people in Africa will instantly recognise the space 'under the tree' to which Azonhiho alludes; where, in a cool shaded area, away from the punishing rays of the sun, discussions take place and consensus is hammered out. But many, like me, will not easily recognise that concept of 'ownership' by the chiefs that Azonhiho so eloquently describes and demands. The space is rarely as authoritarian as he implies unless something has gone dramatically wrong. Perhaps it could just be that something had already gone badly wrong in Benin, and Azonhiho, as the accomplice of a long-running military dictator, had simply distorted the checks and balances of his own traditions, for the sake of power. So what happens 'under the tree' in the village square in the part of Benin where he comes from might in fact not be too dissimilar to what happens to the assembly where I come from, but which is normally more democratic; involving as it does all village members of marriageable age in the discussions, and where the chief is merely the first among equals.

It could also be that Azonhiho speaks truthfully from within his own tradition, which is much more hierarchical. In other words, the same tree, but with different things happening underneath it. Whatever the fruits of the tree, sweet or bitter, the important thing to note here is the similarity of the need for the 'talking', the starting point of human exchange and community. 'The tree' merely represents a cool space of discussion and negotiation about all sorts of things – power relations, land disputes, conflict resolution, gender relations, exchange of goods, identity, etc.

Over the years too much attention has been paid to the architecture of the space, its grandeur, trappings, and how it has been furnished with different and sometimes confusing terminology. Not enough attention has been paid to its core function – how effectively it facilitates dialogue. Rarely are people as successful as the Dogon of Mali, who, by changing the physical architecture of the 'talking space', affected a change in the tone of the dialogue. In Dogon 'talking spaces' people enter a waist-high shaded area, by bowing. To remain inside for the duration of the meeting they have to be seated because the roof is so low. It encourages calm and subdued discussion of issues, as the angry, outlandish grandstanders only knock their heads on the ceiling.

So while we all start from the same spot, Azonhiho's and the Dogon story remind us that there are differences of history and culture, from which we can all learn, and which need to be listened to because Africa is complicated. Those differences make people behave differently. It seems trite and obvious, when put like that, but important nevertheless to state so explicitly – given how often people providing 'solutions' for Africa constantly reduce the continent to one reality and expect everybody to conform to that one reality. The Benin Sovereign National Conference did eventually get rid of Kérékou, the dictator, and it worked for reasons specific to Benin. It was difficult to reproduce the model elsewhere, where those conditions were not present.

The examples of leadership and strategies discussed in *Under the Tree of Talking* are obviously not exhaustive nor the end of the story – the contradictions in Africa, where ethnicity, gender and class are frequently, but not always, linked, are too deep for that. The struggles for transformation, and for better societies continue at all times against this background, which explains why ruling elites whose action and decisions have reduced their country to penury are frequently given power again. Such societies are sometimes faced with limited options as they seek ways to tame their elites, which they know frequently perform more for their own selfish ends and on behalf of outside powers than for their own domestic population. But the contributors in our narratives realise that change is frequently a slow process, rather than a snappy slogan.

Finally, *Under the Tree of Talking* is about the choices people make and how those choices either improve a situation or retard it. So it is about how people take control of their situation, inspire others and move mountains by becoming 'leaders'.

The process of leadership

Through this kind of exploration, I hope the book implicitly throws light on more universal issues that continue to dog the area of leadership scholarship. Are leaders born or made? Do they derive their authority from status and positioning or do they create their authority through vision, charisma, trust?

In various management studies, where the most intense research on leadership has been undertaken, leadership is seen simply as achieving collective goals by winning hearts and minds, and is mainly linked to issues of management, i.e. good leadership equals good management (for example, achieving a rise in profits, share price or whatever other targets are aimed for). In the realm of political science it is sometimes connected to the full panoply of governance issues (democracy, separation of powers, rule of law, etc). At other times it is about vision, or legitimacy, control and authority.

Leadership is about all these things, and perhaps it might be better thought of as a process, the critical elements of which flow in the following way:

- collective vision or sense of purpose which inspires
- structures for delivering/implementing on the vision or constraining the visionaries
- management of the scarce resources for delivering the vision
- monitoring, evaluation and measurement of the legacy of the vision.

This process is a part of everything, and can be found in places small and big, virtual and real, in political, cultural, social and economic spaces. At each stage of the process, those involved in turning the collective vision into concrete achievements need to demonstrate the qualities of creativity and innovation, adaptability, determination and effective co-operation, against the constraints of the real world.

Understanding leadership as a process has some benefits in terms of identifying the appropriate mechanisms for interventions. Corruption, for instance, is a leadership issue. To eradicate it, the processes we obviously need to put in place are the rule of law, honest leaders who can lead by example, and strong institutions and systems to constrain those leaders. Yet these remedies have been attempted again and again in Africa, and found to be woefully inadequate. This assumes that corruption is due simply to the absence of the rule of law, weak systems and dishonesty of leaders, rather than the fact that it might actually be a symptom in the first place of the overall lack of legitimacy of the state. Might it not be better to talk about the *kind* of processes and leadership one needs in navigating through the choppy waters of a corrupt system as one seeks to build a new state that is considered legitimate?

So this book is ultimately about examples of leadership and the processes engaged, sometimes under the most challenging circumstances, and also about instances of change that might inspire others in Africa to undertake transformation in their own societies.

From any given perspective

Beyond this, *Under the Tree of Talking* is divided into sections exploring African leadership 'from' a number of perspectives:

1   From the beginning
2   From the top down
3   From the bottom up
4   From the present to the future
5   From the outside looking in
6   From the inside looking out

1 From the beginning

The historian Chinweizu starts at the beginning with the Egyptians, Africa's, and arguably the world's, first-known political leaders. He examines the state they established, the purposes for which that state existed and why it proved to be so durable so that, despite its many contradictions and being run by different dynasties, it endured for over 4,000 years, becoming the longest lasting state in history. The Egyptian state defined its notion of not only the good life but also the ethical state, and both were intimately related. Its religious and educational system reinforced its ideal values of honesty, social justice, and peace. The Pharaoh as leader of the society became the spiritual and physical embodiment of these values and was supposed to uphold the idealism of the state. Thousands of years later, most of the post-colonial

African states are yet to entrench these basic values in their state structures. Chinweizu argues that societies that do not properly define their values, do not get sufficient buy-in from their people, do not explicitly train their bureaucratic elites to pursue those values, cannot in turn expect those elites to reproduce the values in action or expect those values and idealism to pervade all aspects of those societies.

2 From the top down

Independent Africa disappeared under colonialism. The contributions in the second section explore how African political leaders have managed the post-colonial societies that have emerged since the recovery of independence. In the first of two essays in this collection, the distinguished political scientist Ali Mazrui offers a typology of African leaders who have governed these states, giving an overview of the different styles and ideas that emerged as they sought to deliver on the promises of liberation, democracy and development.

This is followed by a focus on two of these states, Nigeria and South Africa, which, given their size and economic importance, are critical and pivotal states in Africa. If these two states are not working, much of west or southern Africa descends into chaos. Each has suffered its fair share of mismanagement and poor leadership over the last 50 years. Africa's leading novelist, Chinua Achebe, discusses Nigeria, the continent's most populous state, which, since independence 47 years ago, has been mired in corruption and bad governance. In 1983, Achebe wrote *The Trouble with Nigeria*, a searing indictment of his country's leadership. Here he revisits the essay to see how much has changed during the last 24 years, and whether there is, at last, cause for optimism.

William Gumede then considers South Africa, perhaps the most successful, large African state of the last decade. He seeks to understand the role Nelson Mandela and Thabo Mbeki, the country's first two post-apartheid leaders, have played in shaping this extraordinary achievement. They leave a mixed legacy: racial reconciliation and economic growth alongside the continuing poverty and marginalisation of the vast majority of black South Africans who endured the racism, land deprivation and affirmative action of apartheid policies. The next generation of South African leaders have this challenging legacy to ponder as they seek the style of leadership that will suit South Africa's next stage of development.

3 From the bottom up

The third section moves away from political leadership and the state, and explores interactions among African people. It also considers the capacity of ordinary people at all levels to lead, inspire, and evolve solutions to the many challenges that confront them.

In the first essay in this section, Kimani Njogu, who participated in InterAction, a British Council-inspired leadership programme, reflects on the issues that were drawn out of a conference on cultures, leadership and development in Africa, held in Naivasha, Kenya, in February 2006.

Then Ndidi Nwuneli considers why time is a leadership issue. She believes poor time-keeping is a critical factor behind Africa's inability to compete internationally. Martha Chinouya examines the response of grassroots Christian women in a rural community in Zimbabwe to the HIV/AIDs epidemic. New forms of support networks and leadership have emerged among such women, rooted in the traditional concept of *ubuntu*.

Meanwhile, I reflect on leadership in a small African village, the kind of place where the majority of Africans still live, just. Against the background of rapid urbanisation, I explore the relationship between those who govern the village and those who are governed, to test to what degree the umbilical cord that links them has become frayed, and the consequences for Africa if the relationship is in tatters.

After the genocide in Rwanda, when nearly a million Tutsis and moderate Hutus were killed by their neighbours and compatriots, Jean-Bosco Butera returned to Rwanda to help in the task of reconstruction. Most of the institutions were destroyed. Butera's site of engagement was the country's only university, which had employed lecturers who provided the intellectual justification for the genocide. At 37, he became the Vice Rector for Academic Affairs at the university. As he and colleagues began rebuilding the university, they had to design a new purpose for the university and decide how it would assist the broader development agenda for a shattered country. A major preoccupation was also how the knowledge produced in the university could be used to encourage cohesion and a culture of peace.

Eva Dadrian considers the leadership role of the media in North Africa and why it has proved so difficult for the fourth estate to fulfil its conventional constitutional function. The section is concluded by an essay on how we talk to and understand each other on a continent that contains such a huge number of languages and such a diverse people. A message passed around a room of half a dozen people becomes distorted between the first and the last person. If all the people are speaking a different language and all have different cultural backgrounds, the message is liable to be even more confused. Kenyan academic Wangui wa Goro appeals for a network of accurate and transparent translators or 'mediators', who can facilitate badly needed intercultural dialogue on our incredibly diverse continent.

4 From the present to the future

This section focuses on the leaders of tomorrow and their specific challenges.

Faced in South Africa with a tertiary education system which most people cannot afford, and which prepares them for a non-existent job market, Taddy Blecher decided he would create a unique institution, a free university that would train the next generation of African entrepreneurs to provide jobs for themselves and wealth for their communities.

In villages, urban areas and institutions up and down the continent a huge challenge is how to involve women more centrally in leadership positions at all levels of society. Scenario planning is about planning for the future you want to see and avoiding what you don't want. It engages three pictures of the future, a best case, medium case and worst case, looking at what needs to be in place for each scenario to emerge. It allows policy-makers to understand precisely what needs to be done to get the most desirable future. Susan and Juliet Kiguli, lecturers at Uganda's Makerere University, provide scenario plans for 2017: their target is to involve more women in the running of their university, a regional trendsetter.

Parselelo Kantai, a child of Kenya's post-independence generation, ponders the true inheritance of his generation. Disillusionment and tragedy has too often been the lot of his generation, cocooned inside a rigid national identity. He identifies the urgent need for the coming generations to acknowledge a more open and diverse country, and to create spaces where this dialogue can take place.

Marianna Ofuso closes this section, describing her move to Ghana 50 years after Nkrumah won independence. Looking back at the generation who struggled with the post-colonial state, she wonders whether the skills, energy and expertise of young people will finally be allowed to flourish and contribute to a now stable and renascent Ghana.

5 From the outside looking in

The African diaspora numbers over 100 million if we include the diaspora in the Americas and the Caribbean that resulted from the enslavement and trafficking of Africans in the last 400 years. The most recent, the post-Second World War diaspora, that has resulted from globalisation, conflicts, and economic collapse in Africa, still numbers over 20 million. This new diaspora is dispersed both within Africa and all over the world, speaks a range of languages, and includes highly skilled people. It has become a major resource for their home countries. The remittances the diaspora send home are now frequently larger than either overseas development aid or foreign direct investment. Better communications have also increasingly given them the option of playing a more decisive role at home.

Chukwu-Emeka Chikezie reflects on the transnational African communities spread over the world. New types of leadership that truly understand the modern networked community that lives beyond the nation state are going to be needed. If people can vote in Ghanaian elections but work and pay their taxes in London, what kind of power can the authorities in Ghana have over them? Chikezie suggests ideas on how they can be effectively mobilised for national development at home.

Paul Tiyambe Zeleza, a Malawian historian, provides an intimate, insider's account of the creation of this diaspora. So many qualified people outside the continent produce huge 'brain drain' implications for Africa. But the costs and benefits do not just flow one way. Zeleza considers the opportunities that have arisen – a new breed of well-resourced intellectuals, reconnecting with the old diaspora in the Americas, and producing knowledge and skills that can be shared with Africa.

In his second essay, Ali Mazrui considers the issues and challenges that will confront global pan-African leadership in the new millennium.

6 From the inside looking out

Over the last ten years, China, the coming power in the world, has been investing heavily in Africa, both financially and diplomatically. In written Chinese the characters for 'threat' and 'opportunity' share some of the same elements. In this final section I consider the kind of African leadership that might help the continent to maximise the synergies and opportunities of China, while minimising the ability of China to exploit the weak and vulnerable economies of the continent.

A number of important issues have come up again and again throughout these reflections: the glaring shortcomings of the inherited colonial states and how we might reimagine and reconstruct them; pan-Africanism as one response; how we manage the immense diversity of our nations; the importance of involving women and young people in leadership and how we generate African solutions to African problems are some that immediately jump out.

Discussions about these issues and others will go on long after this book, as will discussions on other issues such as science and technology that are not directly addressed here. I want to thank all those contributors who agreed to share the open and democratic talking space under the big African tree, where none was excluded and all took their turn to speak and share their different visions, suggestions, strategies, solutions and examples of service. Under the tree is a place where we do not have to tip-toe slowly and quietly around eggshells, as though too strong a step might crack the shells underfoot and awake the 'chiefs' and 'revolutionaries' who believe they own the property we are quietly negotiating our way around. It is a free space where we say what is on our minds. The order of speaking is not critical, the important thing is how, in arguing back and forth, the discourse develops, and we begin to negotiate a consensus that will allow us to move forward, while embedding common principles of democracy and human rights on our continent.

I also wish to thank the British Council for showing leadership in facilitating the process by providing the shade. They took a seat under the tree, listening in on the proceedings, and though they might not be happy with everything they heard, should nevertheless be inspired by their former Director-General Sir David Green, who has written: 'Listening and demonstrating our commitment to the free and creative interplay of ideas is an indispensable pre-condition for building trust . . . To build trust we must engage in effective, open dialogue . . . Increased mutual understanding based on trust, whether we agree or disagree, is a precious outcome.'

Under the Tree of Talking aims to provide a generation of new leaders with the opportunity and space to explore the resources, ideas, concepts, and institutions that different African societies, cultures and individuals bring to the table in the area of leadership. And there are a lot of resources, ideas and concepts to draw upon if we begin to re-imagine Africa and see within it the sort of chronological and geographic unity that the African Union is seeking to harness as a strength rather than a weakness.

Onyekachi Wambu
London 2007

African leadership: from the beginning

If thou art a leader and command multitudes, strive after every excellence, until there be no fault in thy nature. Truth is good and its worth is lasting, it has not been altered since the day of its creator, whereas he that transgresseth its ordinances is punished. It lieth as a path in front of him that knoweth nothing. Wrong-doing hath never yet brought its venture to port. Evil indeed winneth wealth, but the strength of truth is that it endureth, and is the property of God.

Instructions of Ptahhotep (c. 2370 BCE)

Divine kingship and African governance: the example of Pharaonic Egypt

Chinweizu

Chinweizu is an institutionally unaffiliated Afrocentric scholar. He is a historian and cultural critic, whose book The West and the Rest of Us (1975) is a classic text of anti-imperialist and anti-colonialist scholarship. He has studied and written about African history to determine, as Chinua Achebe famously stated, 'when the rain began to beat us'. He believes that one of the reasons for the dire condition of Africa is the inability of the current leadership and elite to update or build upon the enduring values and the raison d'etre for state formation from the pre-colonial past, in order to better the conditions of their people. He sees these elites as rather more focused on ruling their post-colonial states (or 'bantustans' as he scornfully dubs them) on their own behalf and on behalf of foreign powers.

As we begin to build up a corpus of African bureaucratic and leadership literature that places African realities at the centre of the discourse, Chinweizu has identified many models from that independent, pre-colonial past, which offer interesting ideas and systems of enquiry. His research has taken him back to the earliest known African state – that of Ancient Egypt/Kmt, which produced not only some of the world's first recorded political leaders, but also, at over 4,000 years, probably the longest-lasting state in the world. Given the material conditions at the time to support a largely agricultural society, Chinweizu considers the ideology that inspired the Egyptian state, the role of the Pharaoh within that vision of the state, and the mechanisms for producing an ethically guided leadership that would in turn manage the state in a principled and successful manner in the interests of its

16

people, thus guaranteeing its legitimacy, material survival and succession.

Much of this ideology (rule of law, due process, meritocracy, tax collection, civil service and the notion of the public realm) even now underpins the constitution of many modern states, over 2,000 years after the ancient Egyptian state was overrun and defeated.

Introduction

Before Arab and European invaders came to Africa and violently installed their religions, values and institutions, many African societies were ruled by divine kingship or its derivatives. The comprador-colonial bantustans (erroneously called 'post-colonial states' by Africanist scholarship) that today blight the African landscape were each instituted by European invaders to plunder its territory and its population for the profit of imperialists. At 'independence' they were lured into the dungeons of the UN imperialist system where they have been obliged to obey the dictatorship of the IMF–World Bank–WTO overseers and to pursue objectives designed to serve imperialism and its capitalist masters. Africa's comprador elites – the black colonialists – have been too busy pursuing the imperialist-sponsored objectives of maldevelopment to address questions that are basic to the survival of their societies. In particular, they have not formulated their own concept of good governance, let alone embarked on the quest for devices to effect it.

Unsurprisingly, these comprador-colonial bantustans are cesspools of what even their alarmed imperialist masters now condemn as bad governance. Unlike these exogenous states, the indigenous societies of pre-colonial Africa had coherent and well-thought-out systems and procedures for good governance.

The available evidence, though patchy, suggests that each pre-colonial African society had its own indigenous conception of good governance, especially with respect to resource allocation, decision-making and arbitration, and each had its doctrines on how those discharging these functions should do so for its conception of good governance to be realised.

In the decentralised African societies, such as in Eritrea, Igboland and Botswana, besides consensual decision-making, some typical features of good governance were:

> respect for ancestors, elders, rights of individuals, and community norms and laws. Membership in lineage groups, kinship groups and ethnic groups ensured the protection of the rights of individuals, weak or strong. [Decentralised African societies] rarely had an executive branch of governance with police forces that penetrate communities to enforce laws and rules of society. Rather, members of the community observed the laws, rules and norms of their own

communities primarily because they were party to their making through the consensual decision-making process. The community at large also participates through various means in the enforcement of its rules and norms. Thus, the system in such societies did not create a permanent separation between makers and enforcers of rules or government and society.

(MENGISTEAB, 2003:209)

Though at present we lack details of the doctrines and rules of good governance by which the kings and their provincial and village administrators were guided in Old Ghana, Oyo, Dahomey, Benin, Ashanti, etc., we occasionally find indications of their concepts of conduct not conducive to good governance, as when grounds of social values were adduced for deposing or rebelling against a king or chief.

In the case of Alafin Jayin of Oyo in the 17th century, that veritable lord of misrule was described as 'effeminate and dissolute' and remembered for the debauchery of his court which provoked his forced suicide. And even under British indirect rule, in Ibadan, an offshoot and successor state of the Oyo empire, concerted opposition was mounted in 1941 to block Chief Folarin Solaja's promotion to a very high chieftaincy position, on the grounds that he was a money lender who charged interest, a rich but miserly man, etc. (Adéèkó, 2004:168–169; Adeboye, 2004: 214).

These episodes suggest that in the Oyo empire, debauchery, greed and miserliness were considered traits inappropriate in rulers and, as sources of disorder, were held contrary to their notion of good governance.

In the Ashanti kingdoms it was customary to publicly admonish a chief as follows, especially during his installation ceremony:

> Tell him that
> We do not wish for greediness
> We do not wish that he should curse us
> We do not wish that his ears should be hard of hearing
> We do not wish that he should call people fools
> We do not wish that he should act on his own initiative
> We do not wish things done as in Kumasi
> We do not wish that it should ever be said
>
> 'I have no time, I have no time'
> We do not wish personal abuse
> We do not wish personal violence

(QUOTED IN CHINWEIZU, 1987:229)

This indicates that, among the Ashanti, greed, arbitrariness, arrogance and other such characteristics in chiefs and officials were seen as contrary to good governance.

For deeper insights into African kingships and their governance, our best documented example is the divine kingship of Pharaonic Egypt. Let us now examine its concept and procedures of good governance.

Divine kingship and good governance in Pharaonic Egypt

Pharaonic Egypt (also known as Tawy: the two lands; or Kmt/Kemet: the country of the blacks) was an avowed theocracy. The Pharaonic Egyptians saw theirs as a civilisation founded by gods and ruled by gods for the edification of the gods. According to their historiography, (e.g. Manetho, and the Ramesside, or Turin, Canon) their land/kingdom was first ruled by the gods; after that by 'the demigods and spirits of the dead'. Then began the period of rule by mortal kings which Manetho divided into 31 dynasties. Manetho gave 39,525 years as the total duration of the three phases of Pharaonic Egyptian kingship (13,900 years by gods and 11,025 years by demigods, and the rest by mortal kings). Another Pharaonic Egyptian source gave a total of 23,000 years (18,000 for gods and heroes plus a little less than 5,000 years for mortal kings) (Hancock & Bauval, 1996:211). Even at a little less than 5,000 years, the phase of mortal kings (the only one recognised by Egyptology) was of long enough duration to make it probably the longest-lasting state so far found in the world's historical record. On the Chinweizu Chronology, Pharaonic Egypt, from the Mena unification to the Persian conquest, lasted from circa 4375 to 525 BCE (see Chinweizu, forthcoming, Vol. II).

What did the Pharaonic Egyptians regard as the purpose of their state? And what ideology (body of beliefs and values) guided its leadership during all those millennia?

The purpose of the Pharaonic state was to maintain and restore *Maat* – rightness in nature and righteousness in society – as normatively instituted in the cosmic order established by the gods in the epoch of the *Zep Tepi*, the First Time or First Occasion, i.e. when they initiated civilisation in Egypt: the epoch, long before the establishment of mortal kingship, when

> the basic principles of life, nature, society were determined by the gods; ... a golden age of absolute perfection -'before rage or clamour or strife or uproar had come about'. No death, disease or disaster occurred in that blissful epoch, known variously as 'the time of Re', 'the time of Osiris', or 'the time of Horus'.
>
> (R. R. RUNDLE CLARK, QUOTED IN HANCOCK & BAUVAL, 1996:140,141)

The divine kingship was the glue that held the Pharaonic Egyptian state together. State doctrine maintained that the Pharaoh was the divine and incarnate son of the Sun-god Ra, i.e. an avatar of Heru (Horus). He was believed to be born of woman by immaculate conception and, on his bodily death, his spirit rejoined his father Re and the other immortal gods. As the mediator between society and the forces of nature, his function was to maintain the cosmic order, *Maat*, by controlling the vital forces of the cosmos for the benefit of his land and its people.

One of his titles, *niswt-bity*, indicated that his spirit, the *bity*, was the living member of the *niswt-bity*, the company of Herus (Horuses), living and dead, of which he and all his predecessors on the throne were members. According to the doctrine, it was the *niswt-bity* that actually ruled Egypt; i.e. the mortal king on the throne at any given time was just the part-human representative of the *niswt-bity*. Thus divine kingship was a collective rulership by gods, specifically the current king and all his predecessors since the First Time when Ausar (Osiris) and Heru (Horus) ruled. (See 'Pharaoh-Eze Nri Correspondences' in Chinweizu, forthcoming, Vol. III.)

The principal affairs of the state (as recorded in the Old Kingdom Annals, also known as The Palermo Stone) were:

- building temples
- establishing festivals for various gods
- making offerings and endowments to divinities and the royal predecessors of the king
- executing large scale construction projects, such as irrigation systems
- tax collection
- census taking
- measuring the annual Nile flood-level.

Irrigation works, tax collection, census-taking and measuring the Nile flood-level were duties dictated by the king's role as 'the living *Heru*, who prospers the Two Lands'. (See 'The Shabaka Text' or 'The Memphite Theology', Lichtheim 1975:52.) But of the activities of the state, 'nothing is more important than reverent service to the gods and the building of monuments in their honour.' (Gardiner, 1964:115)

As the lord and shepherd of the country, the king's job was to maintain *Maat*, the cosmic, ecological and social order that brought peace and happiness to the kingdom. Prosperity was part of *Maat* for, at the *Zep Tepi* when Ausar was king, he taught his subjects law, order and religion and – by introducing cereals, the vine and a superior form of agriculture – made the country prosperous. The king sought to ensure that governance preserved the social and moral order that reflected the divine order of the universe and remained consistent with cosmic regularities. If an element of that order went awry or became disturbed, the system had to be recalibrated to remove disorder and restore *Maat*. For example, when, due to the precession of the equinox, temples and other sacred structures shifted from their original stellar alignments they would be rebuilt and realigned to restore them to their right place in the cosmic order.

Similarly, each year, after the Nile floods receded, the field boundaries that the floods had erased had to be redrawn. And, on a grander scale, after the fragmentation of the kingdom in the First Intermediate Period, and after the monotheist theological heresy of Atenism, a consciously implemented *weheme mesu*, i.e. 'repetition of births' or renaissance was, each time, undertaken to restore the old order of kingship, unity, polytheism and Maatian governance. Thus, as Amenemhat declared at the beginning of the Middle Kingdom, which reunified the kingdom, 'Kingship is again what it was in the past!'

For carrying out his duties, the king had available the institutions of the state. Besides his court (*šnty*/shnty) of companions and counsellors, there was a bureaucracy, headed by a prime minister (*tȝty*/tjaty), and consisting of departments, each of which was headed by an overseer (*Imy-r*/ Amir). By the 5th Dynasty, some 1,000 years after Mena's unification of Egypt, the departments of state were:

- The Great Mansions (The Legal Department and Law courts) headed by the *Imy-r ḥwt wrt*
- The Scribes of the King's Documents, headed by the *Imy-r zš 'nzwt*
- (Public) Works, headed by the *Imy-r kȝt*;
- Granaries, headed by the *Imy-r šnwt*
- Treasuries, headed by the *Imy-r pr-hd*.
  (See Nigel Strudwick, 1985)

What was the Pharaonic Egyptian conception of good governance and how did the state ensure that it was implemented by the king and state officials? And how did the Pharaonic state obtain the corps of officials it needed for its job of upholding *Maat*? Through the schools, the state gave the prospective official a Maatian education; through religion, the state taught the Ausarean beliefs and resurrection rites which encouraged Maatian conduct; and through its administrative and judicial systems, the state discouraged and punished un-Maatian conduct among its officials.

Maat and the Pharaonic doctrines on governance

Establishing, maintaining and restoring *Maat* was the purpose of Pharaonic governance. According to Pharaonic sages, the quality of governance is a function of the quality of office-holders. If righteous men hold office, government will govern righteously. Right-acting and disciplined officials result in a just or Maatian government.

Furthermore, the quality of office-holders is a function of the quality of education. Those entering public office must be imbued with a commitment to right-doing; but as 'no one is born wise', it was necessary to educate the prospective officials and the people to their duties and proper conduct by teaching them the collective wisdom of the country as contained in the *Sebait* – the wisdom texts on official conduct and social values. Hence the use of the *Sebait* as curriculum texts for all children in the schools (see Carruthers, 1986:6–15).

The religion taught everyone the Ausarean beliefs about the afterlife, with its doctrines of resurrection and Judgement Day, with eternal rewards for the soul of the righteous individual and punishment for the soul of the wicked. According to doctrine, the result on Judgement Day depended on how the conduct of the deceased, when alive, measured up against the virtues of the Ausarean Code.

Let us now look briefly at the *Sebait*, Pharaonic education, Ausarism and the administrative and judicial procedures, to see how, together, they formed a system for promoting righteous governance.

Ethical doctrines of the *Sebait*

The principal documents of the *Sebait* that have survived include, *The Instructions of Ptahhotep, The Instructions for Merikare, The Instructions of Amenemhat* and *The Petitions of Khun-Anpu*, from the Old Kingdom and Middle Kingdom periods as well as later works. These separate texts, though of the same type – moral instructions – do not appear ever to have been gathered into one bound volume. To the *Sebait* also belong works like Ipuwer and Neferti which describe the disastrous effects of departure from *Maat*.

The texts of the *Sebait* instructed officials on righteous conduct towards peers (family, friends, colleagues), higher authorities and the general public as well as towards the gods and the ecosystem.

The cardinal virtues, as taught by the *Sebait,* are self-control, moderation, kindness, generosity, justice and truthfulness tempered with discretion. (Lichtheim, 1975:62) In Karenga's view, the cardinal virtues are truth, justice, propriety, harmony, balance, reciprocity and order, these being the various meanings of *Maat* in the sacred texts (Karenga, 1989:391). The cardinal vices are greed, injustice/partiality, oppressing the poor /exploiting the little people, laziness, abuse of authority (see 'The Petitions of Khun-Anpu'/'The Eloquent Peasant', Lichtheim, 1975:169–184).

The virtues are commended on the ground that they are decreed by God and rewarded with status, wealth, friends, family, an everlasting good name on earth and, above all, immortal life among the gods in the hereafter. The vices are condemned as abhorred and punished by God.

Noteworthy precepts in the *Sebait* include the following: On the rule of law, due process and impartiality, 'The Installation of the Prime Minister' says:

> 'See to it that all is done according to law,
> That all is done exactly right... .
> The magistrate's safety is acting by the rule... .
> God abhors partiality...
> Regard one you know like one you don't know'
>
> (LICHTHEIM 1976:22, 23)

On meritocracy, The Merikare says:

> 'Do not prefer the wellborn to the commoner,
> Choose a man on account of his skills.'
>
> (LICHTHEIM, 1975:101)

The *Sebait* urge the enjoyment of life. 'Follow your heart' says Maxim 11 of Ptahhotep, for example. However, they emphasise that wealth is a gift of God and its main purpose is to enable one to be generous to friends and intimates. 'Sustain your friends with what you have, you have it by the grace of god' (Maxim 22); 'Don't be mean toward your friends, they are greater than one's riches . . .' (Maxim 35).

The *Sebait* warn severely against greed:

> Guard against the vice of greed:
> A grievous sickness without cure, ...
> It embroils fathers, mothers,
> And the brothers of the mother,
> It parts wife from husband;
> It is a compound of all evils
>
> (PTAHHOTEP, MAXIM 19, LICHTHEIM, 1975:68–69)

Not for them Maggie Thatcher's 'Greed is good' dictum or the capitalist doctrine of 'private vices, public good, via the invisible hand'. Not for them the capitalist view that a well-ordered society should run according to what Adam Smith called the 'vile maxim of the masters of mankind': 'All for ourselves, and nothing for other people' (see Chomsky, 1993:19, 57).

The *Sebait* also instruct as follows:

'Speaking is stronger than all fighting'
'Do to the doer to make him do.'

(LICHTHEIM, 1975:99,174)

'The Lord prefers the timid to the headstrong man.'
'Do not raise your voice in the house of God. He abhors shouting.'

(LICHTHEIM, 1976:24,137)

'If you do good by a hundred persons and just one of them
acknowledges it, no part of it is lost.'
'Do not do to a man what you dislike, so as to cause another to do it
to you.'
'Do a good deed and throw it in the water and when it dries you will
find it.'

(LICHTHEIM, 1980:170,171,174)

It should be noted that the Pharaonic Egyptians did not share the view of
the Greeks and modern Europeans for whom justice is nothing other than
the interest of the stronger. (For Afrocentric translations and introductory
discussions of the *Sebait*, see Karenga, 1984; Carruthers, 1995; Hilliard et al.,
1987; and Karenga, 1989.)

Pharaonic education for governance

The education system aimed to produce the Maatian ideal-type of person, known
as the *geru-maat* – a literate, numerate paragon of righteous conduct who could
be employed by the state as a priest, administrator or military officer; a person
whose spirit, after the death of the body, would qualify as a blessed soul and be
vindicated/(declared *maakheru*) on Judgement Day before Ausar in the Hall of
Double Maat. Pharaonic education emphasised the development of character
and of the soul, and was seen as the path to immortality and divinity for humans.
Its ultimate goal was divinisation, i.e. to make the resurrected soul of the dead fit
to join the astral company of the immortal gods.

The process of education was not seen primarily as a process of
acquiring knowledge. It was seen as a process of the transformation
of the learner who progressed through successive stages of rebirth
to become more godlike.

(HILLIARD 1985:158)

The Pharaonic system was predicated on a view in which a 'person
was seen as being essentially spiritual whose essence was housed in
a finite body. It was the spirit that had an eternal existence.'

(HILLIARD 1986:138)

> The path to the development of god-like qualities was through the
> development of virtue … Virtue was the antidote to character flaws.
> But virtue could be achieved only through special study and effort.
> (HILLIARD 1986:138

Maatian philosophy held that 'self-cultivation through righteous behaviour is the ultimate goal.' It also held 'learning as essential, even indispensable, to the self-cultivation and self-authentication of the geru-maat'. For 'it is in the development of character that instruction succeeds' (Karenga 1989:389,391).

The character training of the student was principally achieved by saturating his mind with the precepts from the *Sebait*, the wisdom books on which the child was drilled from his first day at school, and from which he absorbed the dos-and-don'ts of the Maatian way of life. The ideal character which education aimed to form the *geru-maat* was: the calm, quiet, controlled, modest, wise, gentle, socially-active, person (Karenga, 1986:94), the righteous, self-mastered person 'whose whole character is infused with Maat' (Karenga, 1989:389). Explicating the concept, using quotations from the *Sebait*, Karenga presents some of the main attributes of the *geru-maat*: The *geru-maat* is one who is true in word, just in deed, diligent as well as generous with his wealth; a man of peace who observes the proprieties in his conduct towards superiors, peers and inferiors; who is balanced or measured and applies the right measure in all good things, and who practices reciprocity. He is calm, self-controlled, kind towards people, humble towards god, and follows in the footsteps of the ancestors (Karenga, 1989: 361–369). The opposite of the *geru-maat* is the 'unrestrained person — hot-mouthed, hot-tempered, aggressive, and generally infused with *isfet*, the opposite of *maat*' (Karenga, 1986:94).

The human person was conceived as consisting of a mortal physical body plus nine non-physical parts. Vindication on Judgement Day was the condition for the person's soul to attain immortality and divinity. Therefore, emphasis was placed on preparing it to become eligible for immortality by teaching him to live by the Ausarean code.

However, since education in any ethical code is not enough to guarantee lifelong practice of it, the Pharaonic official had to be motivated to practise what he had been taught. This was done by equipping him with Ausarean beliefs, which made him desire immortality, but made his attainment of immortality conditional on his life-long practice of Maatian ethics.

Ausarism: religious motivation to life-long righteous conduct

The core of Ausarism was the belief that the soul of the deceased would be examined on Judgement Day. Upon arriving at the Judgement Hall, he had to declare himself innocent of crimes on the Ausarean Code; one to each of the

42 assembled divine assessors. The so-called Pyramid Texts, which were inscribed for the kings of the 5th and 6th Dynasties on the walls of their pyramids, were the original resurrection manuals of Ausarism. Later derivatives would appear in the so-called Coffin Texts, inscribed in the coffins of officials; and in the *Book of Coming Forth by Day*, the so-called *Book of the Dead*, which popularised the manual for everyone. The climax of the resurrection rites, The Declaration of Innocence, went thus (*annotations, in italics and between square brackets, are by Chinweizu*):

> These are words which shall be said on arriving at the Great Hall of Maati, so that one may be separated from all offences he or she may have committed and may behold the faces of the divine ones,

> One says: Homage to you, Great God, Lord of Maati.
> I have come to you O Lord that I may behold your beauty.
> I know you; I know your name;
> I know the names of the forty-two divine beings who live with you in this Hall of Maati, who live on the doers of evil and feed on their blood on the day of taking account of character in the presence of Osiris, The Good One.
> Surely, the Two Daughters, the Two Eyes, Lord of Righteousness is your name: Behold, I have come to you.
> I have brought you righteousness and have done away with unrighteousness for you.

[Here begin the Declarations to the 42 divine assessors, each of whom is hailed before a declaration is made to him. The sample declarations below are compiled from several texts. The full list of virtues in the Ausarean Code is not known. If it was ever compiled, it has yet to be found. But the number of distinct virtues found in extant texts exceeds 42. I have arranged the 44 samples below into four thematic groups: social virtues, ecosystem virtues, virtuous acts towards the king and state, and virtuous acts towards the gods.]

Social virtues

1   Hail, Nehau, who comes forth from Restau, I have not mistreated my family and associates.
2   Hail, Sekheriu, who comest forth from Utten, I have not associated with evil or worthless persons.
3   Hail, thou Destroyer, who comest forth from Kesiu, I have not defrauded the poor of their property.
4   Hail, ... , I have not slandered a servant to his superior.
5   Hail, ... , I have not inflicted pain.
6   Hail, ... , I have not caused anyone to be hungry.

7   Hail, ... , I have not made anyone weep.

8   Hail, ... , I have not caused anyone to suffer.

9   Hail, ... , I have not been greedy.

10 Hail, ... , I have not committed fraud.

11 Hail, ... , I have not committed adultery.

12 Hail, ... , I have not coveted others' property.

13 Hail, ... , I have not stolen.

14 Hail, ... , I have not committed murder.

15 Hail, ... , I have not increased or diminished the measure of grain,

16 Hail... . , I have not encroached upon fields of another.

17 Hail, ... , I have not taken milk from the mouth of babes.

18 Hail, ... , I have not told lies.

19 Hail, ... , I have not spoken curses.

20 Hail, ... , I have not been angry without just cause,

21 Hail, ... , I have not terrorised anyone.

22 Hail, ... , I have not been hot-tempered.

23 Hail, ... , I have not been deaf to words of truth.

24 Hail... . , I have not stirred up strife.

25 Hail, ... , I have not been blind to injustice.

26 Hail, ... , I have not engaged in violence.

27 Hail, ... , I have not been quick tempered.

28 Hail, ... , I have not waded in drinking water.

29 Hail, ... , I have not discriminated against others.

30 Hail, ... , I have not been arrogant.

Ecosystem virtues

31 Hail, ... , I have not laid waste the ploughed lands

32 Hail, ... , I have not dammed up water when it should flow.

33 Hail, ... , I have not engaged in unnatural sex.

34 Hail, ... , I have not broken the channel of running water.

Virtues to the king and the state

35 Hail, ... , I have not slandered the Pharaoh.

36 Hail, ... , I have not violated the law.

37 Hail, ... , I have not told lies in the court of law.

38 Hail, ... , I have not worked treason

Virtues to the gods

39 Hail, ... , I have not blasphemed against God.

40 Hail, ... , I have not killed sacred animals.

41 Hail, ... , I have not violated the times of making meat offerings.

42 Hail, . . ., I have not filched that which has been offered in the temples; nor have I purloined the cakes of the gods.

43 Hail, ... , I have not cursed God.

44 Hail, ... , I have not offended the God of my city.

> Behold, I have come to you, empty of evil and devoid of deceit,
> a blameless one, one without a witness against him.
> Therefore, let no case be brought against me.
> I live on Maat, I satisfy myself with the righteousness of my heart.
> For I have done that which men and women request and that which
> pleases God.
> I have found favour with God by doing that which He loves.
> I have given bread to the hungry, water to the thirsty,
> clothes to the naked and a boat to those without one.
> I have made due offerings to God and funeral offerings to the
> departed. Deliver me then, and protect me.
> Make no report against me in the presence of the Great God.
> For I am one whose mouth is pure and whose hands are clean.
> Therefore, let it be said to me: 'Welcome, come in peace'
> by those who shall see me.

*[His heart was then weighed in the balance against the feather of Maat, and
if found pure, i.e. if it was light enough to balance the feather of Maat, he
would be vindicated and admitted to the company of immortals, thus:]*

> Hail, vindicated one. You shall cross the sky and
> travel across the expanse of the heavens; those in the
> winding waterway [*i.e. the Milky Way*] shall revere you and see you
> when you rise on the eastern horizon. You shall come forth
> from the Night-bark of Ra and go aboard the Day-bark
> as Horus, Lord of nobles, himself, commands you.
> Hail, vindicated one. You shall go up on the great
> eastern side of the sky and go down on the great
> western side of the earth among those powers of
> heavens who are in the company of Osiris, the Risen
> Saviour. And you shall go in peace, in peace with Ra,
> who is in the heavens.

(KARENGA, 1984:114)

[The vindicated soul, at its ascension into heaven, would be welcomed thus:]

> The Heavens declare: This royal vindicated one is my
> beloved son in whom I am well pleased, ... my first
> born upon the throne of earth, and Ra has given him
> his heritage in the presence of the Great Powers of

heaven. All the powers of heaven rejoice saying how
blessed is this vindicated one, for his father is greatly
pleased with him.

This culturally instilled craving for immortal life among the gods was a
motive powerful enough to induce most officials to live righteously as they
had been taught. But, as always with codes of conduct, there were those
who, for whatever reasons, strayed from the path of *Maat*. For such, when
caught, there was punishment here on earth, even before the eternal
punishment that was said to await them after death.

The judicial punishment system

For minor infractions of the Maatian code of conduct, an official might be
reprimanded. For more serious transgressions, he might be sacked and have
his property confiscated – as was done to Nemtynakht in the story 'The
Petitions of Khun-Anpu,' or 'The Eloquent Peasant'. For even more serious
transgressions, such as treason, he would be imprisoned, have his nose or
limb cut off, or even be sentenced to death by suicide or starvation—as
happened to those found guilty of conspiracy to make rebellion against King
Ramesses III (see Gardiner, 1964:289–290).

Conscience vs CCTV

Thus did the Pharaonic state organise a three-part system – made up of
education, religious beliefs and judicial punishment – for obtaining the
cadre of righteous leaders it needed to fulfil its Maatian purpose. This
ethical edifice is, in its field, no less impressive than the megalithic edifices,
epitomised by the Great Pyramids, which Pharaonic Egyptians bequeathed
humanity. It helped them to produce what has been called 'one of the best
organised civilisations that the world has ever seen' (Gardiner, 1964:106).

As Karenga points out, in this ethical edifice 'we find a source of the
Ten Commandments and . . . of so many other concepts central to Hebrew
and Christian theology, i.e., resurrection, the Risen Saviour, the Beloved
Son, the Day and Hall of Judgement, immortality of the soul, etc. (Karenga,
1984:103).

What has long been lost sight of is that the doctrines of resurrection,
Judgement Day, paradise and salvation were not propounded as ends in
themselves but, together with immaculate conception, the annunciation,
virgin birth, ascension, etc., were elements in an ideological apparatus
designed to foster good governance here on earth. Christianity, a white power
perversion of Ausarism, severed the quest for immortality in paradise from the
earthly project of good governance and made it a free-standing, other-worldly,
end in itself. With the atheism of the secular bourgeois capitalism of the last

two centuries, we have found out from hard experience that fear of Judgement Day, when internalised as conscience, is a more effective deterrent to misconduct and crime than fear of human watchers, social censure, police, judges, prisons, hangmen and Orwell's Big Brother's CCTV.

Conclusion

The inability of black Africa's comprador-colonial bantustans to satisfy or pacify their populations, whether under one-party, multi-party or military rule, has manifested as rebellions and civil wars that threaten an endemic disorder that could obstruct the stable imperialist plunder of Africa. This has alarmed the imperialists into advocating 'good governance' and other nostrums to legitimise the comprador-colonial bantustans, and thereby stave off the collapse of the comprador-colonial system. It has caused them to sponsor a search by Africanist scholarship (ever the ready handmaid of imperialism) to find ways to integrate aspects of African indigenous governance systems into the structures of comprador colonialism so as to give these outlandish, barbarous and anti-African states -with their brazenly greedy black colonialist officials—legitimacy in the eyes of their victim populations, and hopefully save them from being violently overthrown and scrapped altogether.

Notes

Adélékè Adéèko (2004), 'Political Appellation in Yoruba Literature' in Olufemi Vaughan ed., *Indigenous Political Structure and Governance in Nigeria*, Ibadan: Bookcraft, pp.168–194.

O. A. Adeboye (2004), 'Elders-Still-Exist': Socio-cultural Groups and Political Participation in Colonial Ibadan', in Olufemi Vaughan ed., *Indigenous Political Structure and Governance in Nigeria*, Ibadan: Bookcraft, pp.195–230.

Jacob Carruthers (1995), *Mdw Ntr: Divine Speech*, London: Karnak House; Carruthers, eds (1986), pp.3–30.

Chinweizu (forthcoming), *On Kametilogy and Black Egypt: Vol I: Groundworks on Kametilogy: Vol II: Pharaonic Chronology Revisited; Vol III: Igbo-Pharaonic Correspondences; Vol IV: Black Egypt; Vol V: Miscellaneous Studies in Kametilogy.*

Chinweizu (1987), *The West and the Rest of Us (2nd Edition)* Lagos: Pero Press.

Noam Chomsky (1993), *Year 501, The Conquest Continues*, Boston: South End Press.

Alan Gardiner (1964), *Egypt of the Pharaohs*, Oxford: Oxford University Press.

Graham Hancock and Robert Bauval (1996), *The Message of the Sphinx*, New York: Three Rivers Press .

Asa G. Hilliard III (1985), 'Kemetic Concepts in Education' in Ivan Van Sertima ed., *Nile Valley Civilizations*, New Brunswick, NJ: Transaction Books, (1986); 'Pedagogy in Ancient Kemet' in Maulana Karenga and Jacob Carruthers, eds. (1986), pp.131–148.

Asa G. Hilliard III, Larry Williams and Nia Damali, eds. (1987), *The Teachings of Ptahhotep: The Oldest Book in the World*. Atlanta: Blackwood Press.

Maulana Karenga (1989), 'Towards a Sociology of Maatian Ethics: Literature and Context,' in Ivan Van Sertima, ed. *Egypt Revisited*, New Brunswick, NJ: Transaction Publishers, pp. 352–395, (1986) 'Restoration of the Husia: Reviving a Sacred Legacy' in Maulana Karenga and Jacob Carruthers, eds., pp. 83–99; (1984) *Selections from the Husia: Sacred Wisdom of Ancient Egypt*, Los Angeles: Kawaida Publications.

Maulana Karenga and Jacob Carruthers, eds. (1986), *Kemet and the African Worldview*, Los Angeles: University of Sankore Press.

Miriam Lichtheim (1975), *Ancient Egyptian Literature, Vol. I: The Old and Middle Kingdoms*, Berkeley: University of California Press; (1976) *Ancient Egyptian Literature, Vol. II: The New Kingdom*, Berkeley: University of California Press; (1980) *Ancient Egyptian Literature, Vol. III: The Late Period*, Berkeley: University of California Press.

Kidane Mengisteab (2003), 'African Traditional Institutions of Governance: The Case of Eritrea's village *Baito*', in Olufemi Vaughan, ed., *Indigenous Political Structures and Governance in Africa*, Ibadan: Sefer Books, pp. 208–223.

Nigel Strudwick (1985), *The Administration of Egypt in the Old Kingdom*, London: KPI.

African leadership: from the top down

The kingship is a goodly office; it has no son and it has no brother who shall make its monuments endure, yet it is the one person who ennobles the other; a man works for his predecessor, through the desire that what he has done may be embellished by another who shall come after him.

Merikare's father to Merikare (c. 1990 BCE)

Liberation, democracy, development and leadership in Africa

Ali A. Mazrui

Ali A. Mazrui is one of Africa's leading political scientists. He has written widely on African politics, culture and history. His television documentary, The Africans – a Triple Heritage, *remains the most authoritative television programme on African history, 30 years after it was made. He is currently Director of the Institute of Global Cultural Studies and Albert Schweitzer Professor in the Humanities at Binghamton University, State University of New York, USA. He is also the Albert Luthuli Professor-at-Large at the University of Jos, Nigeria; Andrew D. White Professor-at-Large Emeritus and Senior Scholar in Africana Studies at Cornell University, Ithaca, New York; and Chancellor of Jomo Kenyatta University of Agriculture and Technology, Nairobi, Kenya.*

Professor Mazrui has known personally many of the post-colonial African leaders he writes about. Here he offers first a typology of African leaders, and then explores the goals they aimed to achieve. Finally, he identifies a tradition of heroism and martyrdom that has emerged as African leaders have battled for independence and freedom.

Liberation, development, democracy and pan-Africanism in Africa has demanded exceptional leadership. In this essay, I examine the typology of leadership in Africa so far in the post-independence period.

A typology of leadership

The history of leadership in Africa has stood on eight pillars.[1] Were they

34

eight styles of command or eight categories of commanders? At the time of independence there was a lot of discussion about charismatic leadership. This discourse was greatly influenced by the man who led the first black African country to independence – Kwame Nkrumah of Ghana. He himself was a charismatic leader with considerable personal magnetism.[2] I first met him in New York in 1960 and fell under his spell. Nnamdi Azikiwe was also a charismatic personality, but his magnetism waned after the civil war in Nigeria.

I happen to think that Idi Amin Dada of Uganda also had a lot of charisma, which enabled him to survive in power for eight years until a foreign army (Tanzanian) forced him out.[3] Idi Amin (whom I knew well) was a brutal ruler who nevertheless captivated a substantial following, both at home and abroad.

A mobilisation leader is another category. Nkrumah tried to use his charisma for mobilisation, but in reality Nkrumah was not a particularly successful mobilisation leader in Ghana after independence. On the other hand, Julius K. Nyerere in Tanzania was both charismatic and mobilisational. He succeeded in arousing the masses to many of his causes. Gamal Abdel Nasser in Egypt was also both charismatic and mobilisational from the Suez crisis in 1956 until his death in 1970.

A reconciliation leader seeks areas of compromise and consensus from among disparate points of views. Nigeria is a difficult country to govern. So far mobilisation has not worked for long. Reconciliation as a style of leadership is often essential. Both General Yakubu Gowon (who led the Federal side during the civil war in the 1960s) and General Abdulsalami Abubakar (who provided a transition between tyranny and redemocratisation in the 1990s) were reconciliation leaders. They attempted to find areas of compromise in widely divergent Nigerian points of view.

A housekeeping style of political power is minimalist in sense of purpose. There is more governance and less genuine leadership, more verbosity and less vision. The Kenyan political elite since the late 1980s has been at best a housekeeping elite – governing without leading, maintenance without movement.

An African military head of state, Murtala Muhammad, was the best approximation to a disciplinarian leader that Nigeria has had. He was assassinated within months of capturing power from Gowon in the mid 1970s. Muhammad Buhari was also a disciplinarian Nigerian head of state. However, it is not certain that a disciplinarian style is what Nigeria's ethnic and sectarian realities can really sustain for very long.[4] But this option should at least be carefully considered.

A patriarchal system is one in which a father figure emerges, using the symbolism of the elder and the patriarch. Jomo Kenyatta was already about

60 years old when he emerged from a colonial prison in Kenya to assume the reins of power. He carried the title of Mzee, meaning both 'the Elder' and 'the Old Man'. He ruled Kenya from 1963 until he died in 1978.[5] Félix Houphouët-Boigny of the Côte d'Ivoire was also a patriarchal leader who presided over the destiny of independent Côte d'Ivoire from 1960 until his death in 1993.

Nelson Mandela was both a reconciliation leader and a patriarchal figure. His long martyrdom in prison (1964–90) and his advancing years gave him the credentials of the patriarch. His moral style in his old age was a search for legitimate compromises. The latter was a style of reconciliation. Was Nelson Mandela also a charismatic figure? Or was he only a hero in history? That is a more open question.

Ibrahim Babangida played a patriarchal role in his transition programme, but he was too young for such a role. Babangida's constitutional transition could have made him Nigeria's Charles de Gaulle, but the experiment collapsed when Moshood Abiola's election as president was not acknowledged by the military.

Has Africa ever really produced technocratic political leadership? The answer is yes – but rarely at the level of the presidency. Some vice-presidents have been technocrats or potential technocrats. Kenya has had a series of quasi-technocratic vice-presidents, some of whom got 'debased' in office. They include vice-presidents Mwai Kibaki (distinguished economist), Josephat Karanja (former university vice-chancellor) and George Saitoti (former professor). Are Thabo Mbeki and Yoweri Museveni essentially technocratic leaders? Ghana's Jerry Rawlings was part disciplinarian and part technocratic.

Personalistic political style in Africa is sometimes indistinguishable from monarchical political style in our sense. Both entail the personification of power. But the monarchical tendency, which can thus be categorised as a ninth style, goes further and sacralises authority while simultaneously seeking to create an aristocratic impact. Hastings Kamuzu Banda of Malawi was definitely a personalistic political leader, demanding unquestioning political allegiance. But was he also a pseudo-monarch, seeking to give his authority a semblance of sacredness?

More literally, Jean-Bédel Bokassa of the Central African Republic tried to create a new monarchical and imperial dynasty, with himself as the first emperor. He even renamed his country the 'Central African Empire'. He held an astonishingly lavish coronation that was supposed to be paradoxically Napoleonic.[6]

A new aspect of the monarchical tendency which is emerging is the dynastic trend in succession. In the Democratic Republic of the Congo Laurent Kabila has been succeeded by his son Josef Kabila. In Zanzibar

Abeid Karume has produced a successor in his son. In Egypt Hosni Mubarak may be grooming his son to succeed him. In Kenya Raila Odinga is trying to follow the *nyayo* (footprints) of his famous father, Oginga Odinga.

In addition to these types and styles of leadership there have been a number of pre-colonial cultural traditions which affected those types and styles. The most obvious was the elder tradition in pre-colonial African culture, which has probably conditioned the patriarchal style since independence. The reverence of Jomo Kenyatta as Mzee in Kenya was substantially the outcome of the pre-colonial elder tradition, still alive and well. Nelson Mandela by the time of his release was also a heroic *mzee*.

Also obvious as a continuing tradition from pre-colonial times was an older version of the monarchical tendency. Even African societies which were not themselves monarchical were influenced by the royal paradigm. Kwame Nkrumah attempted to create a monarchical tradition in independent Ghana by declaring himself life-president, by sacralising his authority with the title of Osagyefo (Redeemer), by surrounding himself with a class of ostentatious consumers passing themselves off as Ghana's new political aristocracy, and by increasingly regarding political opposition to the president as the equivalent of treason (a monarchical version of intolerance).

Less obvious as a pre-colonial conditional factor was the sage tradition. This involved respect for wisdom and expertise. In the modern period the sage tradition was rapidly modernised to include the new products of Western-style high schools, and later Western-style colleges and universities. The sage tradition from the post-colonial period has sometimes resulted in promoting an ostentatious display of Western learning among Africans.

Tapping on modernised versions of the sage tradition a number of founding fathers of independent Africa tried to become philosopher-kings. They attempted to philosophise about man and society and about Africa's place in the global scheme of things. Kwame Nkrumah wrote books and became the most prolific head of state anywhere in the world. Léopold Sédar Senghor of Senegal was a more original political philosopher and poet.[7]

Some leaders attempted to establish whole new ideologies. Julius K. Nyerere of Tanzania inaugurated *ujamaa*, intended to be indigenously authentic African socialism. Kenneth D. Kaunda of Zambia initiated what was called 'humanism'. Gamal Abdel Nasser of Egypt had previously written *The Philosophy of the Revolution* and subsequently attempted the implementation of 'Arab socialism'. Muammar Qaddafy of Libya produced the *Green Book* championing the third way.

The modernised version of the Western tradition also popularised the use of honorary doctorates as regular titles of heads of state. Thus the president of Uganda became 'Dr' Milton Obote, the president of Zambia became 'Dr' Kenneth Kaunda – just as the president of Ghana before them had become 'Dr' Kwame Nkrumah. These had been conferred as honorary doctorates, but they became regular titles used in referring to these heads of state. The sage tradition was attempting to realise itself in a modern veneer. African presidents were trying to become philosopher-kings. After his presidency, Yakubu Gowon took the more difficult route and studied for his PhD at Warwick University in England.

Finally, there was the pre-colonial warrior tradition, emphasising skills of combat, self-defence and manhood.[8] Did this survive into the colonial period and onwards into independence? The Mau Mau fighters in colonial Kenya in the 1950s were greatly influenced by traditional warrior virtues, especially those of the Kikuyu. Even liberation fighters in Rhodesia/ Zimbabwe two decades later, who were using much more modern weapons, were recruited mainly from the countryside and were deeply influenced by traditional concepts of the warrior.

But were African soldiers in regular African state armies part of the continuities of the warrior tradition? Were the Abdulsalami Abubakars fundamentally still old warriors? It largely depends upon how much of the old African cultural values are still part of their attitudes to combat, self-defence and manhood. General Abubakar himself maintained high standards of integrity. But sometimes those old warrior values go awry in a modern military ruler. The warrior tradition went wrong when personified in Idi Amin Dada of Uganda. Idi Amin was a warrior-soldier who was mis-cast as head of state in the modern world. He fluctuated between brute, buffoon and genuinely heroic figure. He courageously took on some of the most powerful forces in the world – and yet pitilessly victimised some of the most powerless individuals in his own country from 1971 to 1979. In Idi Amin the warrior tradition had gone temporarily mad.

Nine types of political leadership and four pre-colonial traditions of political culture have helped to shape post-colonial leadership in the 20th century. The question which now arises is whether the 21st century will either reveal totally new styles of leadership or create new combinations of the old styles and traditions and produce better results than Africa has accomplished so far.

Goals of leadership

Here we must turn from styles of leadership to goals of leadership. We know that the 20th century produced very effective leaders of liberation. Nationalists like Robert Mugabe of Zimbabwe and Sékou Touré of Guinea fought against great odds to gain us independence. There were many other brilliant liberation fighters all over the continent who helped Africa end its colonial bondage.

But leaders of liberation were not necessarily leaders of development. One African leader after another let Africa down in the struggle to improve the material well-being of the African people. Only a few African leaders since independence have demonstrated skills of development on the ground. Considering what a terribly damaged country he had inherited, Yoweri Museveni deserves some credit for raising Uganda from the depths of despair to one of the main regional actors in the Great Lakes region.[9] It is to be hoped that the coming African renaissance will produce more and more leaders skilled in the arts of development.

In addition to leaders of liberation (like Mugabe, Sékou Touré, Samora Machel, Zik and Nkrumah), and leaders of development (like Yoweri Museveni and Habib Bourguiba), has Africa produced leaders of democracy? This is a much tougher agenda. South Africa has the most liberal constitution in the world, and has ended political apartheid. But the wealth of the society is still maldistributed along racial lines. The mines, the best jobs, the best businesses, are still disproportionately held by non-black people. Leaders like Nelson Mandela and Thabo Mbeki have presided over substantial political democratisation, but they have also had to tolerate substantial economic injustice.

In Nigeria, Abdulsalami Abubakar provided a smooth transition from the tyranny of Sani Abacha to a return to democracy and civilian rule. In that democratic return Olusegun Obasanjo was elected the first Nigerian president of the new millennium. It was a very promising choice. After all, in 1979 Olusegun Obasanjo became the first African military ruler to hand over power voluntarily to a freely elected government. In 1979 Obasanjo had also been the first Nigerian military ruler to let political power slip from his own ethnic group without attempting to subvert the process.

However, Olusegun Obasanjo in the new millennium is still being tested. He is confronted with Shariacracy in some northern states, with Yoruba nationalism in some Western states, and with demands for confederation among some of the Igbo nationalists. In style will Obasanjo emerge as a gifted reconciliation leader? In normative Africanity is he a warrior or a sage? And in the ultimate goals for Nigeria, does Olusegun Obasanjo stand a chance of emerging as a successful leader of genuine democratisation?

We know that Africa has been served well by leaders of liberation. We are concerned that we have not produced enough leaders of development. In Nigeria and elsewhere we are also looking for leaders of democracy. Perhaps Abdulsalami Abubakar should in the future entrust his political fate to the Nigerian electorate. They may well elect him to a fuller term as head of state. His humility is one of his greatest assets, as was his readiness to relinquish power voluntarily in 1999.

What about leaders of pan-Africanism and wider transnational solidarity?

39

Clearly this is a fourth goal, beside liberation, development and democracy. (See 'Global pan-African leadership in the new millennium', page 252, for a discussion of how pan-Africanism, alongside the three goals of liberation, development and democracy, may have to be examined in the context of globalisation.)

Heroes and martyrs

But let us now turn to other dimensions of African leadership – heroes and martyrs.

Africa's struggle for independence from 1945 onwards produced many great heroes. Africa's exercise of independence from 1960 onwards produced an impressive array of martyrs.

In our present context, what is the difference between a hero and a martyr? A hero is judged by his or her own performance and by the positive results achieved. A martyr is judged not just by performance and results, but also by the suffering or death that he or she has sustained. The ultimate price a martyr pays is, of course, life itself.

The struggle for independence in Africa produced probably as many martyrs as heroes. On the other hand, as already stated, the post-colonial period has seen some of the former anti-colonial heroes deteriorate into dictators, corrupt leaders, or political weaklings.

Africa's post-colonial conditions have produced fewer great leaders than were produced by the anti-colonial struggle. On the other hand, the same unstable post-colonial conditions have produced more numerous martyrs than had emerged in earlier years.

The ultimate form of martyrdom is to be killed for one's beliefs, or one's values, or one's heroic actions, or one's honour. Here are some of Africa's political martyrs at the pinnacle of power – ranging from Tom Mboya and Murtala Muhammed to Anwar Sadat and Thomas Sankara, from Olympio to Patrice Lumumba. Edward Mondlane and Steve Biko fell short of ultimate power.

Let us first examine the three most significant quasi-presidential assassinations of Africa's post-colonial era – the deaths of Lumumba, Sadat and Murtala Muhammed. We shall then broaden the scope of comparative martyrdom, and include the impact of freedom fighters who had yet to capture power.

Lumumba, Sadat and Murtala

The three most significant quasi-presidential assassinations in post-colonial Africa occurred in three of the largest countries in the continent – Nigeria, Egypt and the former Belgian Congo (now Democratic Republic of Congo). As it happens, the three countries are also linguistically different – anglophone Nigeria, Arabic-speaking Egypt, and francophone Congo.

But why are these three assassinations particularly significant? Partly because of the ideals for which the martyrs were sacrificed. Patrice Lumumba died in defence of the sovereign integrity of his country. The Congo had just become independent of Belgian rule. Two events threatened this newly won independence. The army of the new state mutinied and threatened to plunge the country into chaos.

The army mutiny was soon followed by a secessionist declaration from one of the richest parts of the country – the Katanga province. The Western powers were soon scrambling to fish in these troubled waters and fragment the country. Patrice Lumumba was Prime Minister (head of government) and Josef Kasavubu was President (head of state). Belgium, the former colonial master, led the way in trying to consolidate Katanga's secession.

When Lumumba sought the assistance of the Soviet Union, the United States acted quickly to prevent a potential Soviet take-over of the Congo. The United States engineered a situation under which the United Nations could then take the leadership in reconciliation. Very briefly the Congo became a United Nations trusteeship.

Patrice Lumumba fought hard to prevent both the fragmentation of the Congo and the great dilution of the Congo's independence. Unfortunately, the United Nations did little to help him. He was captured by his Congolese enemies in front of the United Nations troops – and taken to separatist Katanga to be murdered by Katangese with Belgium's complicity.

There are different reasons why the larger Congo has remained one country until today. But a crucial factor in saving the Congo's territorial integrity was Lumumba's internationalisation of the Katanga crisis from the outset. It forced both the United Nations and the United States to commit themselves to the territorial integrity of the Congo.

If Lumumba had been a martyr to the sovereign integrity of his country, Anwar Sadat was a martyr to the principle of peace in Arab–Israeli relations. Sadat made the spectacular visit to Jerusalem to be received by the Israeli Prime Minister, Menachem Begin. It was one of the most sensational events of the 20th century. Sadat's visit to Jerusalem subsequently led to the Camp David negotiations between Egypt, Israel and the United States – culminating in the Camp David Peace Accords between Israel and Egypt. With those accords, Anwar Sadat signed his death warrant. He was assassinated in 1982 by militant Egyptian nationalists and Islamists opposed to the peace treaty with Israel. Sadat died for peace; his assassins died for justice. Sadat had negotiated peace without justice.

If Lumumba was a martyr to the sovereign integrity of the Congo, and Sadat was a martyr to regional peace in the Middle East, Murtala Muhammed was a martyr to the cause of disciplining Africa's largest national population – the Nigerians. The most persistent of all social and political pathologies of

Africa as a whole is corruption. Some African countries suffer from law and order problems, seeking a more effective system of law enforcement. Other African countries suffer from acute proneness to militarisation – with the armed forces repeatedly intervening in civilian politics. A third category of African countries suffers from a form of leadership without a sense of direction. But the most persistent of all post-colonial maladies in governance has been corruption. Unfortunately, Nigeria has often been ranked among the most corrupt of all countries in the world.

Murtala Muhammed entered this stage of history as a warrior against corruption. In the war against Biafra, he had been a man of action, but not necessarily a man of vision. But in Nigeria's war against corruption and indiscipline, Murtala Muhammed was a man of vision as well as action.

In this second war against indiscipline, Murtala Muhammed was not always committed to due process or to procedural fairness. It has been estimated that more than 10,000 public officials and public employees were sacked without benefits. Some were dismissed because of age or health, accused of being 'dead wood'. But more were dismissed for corruption, malpractice or incompetence. The axe was not limited to the civil service. There were purges in the armed forces, the police, the judiciary and the diplomatic service. There were trials on charges of corruption, and at least one state governor was executed for gross misconduct while in office.

Murtala Muhammed sought to rescue the Nigerian currency from the consequences of massive government expenditure on public works. He initiated the process of reducing the money supply, partly in order to keep inflation in check and partly to monitor money laundering.

Murtala Muhammed also recognised the fact that the public sector of the economy was a great source of corruption. One solution was to make the Nigerian economy more competitive in the hope of promoting efficiency and cost-effectiveness. He started encouraging the expansion of the private sector, both in new areas and in areas previously monopolised by public corporations.

Last, but not least, Murtala initiated the process of building a new capital for Nigeria: Abuja. Some may regard Abuja as his greatest monument.

And then, on 13 February 1976, Murtala Muhammed was assassinated while sitting in his car on a Lagos street. A prophet of discipline was silenced forever. The controversial hero entered the gates of martyrdom. Since then, an airport has been named after Murtala, schools have been named after him, an annual lecture was established, and even in the neighbouring Republic of Niger songs and poems were composed in the sacred memory of Murtala Muhammed. His face and name adorn the 20 *naira* note of the Nigerian currency.

But what is the significance of such heroic deeds and violent martyrdom in Africa's experience? How do these fluctuating fortunes affect the evolution of codes of conduct in post-colonial Africa? Let us now compare three heroes and martyrs in a narrow perspective, with a particular focus on Steve Biko.

Mandela, Lumumba and Biko

Since independence where have all the super-heroes gone? Great liberation fighters were not necessarily great nation-builders. The lustre has often faded from our super-heroes for two main reasons – first, most of the leaders, with honourable exceptions, were not as impressive in dealing with problems of independence as they had been in fighting for that independence.

After independence Africa produced a whole generation of young people deprived of super-heroes in the political domain. Africa has had heroes, but fewer and fewer super-heroes since the last years of colonial struggle – figures much larger than life were more common then than now. The one single towering political super-hero of the last years of the 20th century was Nelson Mandela, who has been in a class almost by himself.

What Africa produced instead of super-heroes in the last few decades of the 20th century was super-martyrs. Heroes are symbols of achievement – martyrs are symbols of sacrifice. Heroes are ultimate victors; martyrs are ultimate victims. Steve Biko and J.M. Kariuki were victims; Nelson Mandela survived to be a victor. Biko was a symbol of anguish; Mandela became a symbol of achievement.

What is different about Steve Biko in the annals of political martyrdom in Africa was that he was not a head of government like Patrice Lumumba or head of state like Sadat and Murtala, or even a high-ranking minister like Tom Mboya in Kenya. Steve Biko was just a liberation fighter in the vortex of racial politics.

But in his martyrdom Steve Biko can still be compared with a head of government like Patrice Lumumba or a head of state like Nelson Mandela.

Comparing Biko with Lumumba

Patrice Lumumba	Steve Biko
■ Patrice Lumumba was defending the territorial integrity of the Congo by opposing Katanga's secession under Moise Tshombe.	■ Steve Biko was defending the national and territorial integrity of South Africa by opposing the trend towards bantustans.
■ Lumumba was tortured and brought down by the forces of international imperialism and the conspiracies of Belgium, the United States and Moise Tshombe.	■ Biko was tortured and brought down by the forces of internalised racial colonisation of the apartheid era.
■ Lumumba, a pan-African leader of a country which was itself *not* pan-Africanist in either commitment or orientation.	■ Steve Biko was a tragic pan-African figure fighting for a country which was not yet pan-Africanist in either commitment or orientation.

Comparing Biko with Mandela

Nelson Mandela	Steve Biko
■ Mandela's martyrdom was by incarceration. He suffered more a life sentence in jail rather than a death sentence by execution.	■ Steve Biko's martyrdom was by physical elimination. He suffered a death sentence by execution rather than a life sentence without parole.
■ Martyrdom by imprisonment has the advantage of continuous mobilisation of supporters fighting for Mandela's release.	■ Martrydom by physical elimination has a greater shock effect at the time of death, but has reduced effectiveness in continuous capacity for mobilisation of supporters.
■ Imprisonment is a condition and not merely an event.	■ Murder is an event, not a condition.

- Mandela's 27 years in jail were bad for the leadership void of the internal struggle in South Africa, but good in giving the global struggle against apartheid a human focus of continuing martyrdom.

- Nelson Mandela's prolonged martyrdom encouraged pan-Africanism in others but he himself was more of a globalist than a pan-Africanist.

- When all is said and done, Mandela was a martyr to the struggle for multiculturalism and inter-racialism.

- Mandela lived long enough to transcend hate and racial hostility. He came to illustrate Africa's short memory of hatred.

- Steve Biko's torture and murder provided inspiration for the internal struggle against apartheid but relatively brief impact on the long-term global struggle against apartheid.

- Steve Biko was a pan-Africanist and not a globalist. Because of Biko's sensitivity to black unity, he might well be regarded as the first great South African pan-Africanist of the anti-apartheid struggle.

- When all is said and done, Steve Biko was a martyr to black nationalism and the struggle for black authenticity.

- The brutal treatment of Steve Biko as he was slowly tortured to death was a prescription for racial outrage. We shall never know for certain if Biko would have transcended it and illustrated Africa's short memory of hatred.

Conclusion

Outstanding political performance can be judged either by towering effort or by supreme sacrifice. Towering effort in pursuit of worthy goals produces heroes. Readiness to make a supreme sacrifice for great goals sometimes produces martyrs. In this paper we have compared and contrasted heroes and martyrs in the African experience, especially since the end of the Second World War in 1945.

The final decades of European colonialism in Africa produced a disproportionate number of heroes of liberation – from Kwame Nkrumah to Patrice Lumumba, from Léopold Senghor to Gamal Abdel Nasser, from Nnamdi Azikiwe to Joshua Nkomo. These leaders can be categorised under nine styles of leadership: charismatic, mobilisational, reconciliatory, disciplinarian, personalistic/monarchical, technocratic, housekeeping, and patriarchal. They also drew on four older cultural traditions of leadership in Africa: elder, monarchical, sage, and warrior traditions.

But not all great heroes of liberation were great nation-builders after independence. Many deteriorated into either weaklings or tyrants.

On the other hand, the post-colonial conditions in Africa produced a disproportionate number of martyrs – some were assassinated, others were victimised. Among those who were assassinated was Murtala Muhammed. Little more than 15 years after independence, he was the third Nigerian head of government to be killed. Steve Biko was a hero short of the pinnacle of power.

On balance, the anti-colonial struggle produced more heroes than has post-colonial Africa. But post-colonial Africa has produced more martyrs than did the last years of colonial rule.

There have been martyrs who have defended the sovereign integrity of their countries – among whom Steve Biko against South Africa's fragmentation and Patrice Lumumba of the larger Congolese republic are supreme examples. There have also been martyrs in the quest for peace – among whom Anwar Sadat is a controversial example of a quest for peace without a quest for justice.

Murtala Muhammed is almost unique as a martyr to discipline, one of the rarest commodities in post-colonial Africa. Some people regard Nigeria as the nearest African equivalent to the United States in size, legacy of federalism and market militancy. Murtala attacked corruption, indiscipline, and rank parasitism among the different sectors of the Nigerian elite. It is arguable that he was the greatest social reformer Nigeria has produced. In less than a year he shook Nigeria to the core in the quest for a more disciplined society.

Notes

1 For one analysis of comparative African leadership, see A. B. Assensoh (1998), *African Political Leadership: Jomo Kenyatta, Kwame Nkrumah and Julius K. Nyerere,* Malabar, FL: Krieger.

2 A Weberian discussion of Nkrumah as a charismatic leader may be found in E. O. Addo (1997) *Kwame Nkrumah: A Case Study of Religion and Politics in Ghana,* Lanham, MD: University Press of America, especially pp. 22–23 and pp. 99–122.

3 See Gordon Matatu, 'The End of Uganda's Nightmare,' in *Africa,* May 1979, pp. 10–16.

4 These divisions make Nigeria difficult to govern; see Simeon O. Ilesanmi (1997), *Religious Pluralism and the Nigerian State,* Athens, OH: Ohio University Center for International Studies, and Joseph A. Umoren (1996), *Democracy and Ethnic Diversity In Nigeria,* Lanham, MD: University Press of America.

5 For a biography, see Dennis Wepman (1985), *Jomo Kenyatta,* New York: Chelsea House Publishers.

6 A portrait of this leader may be found in Brian Titley (1997), *Dark Age: The Political Odyssey of Emperor Bokassa,* Montreal; Buffalo: McGill-Queen's University Press.

7 For a biography of Senghor, see Janet G. Vaillant (1990), *Black, French and African: A Life of Léopold Sédar Senghor,* Cambridge, MA: Harvard University Press.

8 See Ali A. Mazrui (1977), *The Warrior Tradition in Modern Africa,* Leiden: Brill.

9 Politically, Uganda has been involved in the Great Lakes crisis; see *The Economist,* 23 September, 2000, pp. 51–52. Economically, before the intervention, it appeared that Uganda may have good economic prospects under Museveni; see Robert L. Sharer, Hemar R. De Zoysa and Calvin A. McDonald (1995), *Uganda: Adjustment With Growth, 1987–94,* Washington, DC: IMF.

The Trouble with Nigeria revisited

Chinua Achebe

Chinua Achebe is the father of the African novel and one of the continent's leading intellectuals. His generation inherited the post-colonial African state. Through his works of fiction (Things Fall Apart, No Longer at Ease, Arrow of God, Man of the People, *and* Anthills of the Savannah) *he has explored how Africans moved from their pre-colonial societies, to being dominated by the colonial order, and then to managing the various states of freedom that came with independence.*

Watching, with growing anger, the never-ending crises – political instability and a coup in 1966, the Biafran war a year later, followed by rampant corruption in the 1970s – he offered his fellow countrymen a trenchant analysis of their condition in the short but pithy 1983 essay, The Trouble with Nigeria. *The book identified a number of issues that had prevented a country with vast potential from becoming the African superpower that Achebe saw as its destiny. In Achebe's view, Nigeria had already lost its way in the 20th century because of the evils of corruption, tribalism, social injustice, indiscipline, arrogance, mediocrity, lack of patriotism, lack of national purpose, and, above all – and linking all of these – a lack of leadership.*

Onyekachi Wambu met him 23 years later, in upstate New York where Achebe lives and works, to reflect on these issues and the wider conundrum of leadership in post-colonial Africa.

Onyekachi Wambu

In 1983 you wrote *The Trouble with Nigeria*. I wanted to see, after 23 years reflecting on it, whether some of the main problems you had identified that underpinned poor leadership were still pertinent. You talked about the group of people that led Nigeria to independence – and identified at least two of them, the nationalist leaders – Nnamdi Azikiwe ('Zik of Africa') and Obafemi Awolowo – as being 'self-centred and pedestrian'. You talked about them possessing a 'pious materialistic woolliness' at a time Nigeria needed 'intellectual rigour and objectivity' in her leaders. Do you still think that that was one of the major problems regarding Nigeria's current lack of development – that the people who led us into independence were not of the right calibre?

Chinua Achebe

We have been victims of a history that we did not make – the history of colonisation and the merging of peoples that was not at their own initiative. It was the initiative of the coloniser to make things easier for himself. It was a coloniser who was quite greedy – who wanted their colony to grow as big as possible – as big as India. So we got Nigeria, and we can't just get up one morning and say we don't want this any more. We are stuck with it.

There are so many things that have happened that we cannot change.

One of the most fundamental is that age no longer confers any authority on anybody. It took our people quite a while to get used to this: that young people have inherited the power of leadership. In one of my novels it is hinted at – or perhaps even more clearly than hinted at – it is mentioned that things are now done not in the name of the father, but in the name of the son who goes to school. So the time was foreseen when the old people would become irrelevant and would learn to seek permission from their sons. There is nowhere that I know where people deliberately created such a system for themselves. This was imposed by the demand of colonisation – that what counts is whether you speak English, whether you read and write and so on. We have been struggling with that. But how do you select a leader in this context? The next thing they gave us were elections which produced the Ziks and the Awolowos.

Now, what I am suggesting is that the basis for this selection was flawed. How do you select the best person for this rather confusing situation that we were in – there is real confusion. This is not something that has a simple answer that I can get up and say the answer is one, two, three and that would be it. A people's whole lifestyle has been changed over their heads and they find themselves ruled by people they did not really choose. Just standing in line somewhere and putting paper in a box is a system that is, of course, very easily corrupted – and it produced the people we have to this day. So what we are struggling to achieve is how to make this acceptable, because we can't achieve the optimum, the best in this kind of situation. How can we find a way to be managing this very difficult situation so that it does not get completely out of control?

OW

There is a sense in which we are all disappointed with progress in Nigeria. But the ambition of trying to pull Nigeria together is a huge, huge job. In fact every day that Nigeria stays together is a miracle. So I have become a little bit more humble about the enormity of what is going on. In the UK at the moment, I think two to four per cent of the population are Muslims, and the place is nearly going mad trying to hold things together – trying to find a consensus that everybody can live under. In Nigeria, with about a 50/50 split between Christians and Muslims, there are different ways of organising communities – in the north the Caliphate system, in the west the Yoruba system, in the mid west the Benin system, in the middle north the Tiv, and in the east the Igbo system, plus many others – and one is trying to bring all this together to find a common system for selecting and electing leadership. Is this period of transition itself really the reason for the frustrations and the disappointment? Or is the real failure that of leadership, perhaps because somebody with sufficient vision has not come along and knitted all of these peoples together and articulated a way forward?

CA

It is a miracle to get any kind of stability from the mixture that is Nigeria. Nigerians are not alone, though, in getting credit for this. Senegal has 90 per cent or more Muslims. And yet the first President Léopold Senghor, a highly educated man, a poet, was able to lead it into independence. He was a Roman Catholic who left the seminary at the last moment. He was French, virtually. And yet he was able to keep Senegal together to achieve independence from France. So we can ask ourselves why it is possible there, and why Nigeria is not as marvellous as Senegal? Senghor did not get there by rigged elections but simply by making the Senegalese feel safe and not threatened by religion or by ethnicity. He came from a tiny protectorate of the French – a kingdom apart from the big population of Senegal. Those are examples we can use.

This is why the story of Nigeria did not stay as impressive as it ought to have been. Since the achievement of independence, given the wealth, human resources, the country of great potential – why don't we move to the next stage? We seem to be stuck. Nigeria should not be regarded today in terms of Third-World, bottom-of-the-line in anything – whether it is democracy or whatever. We have had enough experience to have taken one or two steps you can count on. I thought we could count on stable transitions from regime to regime – I thought we had got there. But what is going on today (ahead of the 2007 presidential elections) is a clearly planned intention to make the concept of stability of transition a myth just as (the military dictator) Babangida had done in 1993.

OW

You talked about Senghor – yes, he did remove people's fears concerning religion. Yes, he did create some kind of stability – and he stayed in power for a long time – but eventually he went, so the transition was possible. But the other thing he seemed to have was a vision for Senegal. How important was that? At one point in *The Trouble with Nigeria.* you talked about Nigeria being a providential state: Here's what you said: '[There are] individuals as well as nations, who on account of peculiar gifts and circumstances, are commandeered by history to facilitate mankind's advancement. Nigeria is such a nation.' You talked about Nigeria in that sense. But none of the leaders that have emerged from Nigeria seem to have had a sense of that purpose.

CA

That's my anger. That is what I am complaining about. That is why I mentioned Senghor. I can give a thousand reasons why he didn't do the right thing at different points and so on but you do need this one central vision of '*my people*' – these are *my people* – no matter whether Christians or Muslims, these are *my people*, no matter whether they are Yoruba, Hausa, or Ibibio – someone who will come out and declare that stand and be credible. Everybody declares it – which is another problem – but we don't speak the truth about this. It is hard and difficult to run a place like Nigeria. It is hard – but you must begin from the conviction that these are *my people* – that they have lived together as neighbours, even though they were not called Nigerians, for thousands of years. We are not told that they were fighting wars every single day in that area known as Nigeria today. So they were neighbours. We lack that vision. It is part of the lack of knowledge of the youth – because they took over from the old people. The vision that they should have brought from their education seems not to be there.

OW

But if they went to mission schools (or the modern schools), who was going to give them that vision? One of the interesting things that we got from you, those of us who read you and for whom you have provided an incredible example, is that even though you went to the mission school – you also looked at the traditional structures. And most of us only understand the traditional structures through your work. And I don't mean what we usually see in our villages – a group of men and women carrying out unfathomable rituals – but you allowed us to understand the deeper meaning behind the rituals. Being able to look at that space as a real political space – not just that your uncle is dressed up and chanting endless proverbs – but that he is somebody who is doing something very important. However, these other young people they went into the mission schools or other schools influenced by the philosophy of the mission, but didn't seem to come out with a sense that their own communities were important – that these should have been the very foundation or template. You never see that understanding translated into reality – certainly not with the military leaders who ruled Nigeria. You never get that sense of this deeper community.

CA

Well this is why we are where we are. I am not sure what the magic was or should be for making education really important – it is not merely to acquire the ability to read and write but to move to the next stage – of humane and progressive awareness of what makes a civilised society work. There is a sense in which a mission school can kill somebody – kill because it can give a sense of righteousness, you know – we are the good people, the people of God and the others, as my people say, are the people of nothing. '*Ndi Nkiti*', that's what we called them, the Heathen. That is the danger spot. If education does not address that issue – then having children take over from their fathers will be a real disaster. Because their fathers didn't quite have that vision but they had an equivalent vision of *my people* based on kinship – blood is sacred! They had things like that they would almost – and I hate to quote Conrad – '*bow down to*'. This is why you feel you have to blame somebody – the person who offers himself as a leader. How do you accept such a person, what conditions are necessary? What does he or she have to fulfil before you say be my leader, be my ruler? All that for us is quite chaotic today.

OW

In your novel *Arrow of God*, which I have always loved and found incredibly profound, there is a moment when the six villages that form the universe of the novel are menaced by the Abam head-hunters. In the face of this new menace the villages come together and actually create a new political community, and they create a new leader, essentially the priest at the centre of the novel. But they deliberately select this priest from the weakest village.

CA

Which is interesting because look at the leaders in Africa who come from the smallest group – we talked about Senghor. Nyerere is another, in Tanzania, from the small ethnic group that does not threaten anybody – it is the same thing those in Umuaro (the new enlarged community in *Arrow of God*) were doing – let's give it to those who are not going to swallow us.

OW

So we have always been able, through peaceful means, to create these larger political communities and economies – in that instance in *Arrow of God* (and I know it was fictional) it seemed to work until they were threatened by the arrival of an even bigger menace – the British. However, lots of societies and bigger Igbo towns were created in a similar way – through consensus, while facing a threat. At that moment of creation in *Arrow of God* I thought there was also something magical. I am not sure what it was that they swore on or 'bowed down to' as Conrad put it – but it seems to me that what happens is that a new spirit, *Ulu*, emerges in the land – and literally speaking the priest is the custodian of this new *Ulu* spirit. Everyone bows down before it. How important is that in the context of Nigeria? The flag came down, but there was never a spiritual sense of how you create this new entity which was bigger than everybody. It was never magical in that sense. I don't know whether you know what I mean?

CA

I think I do. I don't know what the answer is. My suspicion is that there was something wrong – that wasn't quite genuine in the making of Nigeria. I felt I was physically there when Ghana achieved its independence in 1957 – the night that the Union Jack came down and the Black Star went up. Nkrumah was shedding tears when they played their national anthem. I was in Lagos then – I remember we stayed up until 1 a.m. – which was something you didn't do – in order to hear Ghana's independence on the radio. It was as if everybody in Lagos was staying up to listen to the moment. I don't know whether Nigerians watched their own independence with the same zeal. There was something magical about Nkrumah's rise to power and his suffering for it, and his strength and conviction. He did make mistakes, as we know. But in Nigeria, the process seemed to have been wangled.

OW

It is interesting that you should mention that again. Look at the similarities between Nkrumah and Senghor, here again was a man with great vision, somebody who wrestled with the big issues of the day and tried to make sense of them in his writing. Nkrumah also came from a small group within Ghana, but inside was this vision. He takes the name Ghana – he has a real idea of history in the context of West Africa, whereas with Nigeria you get the sense that when it was being put together it was pedestrian, as you say. In London people used to be critical and passionless about Prime Minister Blair because initially he ruled through all these focus groups. Nigeria seems to have been put together by focus groups – for example the national anthem decided as a result of a competition, the name suggested by [the former colonial Governor] Lugard's, girlfriend [later wife] Flora Shaw. It does seem to be a space, beyond individual survival, that nobody cares passionately about.

CA

It's a pity. I blame it on the colonialist because I don't think it was at all accidental. You see, when I say wangling I think there was something about the arrangement of Nigeria that was deceitful. People like Sir James Robertson who was flown in from Sudan to be Governor General for the last couple of years – these were people who were very proficient in manoeuvring people leading to where Sudan is today – virtually handing power to the Arabs and sidelining the Africans. This was the man who was sent to fix Nigeria. Britain was constantly comparing Nigeria and Sudan – these were the two critical countries in Africa. So what came out of it, all that manoeuvring, was a country that didn't inspire too much confidence; a country that was inclined to go for the third rate; where we don't really need brilliant philosophers; where anybody can do.

OW

Reading Chinweizu's contribution to this book, one of the concepts he meditates upon is this idea that leaders need to be trying to carry out *something*. They need a purpose. If the state itself has no purpose – then the leaders have no purpose. And according to Chinweizu, even so long ago, the ancient Egyptians were clear about what the purpose of their state was about – *Maat*. I was quite interested in some of the ideas you touched upon in *The Trouble with Nigeria* when you discussed the purpose of leadership. The three main virtues you mentioned were truthfulness, peace and social justice – these are almost the Maatian ideals of the Egyptian state. And the Egyptians also had the notion of the Pharaoh as embodying and carrying out God's law, and these three values were the essence of God's law. I was wondering why after 4,000 years we are still wrestling in Africa with pretty fundamental things. For instance between 4,000 and 5,000 years ago administrator and philosopher Ptahhotep said: 'Be not evil, it is good to be kindly. Cause thy monument to endure through love of thee. Then men thank God on thine account, men praise thy goodness and pray for thine health. Honour the great and prosper thy people; good is it to work for the future.'

We all know this – and we know why there is chaos in Nigeria. You highlight the issues in *The Trouble with Nigeria* – corruption, indiscipline, etc. – but why has this message not been absorbed in terms of the leadership class? Before you answer – the other point that Chinweizu raises is that to ensure *Maat*, there was a need to train the civil servants and the bureaucracy – as the Chinese would have done in terms of the principles of Confucianism. So there was a deliberate policy that in order to produce *Maat* you had to undergo education in *Maat*. I was wondering whether the two things are linked in Nigeria?

CA

They are linked. You have already said so in terms of the vision. Where there is no vision – people don't survive. So 5,000 years ago our people knew about it – it doesn't mean that today 5,000 years later everybody knows – '*knows*' – in quotes, underlined. It is one thing to hear about something – it is something else to 'know'. *To know is really to believe.* It is not something you say to be acceptable. That's not knowledge. If you really know this, if the leaders really knew this – they would believe that social justice and maintenance of peace are linked, and if there is no justice, then peace is out of the window. Our ancestors simplified those things, and made them look easy.

OW

One Nigerian leader you spoke about with real affection in *The Trouble with Nigeria* was Aminu Kano, the radical politician from the North. What qualities made him such an exemplary leader for you?

CA

Aminu Kano's vision of politics and leadership was the promise to empower the common people. Although he was himself of the ruling class in northern Nigeria, his political career was one long struggle against the powerful on behalf of the weak. The Prime Minister of Nigeria, Abubakar Tafawa Balewa once made a comment – half joke and half exasperation – that if Aminu Kano became Prime Minister he would be found the next day leading a demonstration against the government.

Aminu Kano was uncomfortable sitting on the same side of the table as authority. The image of him that I treasure above all others was his appearance at the Kampala Peace Talks, one of the abortive efforts to end the Biafran war. Aminu Kano was on the Federal Government delegation. Or perhaps I should say that his body was on the Federal Government side. I was a member of the Biafran delegation. The two delegations sat staring stonily at each other across the room, while the two leaders held a fruitless debating contest. The leader of the Federal Government delegation was a well-known, rather showy politician, eloquent and condescending. He declared at one point that Biafrans were not a state but a state of mind. The leader of the Biafran delegation was a Chief Justice, a highly respected jurist, careful in his language and restrained in his delivery.

Aminu Kano, who I did not know well, made a very strong impression on me. He was not looking at us, or at anything in the room. He did not seem to be listening to the debate. He was looking outside through a window close to him. He seemed pained and profoundly sad. Quite clearly he was not part of the triumphalist mood of his delegation.

OW

We have focused on political power – but there is a way in which art and artists can influence things by providing vision. Do you think in Nigeria there has been – not a failure perhaps, because I think your generation has done better than mine in terms of thinking, talking or writing about these issues – but do you think that if there is a vision hole in Nigeria, it is perhaps because artists have not projected anything in there?

CA

Yes, well, it is possible for artists to fail in the area of vision. I am not saying we did. I think the artists of my generation did what they were capable of doing – most of them. But it is not something that you do once, it is something which is continuous. In fact I am little suspicious of the generational argument because what is required has not changed – which is that there should be peace, justice, and prosperity in the land. People should be safe.

The easiest failure for the artists is when he begins to say: 'that is politics – what I am doing is art.' Once you get into that I don't really have very much to say to anybody because it seems to me to be a fundamental failure to understand why we are doing what we are doing. Nobody wrote a law to say we should create art – it is something that comes out of us. 'I have a story, I want to tell it, would you like to hear it?' This seems to be one of the marks of humanity. We see the world but that is not enough. It's fine as far as it goes, but we also want to create a world. Or to make this world better. That is another thing Igbos take from their culture – the necessity for continuous development of the world. God did not finish the creation work. He began it but he has been holding conversations with our ancestors when things didn't quite work. When they couldn't eat, didn't find enough food – he gave them yam. He said go and plant it. They planted it and it didn't work because 'the earth then was a swamp', as Eze Duru, still sitting on the anthill, said. And God asked, 'what is happening, I gave you yam?' Eze Duru said: 'the sand is not good'. God said: 'Then go to the blacksmith in Akwa and let them bring their bellows to work on the soil'. And that is how agriculture came into existence, you see. So, no generation has its work done. If there is no work, you invent work.

OW

That is part of the Igbo creation myth. How much of this lack of vision – I come back to it again perhaps because I am becoming obsessed with it – but how much of it is due to the fact that there isn't really a similar creation myth for Nigeria.

CA

I am sure that if you look at the creation myths that are there you will find equivalents in the other cultures in Nigeria.

OW

No, I mean one that everybody buys into. What we have are regional creation myths?

CA

That's because we didn't get to that point [beyond regionalism to nationhood]. The British sort of took over the show quite a while ago and they are still at it. Even if there are things in the myths of different nations that make up Nigeria, I don't know them and there is nobody in hurry to work along those lines as far as I know. It was not in the interest of Britain when she left to say you must learn about each other, on the contrary.

OW

But hasn't that been evolving anyway? For instance, I remember when the great Afro-beat musician, Fela died, we had a wake in London. Everybody gathered (naturally Yorubas, but there were Igbos, Hausas, lots of different Nigerians) around a Nigerian restaurant in Brixton. It was actually quite moving – there were former members of Fela's band and we sang the songs and you realised that we all shared something. And I suddenly saw the possibilities of somebody – again it was an artist – who could hold everybody together inside his own story. And I am not suggesting that Fela is this person, but it seems to me that something has been quietly happening over the last 46 years and some of those stories – the Biafran war, the Niger Delta tragedy, the hanging of Ken Saro-Wiwa, in 1993, and the cancelling of the elections by President Babaginda – mean something to those of us who are Nigerian. We are creating a common Nigerian story but there is a sense in which it is still fragmentary – one doesn't feel it is yet tangible.

CA

It has to be that way to begin with. One thing I would advise is that we must not be too impatient. A certain impatience is appropriate – but not when it moves into despair – at that point it ceases to work. If there is a genuine moment in our history which should be remembered and honoured we should talk about it. Leadership comes into this – because it is not the men in the street who arrange these things. We should celebrate moments of success in this experiment called Nigeria. I don't go as far as some people who have virtually come to the conclusion that Nigeria should be dissolved. I come close now and again but I like to think that we shouldn't really fail because the experiment does not seem so difficult – just respect your next door neighbour, be fair, don't carry the wealth of the nation and send it abroad, outsourcing Nigeria's wealth. Put in place a few fundamentals – we should not give up yet.

OW

There have been a lot of experiments to find ways of selecting/electing the leader. One may cynically call the first coup an experiment of sorts. Then with the return to civilian rule in 1979, we abandoned the British parliamentary system of first past the post, within a regional framework. Now we are trying the American presidential system, within a federal framework of 36 states; we are now talking about a power shift, the rotation of the presidency around – I don't know whether it would be six zones, or two zones (the north and the south) – who knows how many natural zones there really are in the country? The country has been trying different experiments – which of the models do you think might endure?

CA

I think that whatever will remove the almost obsessive hold that power has for the leader. Anything that downgrades the importance of the presidency. It is not the president that is the centre of life in the country, it is the people. Therefore anything that makes the office of the president less attractive, I welcome. I know I am putting it badly but all I am trying to emphasise is, can we just elect a president and move on to other things.

OW

How much is this model of a weak president to do with your own Igbo background and the system of a council of elders where the king or chief is not seen as particularly important, but is sort of a first among elders?

CA

It probably is to do with it – but it's part of the human experience. And if it is helpful to anybody, anywhere, they should use it. Don't be obsessed by the power of the presidency, and the way to achieve that is to spread out the power. The president doesn't have to be minister of oil. He does not have to control the treasury, it is not his money. There are so many other people and institutions that can handle other areas of our need. That to me is what to look for. And this, of course, is what everybody who wants to be president wants to keep, so that he can become a dictator, even if he is going around calling himself a democrat. Democracy is really important. It is important – it is not a joke.

As for the Igbos they looked at size, the size of the community. They did not look for an empire. They did not even admire kingdoms that much. They wanted something they could handle. They came to the conclusion that the optimum size was the size of the village as they constructed it throughout Igbo land.. I don't know how many there are, but the size of the village is not something huge. They knew about huge places – they knew about the neighbouring Benin Empire, and its soldiers. The villagers did not want soldiers. That is something we should look at. Why did they choose a village?

The Igbo people went far in establishing the uniqueness of the village. Each village was created by God. It is not related to the next one. I was absolutely staggered when I realised that – that God went around creating village after village. In my town, God created one man, Ezeochupuagha, 'the king that drives away war'. And then he went further. He walked some distance and created another man – the man who founded the town of Ukwele – novelist Cyprian Ekwensi's people, *Ukwele Uzumaaka*. So the man who God created there was *Uzuma aka*. Then God created the river Nkisi between them as a boundary. So the planning of the world in the view of the Igbos is not on a vast scale, but on a small scale. They know about kings – they probably played around with kings sometime in their history. But they found the best arrangement was this one, where you knew everybody, and you could have direct democracy, where you meet all the time. Even if you don't call it a meeting there is a conversation going on all the time. If we can capture that idea of making everybody count in Nigeria – because that is what it amounts to – then it would be good. When the meeting is on everybody can go. It is not a secret affair, what is discussed is of importance to everybody.

OW

A lot of our talk about leadership has been about men. How important is it to bring women into leadership in Africa? I know you have talked and written about this quite a lot recently. How important would having a female leader change the dynamics of these issues?

CA

Women are entitled to become leaders without any reason – they are there. They are more than 50 per cent of the population. So they should be represented accordingly unless they don't want to – I have known women, especially old woman, who more or else felt about politics – 'I have something more important to do'. And if you look at the nature of the world, you sometimes think that God intended woman to be more serious than the men. There is a part of Igboland that has a story about how God left the world because he was being bothered. In the first case the trouble he had was being invaded very early in the morning by the community, crying about something they wanted him to do. First, somebody's cow had died and it was the only cow, and God said OK and brought the cow back to life. The next day it was a chicken. The chicken was the thing that broke the camel's back. God packed up and left his house in the middle of the village. But before he left, he appointed the village women to look after his shrine. And his shrine was four trees, Ogili seeds, a sacred tree, very slim, not a huge tree, and it is the women he put in charge. Very simple, four trees, not a cathedral.

So, when we say what role will we give women, it is not really up to us to give women any roles. They will take what roles they want. I don't think we should say every other president must be a woman. It may not work, but we can't say a woman cannot be president, that is stupid. What they want, they are entitled to have as citizens like everybody else. If this takes them into business or politics, so be it. The example of Liberia [the election of Ellen Johnson-Sirleaf in 2005] is really one that we should treasure. The fact that it happened is really a miracle. Africa, in spite of bad news, occasionally throws up something which is miraculous.

OW

Nigeria is about to relaunch itself. There is a big campaign where the country will rebrand itself as the 'Heart of Africa'.

CA

I hadn't heard that . . . but the thing about Nigeria is surviving the good intentions. I will deviate slightly. Occasionally I have had to say to my countrymen that something is a wonderful idea – I hope we can keep it and keep doing it. But there are too many examples where this did not happen. For example when I visited Nigeria in 1999 I was honoured for my contribution to the Arts and given a prize in money, I said in the acceptance speech – 'I hope this will go on to recognise artists every year'. And the minister said, 'no, this is not a guarantee – only if there is a good one'. I said there will be a good artist every year to give a prize to. But they never continued. That was the second time – the first time I got the Governor General's prize for my second novel, *No Longer at Ease*, from Zik, and there was maybe one more Governor General's prize and that was it. We must learn to stay the course, if we select something and say this is good, let's try and remember it. If we do it once a year let's do it. We tend to be full of enthusiasm, but only for a short time.

So, back to the Heart of Africa. Nigeria is big enough to call itself anything it wants. It is no joke to have a quarter of the population of Africa living in one country, no joke to have a country with the traditions and art of Nok alone, the bronzes not only of Ife, but Benin. We can call ourselves Heart of Africa – but let's mean it.

OW

I was just interested in this because I have felt this as a Nigerian – that sometimes you are quite reticent about putting yourself out. I remember I had to do a meeting recently in London and the subject was 'Is Nigeria an obstacle to pan-Africanism?' So I went along and there was this general disappointment with Nigeria. My speech was a conceit, namely that if most Africans in one space are in Nigeria and Nigeria is trying an experiment to bring them together, it cannot be an obstacle to pan-Africanism, it can only be furthering the pan-African vision. I thought I detected some defensiveness from some of the audience. On the one hand other Africans want Nigeria to play a big role, but immediately you take the role of leadership seriously, people get fearful of a 'big Nigeria', which might want to dominate them. So is there a sense that Nigerians themselves get quite timid about projecting the potential of this huge country and the leadership thing is part of this crisis of timidity? I mean somebody stood up and said that the first Nigerian Prime Minister Tafawa Balewa was a traitor to pan-Africanism because he said at independence he would rather concentrate on building Nigeria than the Nkrumahist vision of uniting the continent.

CA

There was that problem. That is part of what I was thinking about when I said this thing was fixed. Britain was very much behind the separation of Ghana and Nigeria. Ghana was too troublesome. People like Balewa were just right for Britain. It took strikes and marches by students at the University of Ibadan to get rid of a British Permanent Secretary for Balewa. There is rivalry – Nigeria is big and Ghana may be a bit resentful. So some said we know Nigeria is bigger than Ghana but in the same way that one penny is bigger than three pence!

OW

Having talked briefly about Nigeria within Africa, I was going to ask you more broadly about Africa, the West, China and India – but I think that is another conversation for another day. Thank you for your thoughts on leadership.

Mandela and Mbeki: contrasting leadership styles, but shared visions for Africa's renaissance

William Gumede

William Gumede is the author of the ground-breaking book, Thabo Mbeki and the Battle for the Soul of the ANC. *He is a former Deputy Editor of* The Sowetan, *the largest-selling newspaper in South Africa. And as a journalist, he has chronicled the achievements of the post-apartheid African National Congress governments, led since 1994 by Nelson Mandela and Thabo Mbeki. Inspired by the vision of an African renaissance, these governments have arguably become the most respected and successful African governments of recent years, in a short period establishing a non-racial democracy with effective checks and balances, a stable economy, and programmes of social justice that have housed and empowered millions. Gumede explores the differing leadership styles of Mandela and Mbeki, and looks at the legacy the two 'Ms' leave for those who will take over the mantle of leadership in the future.*

Vision

Nelson Mandela and Thabo Mbeki, though having contrasting leadership styles, have both tried to use individual exemplary leadership to take their country from the ashes of the crippling racial divisions and inequality of apartheid to the uplands of unity, peace and economic development that would match the industrial West.

Furthermore, both hoped that through such exemplary individual leadership, they would set a new gold standard for African leadership, not only one that others might emulate, but one that would bring to an end the widely held negative perceptions of African political leadership both on the continent and in the West.

Nelson Mandela and Thabo Mbeki shared similar visions for their country and their continent. Both believed that they were not only leaders of South Africa, but were destined to provide leadership to the whole of Africa and the developing world, by virtue of South Africa's unique experience of achieving peace and democracy – on a continent not viewed as a beacon of peace – and where 'Balkanisation' appeared to be the norm elsewhere. Both Mandela and Mbeki argued that the end of apartheid in South Africa would be the beginning of an African political, economic, cultural and social awakening that would spread through the continent, and once and for all would slay the perception of the continent as 'lost', and indeed, would trigger an African renaissance.

Both Mandela and Mbeki believed that a predominantly black leadership in South Africa should also give moral and political leadership to other developing countries, beyond Africa. Mbeki made lobbying for a just world for Africa and developing countries into a pillar of his presidency: giving more voice to African and developing countries in international bodies such as the UN. His aim was to make the international trade and financial regimes – skewed in favour of the rich industrial West and against poor developing countries – more equitable. Mbeki was one of the key drivers in organising developing countries into the G20 bloc. Here for the first time they became a force in global trade negotiations against the hypocrisy of the West, which argues that developing countries should practise free trade, while at the same time refusing to lift impregnable trade barriers to products from the developing world. Beyond trade, Mandela and Mbeki often publicly criticised unilateral US action, for example in Iraq or against Cuba. Both argued rightly for greater democracy rather than unilateralism in global decision-making, including over ways to resolve threats to international security.

Upon taking power Mandela and Mbeki were intent on disproving negative perceptions of Africans and Africa both by whites within South Africa and the 'white' West. Successive white apartheid governments claimed if blacks came to power, the economy would be mismanaged. They frequently pointed to mismanagement north of the Limpopo – the river border between South Africa and its northern neighbours. Mandela and Mbeki went out of their way to prove the African National Congress (ANC) to be a black government that could manage the country's economy prudently. During the first decade of South Africa's democracy the ANC was so intent on pursuing orthodox economics to prove its sensible economic management credentials that, even though it had the financial capacity, it cut social spending to its expectant supporters – leaving them destitute – rather than expand welfare and risk being tarnished by the brush of profligacy often associated with many African countries. Indeed, the ANC under Mbeki has now gained a reputation for economic efficiency, after restoring macro-economic stability to a country that was on its knees following decades of Nationalist Party misrule. But in so doing, it has postponed making a frontal assault on the terrible legacy of apartheid by focusing on redistribution and extending welfare services to South Africa's expectant poor black people, instead perpetuating the huge inequality between a predominantly rich white elite and poor black majority.

Mbeki has worked extremely hard on changing negative perceptions of African economic management that plagued the continent. A few months into his presidency in 1999, he launched the New Partnership for Africa's Development (NEPAD), a continent-wide policy blueprint based on good governance, democracy and human rights. So a central ambition for Mbeki is to slay the dragon of Afro-pessimism by engineering an internal change in the governance culture of Africa – and so portray a more positive image of the continent. Underlying this is the idea that Africans themselves should take the initiative to resolve their problems – 'African solutions for Africa's problems'. In both his philosophy of the African renaissance and its policy platform (NEPAD) the basic tenet is not to reinvent new ideas, but to combine African institutions and policies that work with relevant ones from the West. Furthermore, Mbeki argues that since the end of the Cold War there has been a growing international consensus on human rights and good governance. NEPAD is an attempt to secure wide Africa buy-in to the consensus and to link the marginal continent back into the global political and economic market chain. Africa will be lifted up to the level of the developed world, by using globalisation to its advantage and piggy-backing on existing technology such as IT, and also by better utilisation of Africa's own resources.

Mandela made a point of limiting his presidency to one term. This was a message to other African leaders that overstaying their welcome has created a major problem of African leadership and has certainly contributed to negative perceptions of the continent. Mandela was deeply disappointed in Zimbabwe's Robert Mugabe for not taking this important lesson to heart and to insist on staying on, so reinforcing the ugly perception of African leaders as preferring to die in power rather than relinquish it. Mbeki has made it clear that he will not extend his presidential stay beyond two terms. White opposition parties in South Africa have tried to show that Mbeki is likely to follow other African leaders and change the constitution to stay on beyond his two terms. This is precisely the negative perception of many white South Africans and the West that Mbeki has been trying to prove wrong. He has therefore lobbied many African leaders, including Zambia's Frederick Chiluba, Nigeria's Olusegun Obasanjo, Mozambique's Joaquim Chissano and Namibia's Sam Nujoma, not to overstay their terms in government.

Both Mbeki and Mandela have exhibited great political flexibility. Mandela was the first to abandon the ANC's bedrock of nationalisation when it became an albatross around the movement's neck in the early 1990s. He did so when most of the ANC's membership was not in favour of dropping it. Similarly, Mbeki was one of the strongest proponents of the ANC to abandon the armed struggle when it prepared for negotiations with the apartheid regime. At the time the ANC's militant wing demanded the continuation of the armed struggle. Years before, Mbeki was among the first ANC leaders who, in the mid 1980s, began talking to white leaders and businessmen linked to the apartheid regime to sound them out about negotiations for a democratic South Africa. Many ANC cadres attacked Mbeki on both occasions as 'soft' and a 'sell-out'. Indeed, Mbeki most probably set a great example in South African leadership, showing that leadership does not mean populism or demagogy and that there is a place for a leader without charisma and popular appeal.

Gandhi and Nehru

Mandela and Mbeki have had a complex relationship with each other, partly due to their often contrasting leadership styles. For the closest historical parallel, one has to jump continents: the relationship between Mahatma (Great Soul) Gandhi and Jawaharlal Nehru, India's Prime Minister at independence.[1] Mandela admits to having drawn inspiration from Gandhi. Gandhi pushed Nehru to the top of the Indian Congress Party. Mandela's blessing of Mbeki – even if reluctant, as it turned out later – sealed his rise to the presidency against very formidable rivals such as Cyril Ramaphosa, Mathews Phosa and Tokyo Sexwale.

All over the world the figure of Mandela has become the grand symbol of South Africa's transition from the brutalities of apartheid to that of a liberal, non-racial democracy. Often, the transition is described as a political miracle: many believed the conflict in South Africa was so intractable that a peaceful solution and reconciliation between black and white was nigh impossible. Mandela, who spent almost three decades imprisoned by the apartheid regime for his political activism against the brutal system, became a symbol of the 'miracle' transition. His ability to seemingly forgive and to look towards the future was symbolic of the incredibly 'fairy-tale' foundations of the new democracy.

Mandela's historic contribution to the infant democracy was to help cobble together a broad-based consent for the new democratic order. His purpose was to 'carve out a new breathing space where pulses could settle, enmities subdue, and affinities become recast'.[2] So, the Mandela era would be indelibly associated with the early formative years of the new democracy: the new policy-making process, building the new institutions, the legislative overhauls, and the early trust building – so essential – between the different groups who once stared at each other over the barrel of a gun. Throughout the transition, his leadership helped to maintain the majority black poor's trust and loyalty towards the ANC, as well as ease the fears of the predominantly white middle class, pampered and pandered to during white rule, and frightened of black majority rule.[3]

Mandela, like Mbeki, is very conscious of his position in history. He wants to be remembered by future generations as the amazing man who emerged from 27 years in prison, without rancour, to lead a divided South Africa to racial reconciliation. Mandela said as much when he addressed mainly students at the University of Potchefstroom in February 1996. 'I will pass through this world but once,'[4] he said. 'And I do not want to divert my attention from my task – which is to unite the nation.' Even more revealing was Mandela's next sentence in that address. 'I am writing my own testament because I am nearing my end. I want to be able to sleep till eternity with a broad smile on my face knowing that the youth, opinion-makers and everybody is stretching across the divide, trying to unite the nation.'[5]

Mandela's leadership comes from his moral authority. Indeed, Mandela's broad societal authority was akin to that of a benign patriarch, guided by the principles of inclusivity. For Mandela the moral integrity of a leader is crucial. Through moral integrity, he believes the real leader exercises leadership and is able to lead people to a consensus. Mandela broadly centred his presidency on the concept of a traditional chief presiding over his community. The South African public law expert George Devenish writes that although the common view is often that the chief 'possessed unlimited power and was able to impose any tyranny he wished', the reality was 'vastly different'.[6] 'The chief was accountable and his power subject to checks and balances ... An important safeguard against the abuse of power by the chief was the influence of his group of councillors, the *amapakati* or middle ones. The chief governed on their advice. Although he was head, 'he dared not veto a decision of his court except at the peril of his reputation and authority'. Devenish calls it 'ubuntu-style management': 'its emphasis not on differences, but on accommodating these'.

Mbeki also on occasion looked towards the more enlightened elements of African tradition, norms and values. When he was criticised – even by Mandela – for not being consultative enough Mbeki adopted the policy of holding *lekgotlas*, or traditional community forums, where ordinary citizens in far-flung rural areas and townships could petition him in person on government policies. During his second term, he visibly softened his presidential style and tried to become more inclusive, warmer in public and more consensual. He started to refer to the values of *ubuntu* as conceptual frameworks, particularly when the public started criticising the values of enrichment at all costs, fostered in part by Mbeki's emphasis on black economic empowerment and rapidly expanding the black middle class, creating black business tycoons and entrepreneurs.

Mandela is close in sentiment and experience to the generation of post-independence African leaders such as Ghana's Kwame Nkrumah, Tanzania's Julius Nyerere and Zambia's Kenneth Kaunda – they were symbolic leaders, the personification of father figures. The political views of Mandela's generation of black nationalists in South Africa were deeply shaped by the anti-imperialist struggles waged by Africans against colonial occupiers. Moreover, Mandela's generation viewed leadership as something like that of Winston Churchill or Franklin D. Roosevelt – grand statesmanship that by individual example could galvanise the energies of their people into collective action. For Mbeki's generation of black South African anti-apartheid intellectuals – many of whom were influenced by British and Soviet leaders – the British Labour Party's Harold Wilson and the Soviet leader Nikita Khrushchev were the heroes. Both represented the quieter, practical, behind-the-scenes leadership and 'leading from behind' rather than the brash, larger-than-life styles of a Churchill or a Roosevelt.

Although Mbeki is not in the mould of the 'founding-father' leaders of post-independence Africa, his style has tended towards the philosopher-king styles personified by the likes of Nkrumah and Nyerere. Many of these leaders constructed intellectual frameworks that defined the debates of their era: Nyerere with *Ujamaa*, Kaunda with Humanism and Nkrumah with Nkrumaism. Mbeki ushered in the concept of the African renaissance – or at least redefined and brought it to life again. Furthermore, he established his presidency on the philosophy of 'African solutions for Africa's problems'. Mbeki has based a large part of his presidency on that of Pixley Ka Isaka Seme, one of the founders of the ANC (ANC president 1930–37) and a big proponent of the mix of pan-Africanism and African 'self-help' philosophy – both in economic development and in searching for solutions for social and political problems. The problem with presidents being philosopher-intellectuals emerges when they set out their policies as 'authoritative pronouncements' that carry the weight and legitimacy of the highest office in the country. This in itself can limit and stifle public debate and engagement – as Raymond Suttner, a leading ANC member, has argued.[7]

However, most of the time Mbeki's image is commonly associated with that of a visionary 'can-do' politician. Goals are set out and the path towards them more clearly mapped out. The erudite analyst Hein Marais[8] says that whereas Mandela's major accomplishment was to 'rearrange' the political stage, and to get the actors used to the new arrangement where the stage is

South Africa's political map, the role then of Mbeki would be to direct the actors to start acting out their new roles. The change from Mandela to the Mbeki era was from a focus on reconciliation, compromise and forging new symbols emphasising unity, to the much more hands-on governance and management, and fine-tuning new institutions. It also represents an era in which new configurations of power and political relations are being established and entrenched.[9]

Black empowerment

Indeed, the Mandela era was about soothing the fears of minority groups and other powerful interests (such as the still influential white right wing or conservative black traditional leaders) on the one hand, while maintaining the cohesion and unity of the liberation movement on the other, as the change from opposition movement to governing party brought its own internal turmoil in the ANC. Mbeki's era is also about building, realigning and consolidating powerful new forces, from the old liberation movement (and new or other forces not necessarily associated with the liberation movement) into the ruling bloc of democratic South Africa.

Mbeki still has to find his way through the same fragile path between black hope and white fear.[10] So while he also emphasises racial reconciliation, he has focused much more on transforming the apartheid economy and bringing blacks into the mainstream economy. Mbeki would like to be remembered as the person who brought economic benefits and equality to black South Africans and who led a change in the economic fortunes of the African continent. For sure, Mbeki is diligent about reassuring whites that they belong on South African soil. But not for him the hackneyed argument that whites have already done enough: he makes it clear that this means they also have their obligations.[11]

Ironically, it was Mbeki who wrote most of Mandela's major speeches during the Mandela presidency, and who coined many of the reconciliatory words spoken by Mandela. For example, his fingerprints are all over Mandela's much-quoted first speech to the Organization of African Unity in June 1994, where he outlined his vision of a 'non-racial society whose very being would assert the ancient African values of respect for every person and commitment to the elevation of human dignity regardless of colour or race'. In August 2006, Mbeki volunteered himself to the ANC's provincial executive committee in the Western Cape following racial tensions there. Mbeki thinks that racial unity is so important that he will personally see that it is achieved if the local ANC leadership fails in their efforts to heal racial divisions. Indeed, both Mbeki and Mandela have studiously tried to pursue a nationalism for South Africa that is all-inclusive, based on a common geographical space, and a development project that will not only bring South

Africa's disadvantaged majority on a par with its white, predominantly well-off, community, but also bring South Africa on a par with developed countries, to make it 'modern'.

Mandela often publicly lambasted white South Africans, but his warnings were softened because of his smiles and hugs.[12] Mandela is a great proponent of the description of South Africa, coined by Archbishop Desmond Tutu, as a 'rainbow nation', with a diversity of people, unmatched in the world, who can live together, using their differences as strength rather than as a source of divisions. To Mbeki citizenship is defined by civic and universal, rather than ethnic, criteria, and is inherently inclusive. There are certain parallels in Mbeki's use of the state as a tool to forge a new nation and that of India's Nehru. Nehru saw the distinctive model of the Indian state as an important framework for identity: a model committed to protecting cultural and religious differences rather than imposing a uniform 'Indianness'.[13]

Mbeki views the state as an important matrix for a new South African identity based on diversity. The peaceful transition from apartheid to democracy is seen as unique, as are the Constitution, the Bill of Rights and the early government of national unity, all deemed worthy of export to other conflict zones, much as the French Revolution gave rise to the idea of France being a unique carrier of civilisation to other parts of the world. Mbeki has been attempting to cobble together a political consensus in South Africa based on the post-war political consensus in post-Second World War Germany, where the opposing political parties agree on a vision for their country, but still have different political views. Mbeki has worked hard to woo whites and blacks who have never voted for the ANC and opposition parties and groups to strike strategic alliances with the ANC. That is not bad, but it has often meant that those not sharing in the centrist consensus have been pushed to the margins, with no access to the policy-making process – raising the spectre of people feeling so excluded they seek political redress through violence and other means.

Party experience

The difference in leadership style between Mbeki and Mandela is also connected to their different experiences of the ANC. It is not only that they represent two totally different generations of the ANC, but their personalities are totally different. Mbeki's experience of the ANC was of an exile movement, where its armed wing, Umkhonto we Sizwe, was its hope and mantra, and where obedience to rules and discipline from the top was essential for survival. The ever-present danger of infiltration by apartheid agents meant that decisions were made in highly secretive ways by a select few and information was shared on a need-to-know basis only, lest it fall into the wrong hands. Largely for security reasons, among the ANC in exile, consultation happened only among the top leadership, and lower-level members were simply expected to accept and obey.[14] Mbeki treats relationships in terms of power and ascendancy and often divides people into those to be cajoled and those to be stared down. He even sees his own political career as a chess game, where opponents need to be checkmated.

Mandela, meanwhile, lived for 27 years in prison, where consultation and co-operation were key ingredients of the political culture. Moreover, in the ANC of the 1940s, 50s and early 60s – in which Mandela cut his political teeth – the democratic spirit was premium. ANC political prisoners at Robben Island took their cue from that tradition of the ANC, and developed it further into a complex but effective network of consultation, negotiation, discussion and decision-making that recognised the equity of all, with an aversion to one person having overriding authority.[15] The black student movement that emerged was re-energised in the 1970s, after the formation of the Steve Biko inspired South African Students' Organisation (SASO) in 1969, which also rested firmly on a leadership culture that valued consultation. 'This did not mean only the consultation to win over a proposal but the creation of an atmosphere where individual opinions were considered and taken seriously. They were valued equally.'[16] Furthermore, individual members were encouraged not only to express their views freely but were allowed 'much scope for independent initiative'.[17] SASO's successor – formed in 1979 after SASO was banned by the apartheid regime two years before – the South African National Students' Congress (SANSCO), was also based on the same pillars.

Furthermore, the trade union movement that re-emerged in the 1970s, and was consolidated in 1985 by the formation of the Congress of South African Trade Unions (Cosatu) from new unions and old ones that survived apartheid oppression, also had widespread consultation, debate and an atmosphere that encouraged differing viewpoints, as its pillars. So too did the United Democratic Front (UDF), formed in 1983. I came from a generation whose political culture was influenced by the trade unions, student movements and the UDF. Not surprisingly, the political culture that has been associated with Mbeki, whereby the president and the top leadership decide policies and ordinary members and citizens are instructed to follow unquestionably, is quite frustrating. Moreover, South Africa's representative and participatory democracy not only demands full participation by citizens in all decision-making, but the idea that there are limits to the power of the state, and that the state and public leaders must defer to ordinary citizens, and not the other way round, is an important underlying principle. Indeed, citizens and watchdog bodies, such as parliament, the judiciary and Chapter 9 institutions such as the Human Rights Commission, serve as checks and balances against the overweening power of the state and executive. Worryingly, the very opposite has been the case during the Mbeki presidency.

Nevertheless, to paraphrase Jeremy Cronin, one of the main theoreticians of the Left in South Africa, the real contrast between the leadership of Mbeki and Mandela lies between 'the leadership of example' and 'the leadership as a vision'. 'Mandela leads by example. What he does is the leadership he offers. Mbeki leads by seeking to articulate a vision.'[18] Mbeki is the quintessential behind-the-scenes man. He prefers to lead from the 'back', rather than the front, in a bold, populist way. Critics often use Mbeki's rather secretive style to support their assessment of him as a conniving, ruthless politician, but he often acts as a prophet in the wilderness.[19] At the height of the struggle he engaged in such taboos as talking to white South African businessmen to lure them to the side of negotiations and compromise. He called on the ANC to formally end the armed struggle, without securing any guarantees in return from former President F. W. de Klerk's government. This when the armed struggle was the symbol of the ANC's resistance to apartheid and many believed that ending it was premature and nothing less than meek capitulation to the enemy.

Mbeki's upbringing was also instructive of his later political style. To start with, he comes from a powerful ANC family dynasty. His father, Govan Mbeki, was a pioneering African communist and intellect. Interestingly, in 1952, Govan Mbeki was narrowly defeated by Chief Albert Luthuli for the presidency of the ANC. The ANC's Left had nominated him for the presidency, but the centrist – and Christian Democratic – wing of the ANC, including the likes of Mandela, pushed for Luthuli, who won. Perhaps, his father's narrow loss of the ANC presidency made Mbeki more determined to succeed where his father faltered. Mbeki's upbringing certainly made him stand out as a potential future leader.

Sartorial symbolism

The differences between the leadership styles of Mbeki and Mandela are evident even in their respective sartorial styles. Mbeki is very formal, Mandela is informal. A typical Mbeki, when addressing a rally, would look as if he is ready for a corporate board meeting: he would be wearing flannel trousers, a starched shirt with a white collar and a tie. He smiles professionally and seldom laughs aloud spontaneously. Though his sharp suits and cosmopolitan air charm outsiders, he looks an awkward figure in the rough-and-tumble of the townships. When the rest of the ANC dances and sings at rallies he is far happier surveying it all from his chair. For him, rightly, competence is far more important than doses of charisma. He is intensely reclusive, and rarely talks about his private life. Even Mbeki's father often used to get irritated with his son's rather excessive woodenness and formality.

Mandela is tall, he laughs easily – in speeches he often endearingly pokes fun at himself, he wears loose shirts even on formal occasions and he has opened up many aspects of his life, including his messy divorce from Winnie Madikizela-Mandela, to public scrutiny.[20] Mandela has also turned out to be a deft politician. Like Gandhi, he is a master of communication. He has a genius for the simple gesture that speaks to his countrymen's souls.[21] During the 1995 Rugby World Cup, Mandela endeared himself to whites by sporting captain Francois Pienaar's number 6 shirt. In 1996, Mandela gave the national cricket team a surprise 'good luck call'. Though Mandela himself was a child of the pre-television age – he grew up in the golden age of the radio, the newspaper and the telegram – he became what was most probably South Africa's first television president.

Such gestures have always come hard to Mbeki. Early in his presidency his managers worked hard to get him to 'soften' up the image of the president. He then appointed the warm Bheki Khumalo as spokesman, to break down the cast-iron aura of inapproachability that surrounds him, later appointing Mukoni Ratshitanga in a similar role when Khumalo left for the private sector. All of this had an impact and as his confidence soared he started to relax more. However, Mbeki still had to hire image-makers to advise him on securing the 'common' touch, something that comes very naturally to Mandela.

All this has meant that under Mbeki, the stiff, aloof intellectual, the ANC government has come across as 'uncaring' and distant. Mandela's popularity had a lot to do with showing empathy to the worst-off in society and seemingly in deeds making good the ANC's promise of building a caring society. Though Mbeki's aim is to improve the lot of the poor, he comes across as lacking empathy. His statement that he did not know anybody suffering from AIDS, while millions are dying from the disease, is a case in point. His rebuff of the 12-year-old AIDS activist, Nkosi Johnson, who lay dying on his hospital bed, by making a point of not visiting him while everybody else concerned about combating the pandemic did so, portrayed Mbeki as cold and callous. Incredibly, Mbeki allies, such as Finance Minister Trevor Manuel, often contemptuously dismiss calls for a safety net to the poor as promoting a 'culture of dependency'.

Mbeki, extremely confident in his own capabilities, but inherently shy, is a hands-on president, a workaholic, and tends to want to manage even the smallest detail himself – at times overstretching himself. Mandela once even suggested privately that Mbeki take a holiday. Mbeki declined to do so, and when asked if he did not have too much on his plate replied: 'I don't know how much too much is, but there are so many things that needed to be done.'[22] Mbeki, unlike Mandela, cannot draw his authority from either the ANC or the country from warm affection or moral stature. He must stamp it on the party – and indeed does so – which requires stitching together a motley collection of support across the intellectual and interest spectrum of the party. Mbeki came to power when the novelty of having a black government in power for the first time in South Africa had worn thin and criticisms were starting to appear of the government's lack of delivery. And unlike Mandela, Mbeki did not inherit the sainthood that comes with forgiving your jailers after 27 years in jail.

Mbeki has had to fight for the throne, by whatever means, like any other political leader. Though he was the crown prince, he had to keep on fighting to the bitter end. He advanced his career by forcing respect, or at least fear, rather than being loved. Mbeki was the gatekeeper to two great leaders of the ANC, Mandela and Oliver Tambo. He was the one who could advance one's career, or could hold one to account, by virtue of controlling access to the top men. Deal-making is the basis on which Mbeki runs the government. While Mandela operated on the wave of public empathy that greeted his every announcement, Mbeki worked by stealth, assembling a critical mass of constituencies within the ANC to back his refashioning of the party's economic policy into laying the basis of the market-friendly Growth, Employment and Redistribution Strategy (Gear).

Next to a man like Mandela, whose principles and honour are thought to be impeccable, Mbeki's readiness to cut political deals could seem rather underhand. Yet, perhaps, a bit of opportunist deal-making is what South Africa needed to consolidate its infant democracy. Against the instincts of trade unions, communists and most of the ANC's once powerful Left, Mbeki introduced the conservative economic Gear policy in 1996. His success in getting the ANC to adopt the policy, 'kicking and screaming', was due partly to his grasp of the economic detail, partly to his skill at building an alliance of what to the outsider looks like competing groups behind him, and partly to his effectively sidelining those who stood in his way. Mandela, on the other hand, comes out as very saintly with his acts of turning the other cheek, embracing his enemies.

AIDS and gender equality

Both Mbeki and Mandela's leaderships failed on AIDS. When Mandela was in government, the focus was so much on creating political stability, dealing with the economic inequities of apartheid under the cloud of public finances on the verge of collapse because of earlier mismanagement, and getting to grips with the new government, that AIDS was not on the public policy agenda. Mandela often said, when asked about AIDS, that his generation did not talk publicly about sexual matters. However, when out of power, Mandela admitted his paucity on AIDS when in power and started campaigning on the issue. Mbeki on the other hand spent more time

philosophising on the causes of AIDS, and so undermined the fight against
the disease in a country that demanded firm leadership on the issue. In the
end, when criticism against his questioning of whether AIDS is
predominantly transmitted through sexual intercourse reached a peak, he
decided to withdraw from the public debate – thus continuing policy
uncertainty. In contrast, Mandela admits public policy failures much more
easily than Mbeki. In the end, instead of being criticised, admission of his
failures often has the effect of people trusting Mandela more and being more
forgiving. For example, Mbeki has been privately saying that his quiet
diplomacy towards the crisis in Zimbabwe has not been working, but he has
found it difficult to say so publicly.

Mandela – although he was not sexist – could have done much more to
promote gender equality. His generation still saw women's issues as separate.
For example, when his former wife Winnie Madikizela-Mandela challenged
him politically in the early 1990s, he expected her to defer to him as the
leader of the ANC. Furthermore, when Madikizela-Mandela expressed her
ambition to become leader of the ANC in her own right, Mandela did not
think it was the 'right' time.

In spite of his awful gaffe during the 2004 election campaign when he
joked that he would slap his sister if she married a particular opposition
party leader, Mbeki went out of his way to promote women's leadership.
Mbeki appointed a generation of women politicians to his Cabinet, as
provincial premiers and to important public bodies. He also groomed two
women leaders, Foreign Minister Nkosazana Dlamini Zuma and Deputy
President Phumzile Mlambo-Ngcuka, as potential presidential successors.
Although non-sexism and the notion of gender equality were important
objectives of the South African liberation struggle, especially following the
October 1955 women's march to the Union Buildings in Pretoria, in practice
the political culture was highly sexist and male-dominated. This was true
across the liberation movement, from the unions to the student movement.
Even the student movement of the 1980s and early 1990s, where there was an
active effort to build an indigenous African feminist movement, non-sexism
was often only a slogan, its practice was a distant dream. In fact, former
South African Deputy President Jacob Zuma's appalling statement during
his rape trial in 2006 – that he could see by the way a woman dresses that she
was looking for sex – is indicative of a widespread phenomenon of sexism in
society, in spite of South Africa's model constitution that calls for gender
equality. The pervasive sexism in South African society can be seen in the
vigorous opposition by many of the idea of a woman president of the country.

In November 2006, Foreign Minister Nkosazana Dlamini Zuma decried
the *vroue gevaar* – fear of a woman president in the ANC ranks. South
Africa's high rates of violence against women, HIV/AIDS and poverty –

largely related to huge gender inequality – demands that gender equality is not only a slogan, or nice words in the constitution, but that it becomes practice in everyday life.

Managing the opposition

The eminent South African sociologist Sakhela Buhlungu has talked of the shift from 'Madiba magic' to 'Mbeki logic'. Mandela's style was to 'win the voluntary co-operation' of all interest groups (within the alliance). In contrast, Mbeki 'demands co-operation' from the different groups.[23] Mbeki has attempted to contain his biggest trade union critics, by offering them powerful jobs in government or in related areas. Mbhazima Shilowa, the articulate and powerful former general secretary of Cosatu, was made the premier of Gauteng province, South Africa's economic and financial heartland.

Under Mbeki the space for debate has visibly shrunk from what it was under the Mandela presidency. Mbeki generally takes criticism of government policies personally. Often Mbeki 'suspends' internal democracy in the ANC to push through policies that will meet with resistance. This approach has backfired when ANC members rebelled against this kind of leadership and undermining of internal democracy in the ANC. Mandela usually dealt with critics by publicly embracing them, blunting their criticisms. Mandela even hugged his former jail master. It would be indeed hard to persist in attacking an opponent who keeps on holding your hand and embracing you. It is instructive to look at the way Mbeki dealt with two of the ANC alliance's most influential critics of current government policy's failure to create jobs, and to reduce inequality and poverty: Cosatu General Secretary Zwelinzima Vavi and President Willie Madisha. Unfortunately for Mbeki, both have so far been rather resistant to the seduction of government office, in return for muting their criticisms of government policies. Both have, however, been publicly ridiculed and totally marginalised by the President and his allies. For more than two years, Mbeki even refused to meet them.

Mbeki rarely speaks to the media. Mandela, on the other hand, gave interviews liberally. Mandela's openness to the media was also his strength. Negative press was rather rare. Mbeki's dislike of the media and his secrecy has also made him even more vulnerable, as the media are left to speculate. Although under Mandela, the ANC suffered from the same bitter and racist attacks from white expatriates and some Western media, Mandela was never obsessed with countering such negative perceptions. He dealt with it by opening up even more. Mbeki and his strategists are almost obsessed with perceptions, and how to deal with them, rather than just let the government's actions speak for themselves. Unfortunately, in the real world, there is always going to be residual racism against a black government, and it's surely a waste of energy and resources to be preoccupied with combating such negative perceptions.

Mbeki rarely appears in parliament and treats the opposition with contempt. Essop Pahad argues that as President, Mbeki is not an MP, and does not need to be accountable to parliament. Pahad says Mbeki's deputy, Jacob Zuma, is in charge of government business in parliament. Mandela, on the other hand, used every opportunity to put his views across in parliament. Mandela, like India's Nehru, made a determined effort to establish a respect for parliament as a symbol of the new democracy's representative institutions. Nehru[24] went out of his way to show respect for the parliamentary opposition, even if they may have been insignificant, to inculcate a democratic culture in the newly independent India. Mandela did the same during his term as president.

Overall Mbeki has a frosty relationship with opposition party leaders. Mandela, on the other hand, arranged a special forum for parliamentary opposition leaders where they could discuss policy differences with him or where he could listen to their concerns. As a result opposition party leaders were less inclined to aggressively attack Mandela for shortcomings, as they would attack Mbeki during the rare times he appears in parliament. Furthermore, Mandela went out of his way to include opposition groups within his government of national unity. This is one practice continued by Mbeki – and which has been promoted by Mbeki as a policy solution to other African countries trying to make peace after protracted conflicts. Later in his presidency, from 2004 onwards, as his own confidence increased, Mbeki increasingly started to make use of the same reconciliatory public gestures – he emphasised the importance of white South Africans in the rebuilding of the country – so successfully practised by Mandela. Mbeki even praised the efforts of his rival, the acerbic Tony Leon, the leader of the mainly white opposition conservative Democratic Alliance. Furthermore, Mbeki started a recruitment programme to recruit white South Africans who had left the country to return and take jobs in government. Mbeki also started frequently to point to Mandela's example of reconciliation and to point South Africans to the concept of *ubuntu* as a guiding principle his countrymen and women should embrace.

Mbeki ideologically aligns himself with the generation of centre-left leaders including Tony Blair, Gerhard Schroeder and Swedish Social Democratic leader Goran Persson. They use the same ideological theme, the 'Third Way' – less government, using the market to deliver, distancing themselves from the unions, and moving closer to business. Essentially, Mbeki sees his presidency as running a business, South Africa Inc., of which he is CEO, strongly in control of Cabinet and the ANC's governing body, the NEC. The ANC now operates like a highly presidentialised party with power concentrated in the CEO. In contrast, former president Nelson Mandela operated 'more like a ceremonial head of state, more like a constitutional monarch, submitting himself with a strong sense of duty to the disciplines of party democracy through the Cabinet or ANC NEC'.[25]

Mbeki, as CEO, is not someone for the big hall meeting. He excels in cobbling together policy in bilateral meetings of small groups. He would deal with problems by talking separately to conflicting parties, securing separate agreements. Policy is increasingly developed at such bilateral meetings.[26] Mandela made an issue out of consulting with party leaders and supporters – even if not always implementing their proposals. Often those consulted would appreciate being included – and their criticisms when their policy proposals are not implemented would often be muted.

Leadership styles do matter. Mbeki is often accused of technocratic policymaking, rather than wide consultation, lest it would compromise his policies or his ability to embark on them single-handedly because he thinks it is for the greater good of the country and the recipients. Often he would say, 'I've been elected by the people to govern, if the people have problems with me or the party, they will vote me out: if they don't, it means they are happy with my policies'.

The danger with this approach is that in the end, society learns that it can vote for but not choose; legislatures feel they have no role in policy-making; and civil society groups perceive that their voices do not count. This kind of policy style 'tends to undermine representative institutions'.[27] Consultation and negotiation among representative institutions is necessary to channel political conflicts. If decisions are made elsewhere, representative institutions wilt. At his deathbed Nehru realised this – too late. Midway during his presidency, Mbeki appears to have learned that lesson. However, his great challenge now, for the remainder of his presidency, is to convince a sceptical ANC membership and South Africans that he has indeed taken that lesson to heart.

For the leaders who will follow in governing a free and democratic South Africa, the models of Mandela and Mbeki provide an important legacy of achievement and warning.

Notes

1   See Larry Collins and Dominique Lapierre (1997), *Freedom at Midnight: The epic drama of India's struggle for independence*. HarperCollins, London, p xii.

2   Hein Marais (2002), 'The logic of expediency: Post-apartheid shifts in macro-economic policy', in Sean Jacobs and Richard Calland, *Thabo Mbeki's World: The politics and ideology of the South African president*. Pietermaritzburg, Natal University Press, pp.83–103.

3   Sahra Ryklief (2002), 'Does the emperor really have no clothes?: Thabo Mbeki and Ideology', in Sean Jacobs and Richard Calland, *Thabo Mbeki's World: The politics and ideology of the South African president*. Natal University Press, pp.105–120.

4   Nelson Mandela, speech to the students of the University of Potchefstroom. February, 1996.

5   Ibid.

6   George Devenish, 'Understanding true meaning of ubuntu is essential in politics', *Cape Times*, 17 May 2005.

7   Raymond Suttner (2005), 'The character and formation of intellectuals within the ANC-led South African liberation movement' in Thandika Mkandawire, *African Intellectuals: Rethinking Politics, Language, Gender and Development*, Unisa and Zed Books.

8   Hein Marais, op.cit.

9   Sakhela Buhlungu (2002), 'From "Madiba magic" to "Mbeki logic": Mbeki and the ANC's trade union allies', in Sean Jacobs and Richard Calland, *Thabo Mbeki's World: The politics and ideology of the South African president*. Pietermaritzburg, Natal University Press, pp. 179–200.

10 See, for example, Anthony Simpson (1999), *Nelson Mandela: The Authorised Biography*, London, Jonathan Cape.

11 Ibid. See also 'From Mandela to Mbeki', *Houston Chronicle*. 8 July 1996.

12 Anthony Sampson, op.cit.

13 Ibid.

14 See Stephen Ellis and Tsepo Sechaba (1991), *Comrades against Apartheid: The ANC and the South African Communist Party in exile*, Bloomington and London: Indiana University Press and James Currey. Or see Tom Lodge (1987), *Black Politics in South Africa since 1945*, Ravan Press. Johannesburg. See also William M. Gumede (1997), 'The Battle for the Soul of the ANC', *The Sunday Independent*, September.

15 Anthony Sampson, op.cit. Also see Adrian Hadland and Jovial Rantao (1999), *The life and times of Thabo Mbeki*, Zebra Press. Stephen Ellis and Tsepo Sechaba, op.cit. See also Charlene Smith, 'Two Faces of the Struggle', *Saturday Star*, 20 June 1998.

16 Lindy Wilson (1991), 'Bantu Stephen Biko: A Life', in Barney Pityana, Mamphele Ramphele and Malusi Mpumlwana (eds.), *Bounds of possibility: The legacy of Steve Biko and Black Consciousness*, London: Zed Books.

17 Saleem Badat (1999), *Black Student Politics, Higher Education and Apartheid: From Saso to Sansco*, 1968–1990, Human Sciences Research Council, p.111.

18 Author interview with Jeremy Cronin.

19 See Mark Gevisser, 'The 60s anti-hero', *The Sunday Times*, 30 May 1999. But see also Anthony Sampson. 'President select', *Observer*, London, 10 June 2001; or Anthony Sampson, 'Mbeki: The Anglophile With Roots in a Tangle', 18 April 2004.

20 *The Star*, 10 May 1995; Anthony Sampson, op.cit. See also 'From Mandela to Mbeki', *Houston Chronicle*, 8 July 1996.

21   See Larry Collins and Dominique Lapierre, op. cit.

22   *The Star*, 10 May 1995.

23   Sakhela Buhlungu, op. cit.

24   See Sunil Khilnani (2003), *The idea of India*, Penguin. London, 2000 and Judith M. Bro, *Nehru: A Political Life*, Yale University Press.

25   Anthony Sampson, op.cit.

26   Author interview with Moss Ngoasheng, 6 March 2000.

27   Ibid.

3

African leadership: from the bottom up

If thou journey on a road made by thy hands each day, thou wilt arrive at the place where thou wouldst be.

The Maxims of Ani (c. 1300 BCE)

Reflections on Naivasha: cultures, leadership and development

Kimani Njogu

Kimani Njogu is a Kenyan linguist, literary critic and researcher on cultural leadership. He has written and published widely on Kiswahili and other African languages, and their use in national development efforts. He is the Director of Twaweza Communications and a member of the Global Leadership Network.

He was the event director of the British Council's InterAction Programme on Cultures, Leadership and Development, held at Naivasha, Kenya in February 2006. The Naivasha Forum brought together 70 emerging leaders from African countries to discuss culture, leadership and the way these concepts interact with development. Here he reflects on the issues explored in the programme, and the importance of youth to the process of change in Africa.

Sitting on a hill in Naivasha at the centre of the Rift Valley, I admire the beauty of the setting sun in this dry and dusty landscape. Meanwhile, a chain of thoughts runs through my mind – pan-Africanism, the cultural imperative and the development agenda, development as a cultural project, debt management, transformational leadership and the state in Africa, basic needs and basic rights and freedom.

I frown as words in different languages flash through my mind. These thoughts have followed me incessantly for quite some time; since I became increasingly involved in the theme of leadership in Africa. I try to shut them out in order to enjoy the scenery, but fail. In the distance, I hear cattle mooing and goats bleating as they troop home to a Maasai *manyatta*. They are hungry. How does one ensure food security for all in this dry season? How does one keep the flame of hope alive? I hear children singing and laughing as they return home from school. I smile at the resilience and creativity of youth. Maybe therein lies the hope for the continent. But we need to give them high-quality education. All of them. My mind wanders again and I see images of the past and the present intertwined, as if smiling at each other. Do these images provide a glimpse into the future?

Since the 1980s, there has been a visible ascendancy of the global neo-liberal political, economic and cultural approach and this has generated interesting discussions on the role of the state, the market and culture in development. Within the economic sphere, the neo-liberal development paradigm views the state to be the main hindrance to economic advancement. Significantly, the state in post-colonial Africa is seen to be intrusive, extensive and inefficient in the allocation of available resources. Through its bureaucratic bottlenecks, the state is viewed as constraining the emergence of entrepreneurs and a vibrant middle class. Advocates of the neo-liberal approach to development in Africa argue that if the role of the state is reduced drastically and the market is liberalised through, for instance, privatisation of public goods, Africa would realise development. But others have argued (Bujra, 2005) that liberal democracy has its own foundations and challenges. In the West, industrialisation and economic growth became possible with the help of resources forcibly extracted from colonies in Africa and Asia as well as outward migration of surplus population. Additionally, liberal democracy has buttressed economic, political and social inequalities and systematically excluded the masses from participation through manipulation. (Bujra, 2005:8) To what extent is liberal democracy feasible for Africa?

Then there is the neo-Weberian approach that argues that patrimonial practices rooted in African political and economic cultures have contributed to Africa's problems. In the African traditional systems leaders (patrons) extended social and economic benefits to their communities (clients) and as a result gained power and loyalty. The patron-client relationship was thus the basis of hegemony in the post-colonial African state, according to the neo-Weberian perspective. The consequence of the relationship has been personalisation of state structures and concentration of power on individual leaders. The way to deal with this phenomenon, it is asserted, is to entrench market initiatives and employ technocrats to ensure the rationalisation of the economic route, while minimising the rent-seeking tendencies of the patrimonial state.

Other explanations to the situation in Africa demand that global and local tendencies be factored in and that historical, political, ideological, cultural and economic contexts be examined. Furthermore, the gendered nature of the state and market forces has entered the debate. (Sahle, 2006) In the latter case, markets are understood as socially constructed institutions and have a gender dimension, as seen in the way political participation and democratisation take place in many countries.

These discussions are all aimed, in my view, at seeking ways in which 'development' could be realised in Africa. Many explanations have been advanced for the 'failure' of development in Africa, including the colonial legacy, ethno-linguistic diversity, corruption of its leaders, indiscipline in production, absence of entrepreneurial skills, deficiencies in planning and management, inappropriate policies, political intolerance and so on. Whatever the case, the political legacy of colonialism has contributed significantly to the current state of affairs on the continent, given that its structures were not dismantled at independence and the political class has continued to utilise its institutions and philosophies to mobilise and consolidate power. For instance, just as in the colonial days, the state has tended to be absolute, failing to address those issues that limit people's ability to realise their human potential. The political class has continued to seek and consolidate power through mobilisation of national, ethnic and community structures and loyalties. Political leaders have contributed in the perpetuation of economic inequalities and have stifled public participation in those matters that would contribute to their liberation.

According to Amartya Sen (1999), development requires the removal of situations that create unfreedom such as poverty, tyranny, poor economic opportunities, social deprivation, neglect of public facilities and oppression. Individual freedom is essential to development because 'what people can positively achieve is influenced by economic opportunities, political liberties, social powers, and the enabling conditions of good health, basic education, and the encouragement and cultivation of initiatives'. (Sen, 1999:5) Viewed in this way, development becomes a process of expanding people's freedoms as the *path to* and *end* of development. But in Africa the 'premium on power is exceptionally high, and the institutional mechanisms for moderating political competition are lacking'. (Claude Ake, 1996:16) Because the struggle for power is so intense the pursuit for development is put aside and marginalised. If it occurs at all, it is only incidental to the larger pursuits of power.

In addition to the many factors that constrain freedoms in Africa, two of them – culture and leadership – have recently been the subject of important discussions within the continent. Could an invocation of these concepts contribute to the way development would be possible in Africa? In this section, I draw on a workshop organised by the British Council in February 2006, in Naivasha, Kenya, in which I was involved as Event Director. According to David Higgs (2006), the British Council's InterAction for a New Generation of African Leaders programme is about finding and facilitating leadership capacity in Africa.

The Naivasha Forum brought together 70 emerging leaders from different countries to discuss culture, leadership and the interaction of these concepts with development. The British Council recruited active cultural actors with the maturity and skill to sustain positive intent, to make differential judgements in a neutral tone and to contribute to a continuously supportive environment. It was assumed that all participants were willing to accept the challenge to identify fresh thinking from intellectual exchange, and had the capacity not only to activate that thinking, but under time pressure, to capture it in words. These were people interested in looking at real experiences from which they derive their thinking, and had the dynamism to ensure their voice was heard. The gathering was flat and democratic, dispensing with 'keynote speakers' or 'distinguished guests'. Politicians, writers, academicians and activists were given an opportunity to discuss Africa and reignite the spirit of pan-Africanism. The facilitators drawn from Kenya, Ghana and Botswana ensured considerable dynamism in format so that individuals worked in plenary, in small groups and alone at certain points. No papers were presented but instead there were deep conversations about the challenges facing Africa and what could be done to reverse the pattern.

Does culture matter?

Culture is without doubt a complex and elusive concept. However, one can identify certain features around which the concept could be organised. First, culture may be understood as 'the order of life in which human beings construct meaning through practices of symbolic representation'. (Tomlinson, 1999:18). Within the economic sphere, for instance, the cultural dimension might involve the communicative practices that enhance production, exchange, and consumption of goods. In contrast, within the political domain it is the communicative practice for the concentration, distribution, and deployment of power. Culture is a people's way of life; that which defines them and their relationships.

It was appreciated at the Naivasha Forum that culture – the distinctive spiritual, material, intellectual and emotional characteristics that define a society or a social group – is dynamic and is subject to many influences. In addition to the arts and letters, it encompasses ways of life and the fundamental rights of a person, value systems, traditions and beliefs. It could facilitate or impede the realisation of development depending on the ways in which it creates opportunities for the exercise of individual and collective freedoms. Drawing on their own experiences, the Naivasha Forum leaders deliberated on the features of cultural life, its content and the methods used to express it, and it was not just looking at ethnographic culture but culture as a total way of life, including material, spiritual, intellectual, emotional, arts, and value systems.

In order to stay on track and to deepen reflection, participants were encouraged to explore the following culture types:

- traditional social culture: the ethnographic focus
- contemporary socio-political culture: the political and economic focus
- faith-based culture: the religious focus
- organisational related culture: the business focus
- gender and/or family-based culture: the social focus
- linguistic, artistic and other cultural structures based on social activity: the cultural focus
- youth-based culture: the life stage focus.

Communities in Africa operate within a range of social, cultural, economic and political environments. How entrenched are these environments and what role do they play in shaping communities? What are the gender roles and expectations? Which politico-religious structures exist in societies? We recognised that cultures are ever-changing and are responsive to internal and external stimuli.

Discussions on culture took us through factors which define some of our communities as well as 'traditional' power structures, hierarchies and decision-making channels. In the pursuit of nationalism local power structures were either brought on board or ignored as power became centralised. Because access to political power has benefits for individuals and communities, through patronage, an ethnic base is extremely important for political leaders on the continent. Resource allocations and access to opportunities have tended to be linked to the ethnic origins of those in power and one would need to pay attention to ethno-linguistic considerations in contemporary African politics. Without underestimating the role that colonialism played in sharpening regional differences, it is fair to say that these considerations have contributed to glaring inequalities.

Culture could also be a method for making development possible. The media and other cultural forms (song, drama, puppetry, cartoons, dance, poetry, music, video and photography) are used by many development workers. These cultural forms target both the cognitive and affective domains and can play an important role in social change. Culture is also a tool through which we express ourselves; and expression is vital to self-determination, community engagement and to imagining futures. It creates socio-cultural relevance and resonates with the lived experiences of beneficiaries. Instead of imposing perspectives, a cultural approach gives communities an opportunity to think through and question their own lives. They become part of the solution through deep reflection and problem solving, guided by those who may have spent more time working on the issues.

Thus, development work cannot ignore the context and realities of societies in which interventions are implemented. Moreover, it is critically important to identify influential local power structures and pressure groups (religious, cultural, political, legal, and professional) that can be potential allies or adversaries to development and bring them on board. Once 'innovations' have been accepted by community leaders, they tend to spread out. But the acceptability of the innovations could be delayed or subverted if development workers are not sensitive to the tensions and aspirations of community members. They ought to develop culturally acceptable language and communication strategies that resonate with their audience. This is not to say that universally recognised human rights should be sacrificed at the altar of culture; rather, it is to affirm that development workers ought to create an environment in which bridges are established between local cultural values and global values as enshrined in international declarations and conventions.

As I listened to the leaders gathered in Naivasha, I became convinced that what was needed was 'global leadership'. In articulating the concept of global leadership, Link et al. (2006:4–5) assert:

> For too many of us today 'global' simply means projecting our own particular beliefs, values, and perspectives on the world around us. Instead of realizing that 'global' requires awakening a new and integral dimension of reality, we too often assume that we can apply to the world the preconceived attitudes we have inherited from our families and cultures, from our professions or political ideologies. In fact this is not 'global' thinking at all. It is merely applying our own parochial perspectives to a larger geographical scale. Instead we need to hear and learn from each other. In dialogue, we need to find solutions that come from our shared humanity and support our joint sustainability. These solutions must unite us across the potential divides not only of nationality and culture, religion and political beliefs, but also of societal sectors and social classes, professions and types of organizations.

Leaders who contribute to positive social change 'listen to more than their own voices. They accommodate other viewpoints and celebrate knowledge gathered from lived experiences. They are ardent students of community ...' (Njogu, 2006:122) As students, the leaders at the Naivasha Forum visited a Maasai community in an *ilmurua* (homestead) consisting of three families. The visit was facilitated by two Maasai men, Ole Parkire and Ole Tinkoi, who were also participants at the Forum. Before the visit, participants were briefed by Ole Parkire on how to conduct themselves in the community and how the women would *ng'asak*, bow their heads, when greeting the Olnyangusi, the 85-year-old head of the homestead. The *ilmurua* is on a dusty and hot hill overlooking the rapidly disappearing Lake Naivasha.

Until 1984, the Tinkoi family lived in Hell's Gate, famous for its geysers, before it was gazetted as a national park. They were evicted, without compensation, in order to pave the way for conservation-tourism. They were settled by the then Conservation and Management Department on this dusty and waterless hill. The community has no access to the lake because, downhill, the cut flower farms owned by local and international companies have blocked all routes, except two from an original 17. The Maasai are pastoralists who depend on their cattle for survival. They are competing with modernity and losing out. They immensely value their culture, which has been exploited in the pursuit of capital and marginalised by tourism and horticultural farming.

The visit to the Maasai community was in many ways and for most participants the peak of the interaction. It questioned their assumptions and brought home the fact that issues of culture, leadership and development are not abstract but concrete experiences. How will this *ilmurua* ever get the water that the community so desperately needs? How can development be made possible within the context of the cultural integrity of each community, even as practices detrimental to the realisation of human potential are interrogated, eradicated and revised?

Development and peace

In the struggle for independence, most African leaders mobilised communities around a development agenda. But what was its essence? The post-colonial development efforts of the 1960s paid no attention to the democratisation of institutions of governance, management of the environment, rapid urbanisation, decentralisation of decision making, integrity in the performance of public duty. The spirit and dream of pan-Africanism was set aside as national leaders sought to consolidate power within their borders.

The Naivasha Forum brought that spirit back. I felt the energies of these new leaders who shared a dream for the continent: that despite the big challenges facing Africa, there was still hope that things will get better. But what do the African leaders need to do in order to turn the tide? There is an urgent need for African countries to focus on growth, productivity and discipline in public service and to look for ways to engage communities in determining the preferred direction of development. Leaders must regain the trust of communities, engage in dialogue with them, learn new ways of doing things and believe in their ability to bring social transformation. African countries need to co-operate with each other on matters of trade, commerce, the sharing of information and technology and the provision of health care, safe water and food. A new paradigm is needed for Africa. This development paradigm calls for 'people-centeredness' in perspective and action. It is a call for a redefinition of what really matters in the lives of people so that they can live fully and share in the benefits of science and technology. This integrated and comprehensive view of development will, of necessity, draw from indigenous knowledge systems and contextualise them within the contemporary world. Given the adaptive capacity of cultures, this redeeming experience need not be too difficult to fathom. There is a lot that the creativity of youth, now and in the past, can teach us.

Maybe by looking deeply into our cultures and listening to the voices of the past, we may start opening up opportunities for young people to take leadership roles and responsibilities because cultures provide the ground on which a nation can stand. Cultures that are receptive to other voices can provide possibilities for people-centred development because they encourage consultation and consensus building. The circle around which the council of elders sat to deliberate epitomised a unity of purpose and vision; a continuity of co-operative engagement. To be a member of the circle was to accept that one's ideas were not the only possible ones and that they found completion through dialogue and consultation. It is not true that our cultures are a hindrance to development. They are, in fact, a resource that, properly utilised, can provide opportunities available for all to enjoy the rights to health, education, shelter and food. Culture encapsulates life in its totality, embraces the various domains of life, and is not just traditional and ethnographic. Culture finds expression in political and economic activities; in faith-based set-ups; in languages and the arts; in business, family unions, gender interactions; and among the youth. Culture is adaptive and is a vibrant manifestation of our being, of our humanness. When in contact with others, culture shows its adaptability by flexing to receive and appropriate an alien way of expressing life.

But when an alien way of life and interpretation of the world are imposed, as has happened in Africa for years, the result is lack of self-confidence and a superficial allegiance to the external value systems. It is only when we begin to appreciate the large body of ideas, systems, institutions and creativity of the people with whom we engage, that we start having meaningful and action-oriented dialogue on such pertinent issues as culture, leadership and development. This is because culture, leadership and development are intimately embedded and intertwined. A development paradigm that ignores indigenous knowledge systems and spits at the values, interests and aspirations of the people for whom it is intended, is not sustainable. If all human societies have an adaptive capability which makes them appropriate the ways of life of others then it is reasonable to conclude that we all share certain cultural values irrespective of our backgrounds. This shared humanity opens a window for cultural dialogue, stimulation and activity. It allows us to 'un-think' the linear approaches to development and to be more holistic by deliberately integrating its social and ecological tenets.

In the case of Africa, it has become critical that we examine how the various strands of cultures shape the type of leadership we espouse and experience, including the ways in which leaders located outside conventional politics are transforming lives through committed and selfless service to the people. The shared and distributed leadership, as well as the transitional mechanisms and systems of transferring authority from one generation to another practised by communities in the past may, in fact, be the basis on which to build a new governance and leadership ethos in Africa. A deliberate and systematic engagement with communities where we are students may offer a way out of the uninspiring national leadership styles and the politics of patronage that dominate the continent and are perpetuated by the colonial experience.

The development paradigm that dominated African nations in the 1960s, under a general umbrella of nationalism, was wrought with numerous problems. Young people, once viewed as the hope for Africa, have lost status and presence in national affairs and no longer constitute the national priority. No systems are aggressively put in place to ensure their relevance in nation building and throughout the continent we are witnesses to the collapse of learning institutions, especially at the higher levels. Development requires peace and security. Current events in Rwanda suggest that with peace a country can tap the best of its human resources for common good. Peace and security allow citizens to exercise their freedoms, unfettered. Unfortunately, in many parts of our continent, including Sudan, the Democratic Republic of Congo, northern Uganda, Côte d'Ivoire and Somalia, violence is the order of the day. In other countries a sense of the emergence of violence always lurks in the background. People are never quite sure if clan and ethnic tensions will break at the seams and degenerate into violence. The accentuation of ethnic tensions is, in most cases, motivated by politicians bent on safeguarding their personal interests under the guise of protecting the wellbeing of their communities. On occasion they encourage their communities to 'restock' their animals by attacking neighbouring communities. Idle youth are constantly manipulated in the perpetuation of this violence. This tendency can be reversed.

There is also need to urgently address matters related to the environment because it has a bearing on availability of resources, including food and water. And safeguarding the environment is not just protecting trees. It involves looking and acting on the whole ecosystem. Issues of environmental degradation (contaminated water, air pollution, unfavourable mining and logging practices) have a direct bearing on our lives and are too important to ignore. The choices and decisions we make today must champion the cause of a balanced ecology so as to safeguard future generations. As we treat the earth, so we treat each other. Indeed, a peaceful physical environment is a metaphor about our lives with each other. Equally, an imbalance in the environment marks our own imbalance as human beings.

A culture of peace is a state of mind that values partnership and respect. The earth should be viewed in the same way. As the integrity of our natural systems erodes, resources necessary for survival become scarce; land, water, minerals and fossil fuels are turned into battlegrounds. In many African countries, we can clearly see the interconnectedness of nature as one web of life. It cannot hold together if one part is broken. Without peace, the earth ceases as a space of solace and becomes one of pain and anguish. Our national leaders owe it to the citizens to ensure peace and wellbeing. Peace is the ability to engage in humanising work without fear of violence. It can create a conducive environment for good governance, and the accountability of public servants. Unfortunately, governance in many African countries has assumed a peculiarly repressive character that has been the focus of several international human rights organisations. This may be due to hegemony as a relation – not of domination by means of force – but of consensus by means of political and ideological direction. Political parties seek to perpetuate hegemonic relations through distortion of information and manipulation of truth. As has now been generally appreciated, a social group is said to have attained a hegemonic status if it has succeeded in creating an impression of transcending its own corporate interests by taking into account the interests of other social forces in society, linking these with its own interests so as to appear to be their own universal and legitimate representative.

This is the political status that the governing class of every nation strives to attain with respect to the rest of civil society. Yet hegemony does also imply the possibility of resistance and contradictory consciousness manifested through recurrent protests from some sections of society. The ruling class will often respond to its failure by a demonstration of state power, as has happened in most of Africa. Autocratic repressive measures in many African countries are, to some extent, political responses to the perceived hegemonic failure of the governing class.

Conclusion

What lessons do we learn from the Naivasha Forum? First, in the interaction I became convinced that the way to deal with the challenges facing Africa is to revive rigorously and deliberately the spirit of pan-Africanism and provide a framework for the actualisation of that vision. Whereas the ruling class has forums such as the African Union, the Pan-African Parliament and the Africa Peer Review Mechanism, among others, emerging leaders have no such spaces from which they can realise their dreams for the continent.

Second, the continent ought to invest in its young people. Governments and civil society organisations should have deliberate policies that target youth. Young people are creative and, when linked with more experienced leaders, can come up with sustainable political, economic and social solutions to the problems facing the continent. The synergy that can emanate from intergenerational linkages will be able to address issues of poverty, HIV/AIDS, food security, technology, water and sanitation, and the environment.

Third, high-quality leadership does not just happen; it is nurtured and given an opportunity to function. Currently, there are no systematic efforts to grow leadership on the continent through mentoring and role modelling. The image portrayed by the political class is disappointing: the pursuit for power is vicious and warlike. It is devoid of humility, integrity, trust and dialogue. Political culture needs to change so that power is used, not for individual aggrandisement, but for the welfare of communities. This might require a reconsideration of the governance institutions inherited at independence. Because democracy is a process, those institutions that broaden citizens' freedoms out to be established by law and leadership at all levels made accountable to the citizens.

Fourth, because ethnic sentiments are exploited by politicians for the acquisition and consolidation of power and resource allocation, it is urgent that other forms of identity formation be activated. This will ensure that ethno-linguistic difference is not the only tool that is used for political mobilisation. Other identities such as youth, gender, professions, class and so on are equally important and can help reduce the ethnic polarities we currently experience in Africa.

We must move quickly to address these matters. Even as the Naivasha Forum was taking place the lake in front of us was being visibly choked by silt and weeds. The resident hippos, we were told, are fanning out in search of pasture – in much the same way as our best and brightest are emigrating to the West to escape the despair and poverty choking their dreams of a better life.

Notes

Claude Ake (1996), *Democracy and Development in Africa,* Washington: Brookings Institution.

Abdalla Bujra (ed.) (2005), *Democratic Transition in Kenya: The Struggle from Liberal to Social Democracy,* Nairobi: African Centre for Economic Growth.

David Higgs (2006), 'Foreword' to *Cultures, Leadership and Development,* Nairobi: British Council.

Walter Link et al. (2006), *Leadership is Global: Co-Creating a More Humane and Sustainable World,* Global Leadership Network.

Kimani Njogu (2006), 'Harnessing the Power of Language: Understanding How Language Shapes Leadership' in *Leadership is Global: Co-Creating a More Humane and Sustainable World,* Global Leadership Network.

Eunice Njeri Sahle (2006), 'Gender, States and Markets in Africa' in *Studies in Political Economy 77,* Spring.

Amartya Sen (1999), *Development as Freedom,* New York: Alfred A. Knopf.

John Tomlinson (1999), *Globalization and Culture,* Chicago: University of Chicago Press.

Time for change
Ndidi Nwuneli

Ndidi Nwuneli has an MBA from Harvard Business School, and is founder and CEO of LEAP Africa, a non-profit organisation based in Lagos, Nigeria, committed to inspiring, empowering and equipping a new cadre of African leaders. LEAP provides leadership training and coaching for business owners, social entrepreneurs and youth in eight cities across Nigeria. Her contribution below, where she explores why time management is increasingly a leadership issue in Africa, was inspired by her participation in the British Council InterAction Programme on Cultures, Leadership and Development, in Naivasha, Kenya, in February 2006.

Scenario 1

Imagine for a moment that you were being honoured by your community for your contributions to the social, economic and political development of the region. As a member of a select group of people to receive awards from the local government chairman and the traditional rulers in the community, you receive a letter that clearly states that all honourees and their guests must be seated by 10.00 a.m., and that the event will promptly start at 11.00 a.m. Filled with excitement and pride that your quiet contributions are finally being recognised, you prepare for the big day – notifying your family and friends about the event and carefully selecting your favourite traditional outfit. By 9.30 a.m. you make your way to the venue and are promptly seated by 10.00 a.m. As the hours drag on, you kick yourself for believing that just this time, a special day in your life and the lives of other truly exceptional people, things would be different. Unfortunately, they are not. At 12.00 noon, the traditional rulers start trickling in. By 1.00 p.m., the local government chairman and his entourage finally arrive and the event commences, two hours after the scheduled time. There is not a single apology from the organisers. Does this appear far-fetched? This experience was one that I shared with others, when I was fortunate enough to receive a service award from my local community. But here I was not in control of the time or events.

Scenario 2

It is 6.30 a.m. in the city of Lagos. I jump out of my bed, excited about the busy day ahead. I have planned a full day of activities, starting off with a breakfast meeting at 8.00 a.m. with a partner in Lagos; followed by a short day trip to our capital, Abuja to speak at an event at 1.00 p.m., and then ending with a meeting with my staff and the printer at 7.30 p.m., back in Lagos, to review the third draft of the programme of events for the Annual Nigerian Youth Leadership Awards, scheduled to be held in a week. I am being too ambitious for one day, you might ask? Being the eternal optimist, and consummate planner, I do not think so.

My day starts: I scramble through the Lagos traffic, and I am seated at the Sheraton Hotel lobby by 7.50 a.m., awaiting my partner's arrival. As my partner is not known for his lateness, I send him a text message by 8.10 a.m. reminding him about the breakfast meeting and informing him that I am waiting. By 8.30 a.m., I am getting ready to leave the venue for my 10.00 a.m. flight to Abuja, when a phone call informs me that my partner is on his way. Our breakfast meeting finally commences at 9.00 a.m. By this time, I only have 45 minutes to eat and talk. Unfortunately, our conversation is far from being completed before I have to run off to the airport.

I arrive at the airport and check in for the flight. It is already 10.00 a.m. but I am not too late. Before obtaining a seat number, I enquire about whether or not the outbound aircraft has arrived, and I am assured by the airline employees that it has, and that the plane is boarding. Unfortunately, the plane has not actually arrived. It finally lands at 11.00 a.m. and we take off at 11.30 a.m.

By 12.30 p.m. I am in Abuja. I board the first taxi and rush to the venue of the event. By 1.30 p.m. I have arrived at the venue, but the hall is empty. Unfortunately, the event does not commence until 3.00 p.m. and I am finally called for my keynote address at 4.00 p.m. Immediately after my speech, I scramble back to the airport, and catch a 5.30 p.m. flight which departs at 6:00 p.m. I arrive in Lagos at 7.00 p.m. Anticipating the traffic that I will encounter en route to my office, I immediately call my office to inform my staff that I am running a little late for our 7.30 p.m. meeting. They inform me that the meeting has been postponed because the printer has not completed his work on the draft publication.

As I head home, a rush of emotions fills my head! I am frustrated that my day was so inefficient and unproductive. I am saddened by the fact that I had an incomplete meeting with my partner because I was rushing to catch a plane which was late, and that I left the event in Abuja before it ended, missing out on an opportunity to engage in one-on-one discussions with the young people and entrepreneurs. I am upset at the airlines for being inefficient, and I am disappointed in my printer for not prioritising our work. Most importantly, I am saddened by the fact that I devoted four and a half hours of my day to waiting. By 10.00 p.m. I crawl into bed, feeling unfulfilled.

Does this appear far-fetched? This is a typical day in the life of many professionals on the African continent. Indeed, it is not uncommon to arrive at a professional or social event and have to wait for as little as 20 minutes or, as in scenario 1, as many as four hours for it to commence. In some cases, we wait for the 'big' man or woman who is in charge of the meeting, the special guest of honour, the master of ceremonies, the electrician who is in charge of the public address system, the property manager who has the key to the control room, or the musicians who are supposed to provide the entertainment or even the guests, who we hope will arrive in sizeable numbers. All victims of the waiting game at one time or another, many of us gradually become culprits, attending events one to two hours late, just because we know that they will not start on time.

Similarly, we wait for buses and planes that rarely depart exactly on time. We also wait for service providers, suppliers and contractors, who are often late or, in turn, they have to wait for us, to pay them after the job has been completed.

However, it is important to note that unlike me, many Africans are not frustrated or upset by the need to wait. They simply have accepted this phenomenon, popularly called – 'African time' – as a way of life. It's part of their culture!

African time?

There is a range of conflicting views on the history of the 'African time' phenomenon. Some anthropologists argue that prior to the colonial era Africans had a profound respect for time, seasons and years. They knew when to plant and harvest. They religiously awoke before dawn, to clean their compounds and ensure that they reached their farms in the early hours of the morning, when the sun was just rising. They worked until the mid-afternoon and took their lunch and naps in the available shade, when the sun was at its peak. They then continued cultivating the ground until the sun began to set, a clear indication that it was time to head home, before dark.

This school of thought argues that 'African time' emerged as a form of rebellion against the colonialists. Popular folklore recounts incidences in which traditional rulers kept their colonialist administrators waiting. In one instance, when asked about the reason for the delay, the African retorted, 'Three o'clock is when I say it is three o'clock.' This type of behaviour enraged the colonialists, allowing the African to regain some measure of power and dignity.

Other anthropologists argue that the 'African time' phenomenon is a direct outcome of African beliefs and values regarding time itself. According to them, life in African cultures is composed of events, defined by relationships. They state that most African communities view time simply as a component of an event or an activity. The more or faster the activity, the more time flows and when resting or sitting, time is typically conserved.

According to Orville Boyd Jenkins, 'Instead of hours and numerical dates, Africans traditionally rely on emotional marks of time, like when you were born, when you married, when you had you first child, when there was a war. But as far as the future is concerned these marks are still to be made, and the African typically considers his or her influence on that as small.' As a result, he argues that the difference between Western and African time-consciousness is embedded in these statements: the Westerner asks: 'When did your grandfather die?' The answer is '15 years ago'. The African asks: 'When was 15 years ago?' And the answer is 'When your grandfather died'.

Another group of anthropologists simply argue that 'African time' has emerged as a result of the difficulties and uncertainties in the environment. According to them, even though most people start off their day with the best intentions, planning to arrive at meetings and attend to different commitments on time, a range of unplanned events fill up their day. Unexpected visitors show up at their offices and homes; unannounced road construction projects create traffic jams on the roads, adding an additional hour or two to their regular commute; their bus breaks down or is held up by police officers en route to their meeting, and so on. These uncertainties, which are often minimised in more industrialised nations, make it almost impossible to be punctual or to plan accurately.

This reality of existence on the continent is further exacerbated by the absence of consequences for not meeting preset deadlines. There are few consequences of lateness on the part of the 'big' men and women that stall meetings or the providers of products or services who do not meet pre-set deadlines. Indeed, it is not uncommon to experience unexplained delays in departure times for local road or air transport operators, and disappointments from tailors, printers, mechanics, architects, contractors and a range of other providers, many of whom do not even have functioning watches. The reality is that beyond the reputation risk to a select few, who are left with no better alternatives, relationships are rarely damaged because of lateness.

There is also the challenge of saying 'no' to additional commitments or responsibilities or to setting boundaries between the personal and professional life. This often means that many Africans take on additional commitments from the family, community, religious group, or their company, with the best intentions. Unfortunately, given that there are only 24 hours in a day, these tasks prove impossible to accomplish because of their other responsibilities, hence the emergence of the concept of 'African time'.

Regardless of which view cited above you most associate with, it is important to recognise that parts of the Arab world, Latin America, the Caribbean, South Asia and the African American community in the United States appear to share a similar concept of time to Africans, hence the use of the terms 'Arab time', 'Asian time', and 'Coloured people's time'. Indeed what many Africans have come to embrace as a unique part of our culture is actually shared by many other communities.

Sadly, these similarities also highlight a strong correlation between the level of industrialisation in a region and the concept of time in that region. More specifically, communities that view time as an expendable and economic resource are typically wealthier than communities that do not share these perspectives.

Even sceptics, who argue for the preservation of 'African time' because it emphasises the importance of relationships and events, over money, or because the Western concept of time is only a human construct, will not deny the fact that Africa is being increasingly isolated from the global economy because it is not competitive.

While many African CEOs spend half of their day waiting for their account officers or public sector officials, their counterparts in the West hold productive meetings and negotiate deals. While African manufacturers struggle to engage their employees for eight-hour shifts, typically operating at 30 per cent utilisation rates, their peers in China and India operate on a 24-hour basis at 95 per cent utilisation rates. Some even provide back office and call centre operations for companies in the West, capitalising on the differences in time zones. While stock analysts in the United States start their day at 6.30 a.m. to ensure some overlap with the London Stock Exchange, analysts in most sub-Saharan African countries operate in isolation, spending just two to three hours on the trading floor.

If we are serious about African competitiveness, then we have to recognise that culture is dynamic and evolves. While we may need to fight to retain specific aspects of our cultures, we have to be prepared to discard others. We need to urgently assess our current perspectives on time, and be prepared to change our mindsets and behaviour regarding this important component of life.

The way forward

Through our work at LEAP Africa, my colleagues and I have proved that it is possible to change mindsets and behaviour regarding the issue of time, a critical prerequisite for effective leadership. Beyond educating our participants that time is an expendable and quantifiable resource, and assisting them with assessing their current time usage, we also help them recognise that there is an opportunity lost for every minute that is spent waiting for someone or something. We teach them to create to-do lists, and prioritise them, to create work schedules and adhere to them, to create contingency plans to accommodate uncertainties, to address procrastination in their lives, to adopt the art of delegation and the skills required for effective time management.

Beyond the more theoretical aspects of our time management training, which is only a small component of our Youth and Business Leadership Programmes, we actually enforce strict time codes. From their first day on the programme, participants who arrive at the venue after 9.00 a.m. are dismissed from the programme, regardless of the circumstance that led to their late arrival. For the first time in many of our participants' lives, we introduce them to the consequences associated with lateness. This provides a painful, but very important signal to the other participants, and ensures that for the remainder of the programme, and their relationship with LEAP, they remain punctual. This change in behaviour often spills over to other aspects of their lives, as observed by nominators, peers and managers. Many of our entrepreneurs introduce these time management principles to their staff and are able to realise tangible benefits.

It is important to recognise that enforcing these principles also demands an additional burden on the Board, management, staff and volunteers of LEAP, who are required to model the behaviour that they expect in their participants. Indeed, changes in belief systems and behaviour are possible only if the 'change agents' are committed to consistently communicating and acting in a certain manner.

Like LEAP, other organisations in the Nigerian public, private and non-profit sectors are beginning to demonstrate the power of consequences in addressing the 'African time' phenomenon. They have adopted strict time management principles, while striving to preserve the important human relationships that form a critical component of African culture. They have introduced tools to track the time that their employees arrive in the office and when they leave. Some have also instituted daily departmental meetings as early as 6.30 a.m. to ensure that their employees get off to an early start. Lateness at these meetings often attracts a sizeable fine. In addition, companies are extending some of these rules to their suppliers and contractors, who forfeit a portion of their revenues for every single late day, after their predetermined deadline. It is important to recognise that these efforts have yielded extremely positive results, demonstrating that there is a strong correlation between time usage and increased efficiency and profitability.

Indeed, by providing formal training, introducing consequences and modelling behaviour, LEAP and a range of other Nigerian organisations are cultivating a new generation of African leaders and managers who are absorbing time management practices different from the norm. However, it is important to recognise that these leaders and managers still struggle on a daily basis to model this behaviour, given the difficulties associated with life on the continent. As a result, beyond the interventions described above, it is imperative that Africans address the obstacles of poor infrastructure, the rule of law, and governance, in order to create a conducive environment for effective time management, improved productivity and increased global competitiveness.

Conclusion

Imagine for a moment that I could relive the typical days described at the introduction of this article.

Once again, imagine for a moment that in 2008, you are being honoured by your community for your contribution. As you arrive at the venue at 9.30 a.m. and walk beyond the security area, you are greeted by the traditional rulers and the local government chairman. Instantly, you are filled with a sense of humility, and a conviction that those in positions of authority in your region truly value you as a person. After welcoming the honourees, the event commences promptly at 11.00 a.m, as scheduled.

Or that my partner meets me for breakfast exactly at 8.00 a.m. We have an excellent discussion for an hour and a half. My plane for Abuja promptly departs at 10.00 a.m. and I am on it. I arrive at the venue for the speaking engagement at 12.30 p.m. and have enough time to speak with the organisers and other special guests who have arrived on time. I speak at 2.00 p.m., network with the young people and entrepreneurs at the end of the event, by 4.30 p.m. I am on a flight back to Lagos. The printer is at the LEAP office at 7.30 p.m. and we are delighted with his work. All three tasks are accomplished.

This time, as I crawl into bed, I am fulfilled. I have had a productive and efficient day.

Is this a pipe dream? I do not think so.

I believe that everyone in a position of authority – teachers, entrepreneurs, civil servants, politicians, technocrats, traditional leaders and professionals – must be the first to change their mindsets and behaviour regarding time. This will not only demonstrate true leadership but will also send a powerful signal to others in society.

However, regardless of our status in society, it is imperative that we model time-conscious behaviour. Our 10.00 a.m. should mean 10.00 a.m. and 7.00 p.m. should mean 7.00 p.m. Convinced of our commitment and consistency regarding time, others will gradually begin to adopt similar practices. Collectively, we can begin to push Africa one step closer to global competitiveness.

Ubuntu and the helping hands for AIDS

Martha Chinouya

Martha Chinouya is a Zimbabwean social scientist working as a senior research fellow at London Metropolitan University. She has been active in faith-based HIV/AIDS work and has been involved in HIV research in Africa and the UK. She has a particular interest in gender and has studied the impact HIV/AIDS has had on rural communities, especially the response of grassroots Christian women and the new forms of leadership that have emerged among such women, rooted in the traditional concept of ubuntu. *Leadership has been designated as the theme for World AIDS Day 2007 and 2008. Here Martha Chinouya gives a concrete example of such leadership in action and how it has helped mitigate some of the effects of the epidemic, seen as one of the most pressing challenges facing Africa – particularly in how to cope with the millions of children orphaned by the deadly virus.*

> God did not give us hands for glamour: they are there to wash each other
> (LOCAL GRANDMOTHER CARING FOR ORPHANS IN MANICALAND)

Introduction

A six-year-old girl sits at the Anglican Diocesan Orphanage amidst the rolling landscape of mountains in Manicaland, eastern Zimbabwe, playing with an empty container of Mazowe (a local orange drink), which she uses as a toy. Occasionally she fills the container with mud, oblivious to the fact she is among the 15 million children throughout the world orphaned by AIDS. Together with her friends, some as young as two, she shares a home at the Anglican Church orphanage, and is looked after by nuns or sisters.

Traditionally, before the advent of AIDS, the family would have cared for orphaned children. The family, albeit in its extended form, is the institution recognised as the best for bringing up children, including those whose parents have died or those who are abandoned. Reflecting on my own childhood, rather nostalgically, this little girl's childhood stands in tension with what I experienced after my mother died, when I was a little girl, in the 1970s. Growing up as a motherless child, I watched my family mutate, shrinking because of deaths and migration, but expanding with marriages and births, its members including both the kin who shared the same totem as our family and the *sahwira* (those who had strong bonds of friendships with our parents).

I do not remember being referred to as an orphan, as I had my other mothers. The death of my mother was not the death of my being mothered. I was mothered by my biological mother's sisters, whom we referred to as 'younger or older mothers' according to their birth or clan position relative to my mother. Our mothers' brothers were 'male mothers'. I remember visiting my mother's brother, my 'male mother', who remarked that he did not have any breast milk to give, but rather a drink of Mazowe. Using the elastic definition of a family, we often joked as children that our parents and other adults forged kinship bonds with 'anyone' and our relatives seemed infinite. We had many mothers and fathers. But then those were the days when a few Zimbabwean dollars could help a young man marry. (One of my 'younger mothers' told me she was married for Z$50 in the 1950s, but today that money cannot buy a loaf of bread.)

The increasing costs of bringing up children, including school fees and housing, is causing some relatives to shy away from the responsibilities of caring for ever-increasing numbers of orphans in the family. AIDS is killing the breadwinners, mothers, male mothers, and also the *obabakazi* (the female fathers, sisters of our fathers). AIDS is shrinking the numbers of relatives that a child can turn to. But it is not only the cost of raising a child that scares relatives away from the responsibility, there is also the possibility that HIV/AIDS will be affecting their own, closer, family – or indeed themselves.

Nevertheless, here at the Anglican Diocese of Manicaland, as in many local areas all over Zimbabwe, the leadership of women in the Church has evolved in response to the threats to human dignity brought about by HIV. Other multiple challenges have arisen from the complex interplay of HIV/AIDS, patriarchy, and economic factors such as high inflation rates, migration and the brain drain, triggered by the structural adjustment programmes imposed by multilateral bodies in the 1980s and the political crisis in the country. This environment, marked by a shortage of resources, curtails efforts to improve access to both prevention and treatment – particularly anti-retroviral treatment, with home-based care a vital source of support for those unable to have treatment. Despite these difficulties, Zimbabwe is the only country in Southern Africa that has reported a drop in the prevalence of HIV.

Who is the leader? The *ubuntu-hunhu* approach

I grew up in Zimbabwe's second largest city, Bulawayo, and was 'lucky' to be able to master both major national languages – Shona, which we used at home when conversing with our Shona-speaking parents (migrants from Manicaland) and Ndebele, which we used with siblings and friends at school, for ours was a predominantly Ndebele-speaking community. We also had some Zulu speakers, mostly 'migrants' from South Africa, some of them refugees running away from apartheid to independent Zimbabwe. We were taught at school and at home that our behaviour must be guided by the principles of humanity referred to as *hunhu* (Shona) or *ubuntu* (Ndebele), those values that separate human beings from animals, birds and reptiles. Ndebele 'street' descriptions, such as *'uyinja'* (you are dog), are often heard to refer to people who have deviated from such principles (e.g. people who would refuse to share their stockpiles of food with a poor neighbour). The principle of *ubuntu* is encapsulated in phrases such as *'umuntu, ngumuntu ngabanye'* (a person is a person through others) or proverbs such as *'izandla ziyagezana'* (the left hand washes the right hand and the opposite is true), all stressing the importance of communal responsibilities.

Ubuntu-hunhu is the art of being human and belonging to life's networks, where behaviour produces ripple effects on other forms of communal existence. Human social and sexual networks, without internal interventions from within the group or externally from policy-makers, funding agencies and other global forces such as the availability of HIV and sexual health medicine, can shape the burden of disease in a community. Any intervention in these networks creates ripple effects that can change the course of the epidemic from one form to another. As an example, the migration of so-called 'educated' brains from Zimbabwe may have the ripple effect of increasing mother-to-child HIV infections, as there is a diminishing pool of trained staff to offer interventions that could help reduce this transmission. Recognising local grassroots 'hands' as an important resource with a positive role in social care is also likely to shape the course of the HIV/AIDS epidemic and its future.

It is in times of stress such as that presented by AIDS in Zimbabwe that *ubuntu-hunhu* can be a resource for designing interventions. In the UK, when some policy-makers assumed that Africans would easily accept the language of Western notions of research ethics and rights, we used the principles of *ubuntu-hunhu* to set a research agenda that was filtered through our ways of seeing, knowing and interpreting the world, grounded in this art of being human (Chinouya and O'Keefe, forthcoming). *Ubuntu-hunhu* principles are very close to the Christian doctrine that stresses forgiveness, sharing, and loving your neighbour. Indeed proponents of *ubuntu* in South Africa, such as Archbishop Desmond Tutu have used it and religion to calm the storm through the post-apartheid Truth and Reconciliation Commission which he chaired. Archbishop Tutu was like the metaphorical hands that helped other hands to wash themselves at the Commission, using the principles of *ubuntu*.

In Zimbabwe, HIV grassroots heroes of the epidemic emerge as they bring forth their *being* human, promoting communal responsibilities against the HIV/AIDS threats. A local grandmother – 'Gogo' (Ndebele for grandmother) – one of the local 'hands', who cares for six orphans, remarked that we cannot ignore a neighbour dying or suffering from AIDS, because that neighbour is also part of you and me. She asked, 'What are our hands for? Are they not for washing each other?' She added, 'God did not give us these hands for decoration or glamour, they are there to wash each other.' Gogo then posed the question: 'How can I sit in my hut and watch these starving children and not be part of their lives?' She went on, 'What will Mwari [God] think of me as a member of the Mothers' Union if I sit on my hands?' She even asked, 'How can I sleep at night knowing that this child has gone without *sadza* [maize meal food]?' Her words echoed the spirit of *ubuntu-hunhu* in that we are all affected, since our partners and families, to whom we are intricately bound, are living with the virus too. HIV affects all Zimbabweans, and all Africans.

Using *ubuntu-hunhu* as the starting point to ask who is a leader (the hands), it becomes clearer that within the Anglican Church in the Diocese of Manicaland there are many 'hands' at the grassroots emerging and pouring the cooling waters on a community devastated by the HIV epidemic. These 'hands' are women like the grandmothers, the Mothers' Union members, people infected with HIV and the nuns. Traditionally, proximity to the male parish leader, namely the Bishop or priest, gave women automatic leadership status as priests' wives or as leaders of the Mothers' Union in a given parish. The wife of the Bishop is the overall leader of the Mothers' Union for the Diocese. Because of the devastation of HIV, new leaders in the battle against it are emerging within the Church, silently raising their voices to be heard and presented within the Church. Using what I construe as *ubuntu-hunhu* philosophy, the Church is responding to calls from a congregation affected by HIV and increasingly becoming an institution that has embraced the prevention of HIV as part of God's work.

Ignoring God's hands

Leading this army of grassroots 'hands' is the Bishop, the overall head of the Diocese, aided by the priests, the leaders in their respective parishes. However, some funding bodies, policy-makers and planners at both international and local level, often relegate the Church's response, and the 'hands' that lead them, to being part of 'God's work'. Small groups of ordinary community members, caring for orphaned and vulnerable children and in urgent need of financial support, do not receive international funding, as many obstacles exist that prevent resources from reaching grassroots communities (Foster, 2005). This is despite the fact that in poorly resourced communities such as those found in Manicaland, the Church is an important development partner in achieving the interrelated Millennium Development Goals, such as universal primary education by 2015.

The Anglican Church in Zimbabwe manages a number of institutions, such as schools and clinics, in partnership with the Ministries of Education and Health respectively, which ensures a regular audience for HIV education and care. Indeed many Zimbabweans from the Manicaland Eastern Highlands have been educated at one of the Diocesan schools, such as St Augustine's (indeed with some elite members arguing that unless one has passed through St Augustine, one has not yet been to school!). However, expensive school fees often mean that children from poorer households, such as orphans, are unable to access primary school education. Such households often opt to send boys rather than girls to school, thus increasing vulnerability of girls to HIV infection, which has in turn led the local 'hands' to try to help *all* children access education in spite of the rocketing school fees.

The Mothers' Union (MU): hands washing each other

I remember visiting Gogo one time in Manicaland: I sat on her veranda facing the sun setting behind the mountains, drinking Mazowe brought to us by one of the orphaned children she looks after. Gogo is in her 80s (she has no birth certificate to prove her age, let alone identity) and talks passionately about her blue and white (MU) uniform and the day *'randakufekedzwa bachi'* (she was 'clothed in the coat of armour' or ordained) as a member of the MU. She had to undergo some lessons about being a Christian woman, looking after the family within the values of Christ. She tells me that in the 1950s, how you slept with your husband was not discussed at the MU and looks at the sky as she tells me that nowadays the young women are being talked to about *chirwere chemazuva ano* (modern disease, AIDS) in the MU. Gogo tells me that she has overheard two young MU members talking about rubbers (condoms) in the Church grounds! She tells me that a few of the younger MU members have died, and she was not sure if this was from this modern disease. Other women had been widowed. She wonders how the women could have contracted the virus if they had stuck to the doctrine of the Mothers' Union, which promotes monogamy. She spits on the ground and quickly buries the spit with her bare feet and with a shaking voice, now looking intently at the sun, says, *'varume mwangu'* (men, my child!).

Her words point to the gendered tensions that exist in HIV discourses. It is now recognised that the HIV epidemic is a feminised epidemic, particularly in sub-Saharan Africa, where more than half the infections are found among women. According to the Zimbabwe Development Report (2003) an adult prevalence of 33.7 per cent translates into 2 million adults living with HIV and AIDS by 2001, 60 per cent of these infections among women. Gogo's narratives about the MU clearly bring to the fore that being a member of the Mothers' Union in Zimbabwe is a vocation loaded with contradictions, in particular when negotiating the complex public discourse of 'purity' and the private sexualised lives of women, which can be marked by sexually transmitted infections, including HIV. *Kufekedzwa bachi* (to be 'clothed in the coat', i.e. the uniform) was an occasion that marked the transition of being a mere married women to becoming a Christian, 'armoured', 'clothed', monogamous wife and a church-wed mother. In the early 20th century, missionaries in Southern Africa prescribed an ideology of domesticity for Christian women, with housewifery, wifehood and motherhood full-time spiritual vocations (Epprecht, 1993). This discourse, marked by good housewifery, needlework and Christian motherhood, often silenced the private voices of women of Gogo's generation, in particular on matters related to domestic violence, sex and sexual health.

Although originally 'silenced', HIV is now changing the landscape of what this 'clothed army' of Christian women can educate each other about. Silently and painfully HIV is affecting the way women are using their time, once traditionally assigned to sometimes exchanging recipes, reading Bible verses, church flower arrangements, now to visiting the 'sick', attending *'nhamo'* (Shona for 'problem', referring to funerals or wakes), burying the dead, planning for the future of children and, like Gogo, caring for and accommodating orphaned children. Rocking a terrain marked by purity, some MU members are now infected with HIV, a predominantly sexually contracted infection. The private lives of these 'clothed' women are being rocked, pushing them to help each other, to become the hands that wash each other, thereby metaphorically elevating them to leadership positions, guiding the path for others to follow in caring for a community devastated by AIDS. Women, now affected through their intricate link with other MU members and the community they are situated in, have forged spaces for discussing very intimate issues, including widowhood, orphans, unpaid hospital bills, house-building projects left unfinished by their dying husband and, rarely, their own HIV infections. Some now clad for a year in black from head to toe, a mourning ritual for late husbands (bereaved husbands only wear a little black patch, about 2cm square, pinned on their shoulders, which can be covered by a jacket or a cardigan), the young widows are visible among their peers, with questions raised obliquely about the mourning widow's own HIV status. Some 'clothed' members of the Mothers' Union, to whom I spoke while in Manicaland, remark that they are very much affected by HIV and they have no choice but to engage with HIV discussions as part of their biblical studies. In so doing they are taking on a leadership role by changing the direction of the 'path' for Bible study.

Personal communication with the current Mothers' Union President, Mrs Victoria Jakazi in 2007 and the former President, Mrs Ruth Bakare, in 2003, indicated that as presidents they were supporting the women in embracing HIV and AIDS issues as part of their ministries. Indeed in their Bible study called 'Education of Women in God's Field', written by the Evangelism Committee, women are reminded about HIV as part of the education for being a member of the Mothers' Union. In their annual conference, which attracts over 700 women from urban and rural Manicaland, speakers are invited to talk to women about health, including HIV and AIDS.

Mothers' Union leadership has transformed itself in the wake of the HIV epidemic, and has increasingly become a network of peer support for those living with and affected by HIV and AIDS. In the event of a death, members of the Mothers' Union rally together, offering support to their peers, family and members of the community. This army of uniformed women, known locally as the *Ruwadzano Rwemadzimai*, are vital leaders in the support and care of people infected with HIV in their various parishes. Some of the women also form the 'barefoot care-givers', providing care and support to those living with HIV in the remote parts of this mountainous province. As care providers, they receive training that includes HIV awareness and caring for the sick. One member of the Mothers' Union once remarked that it is the gospel that gives them the strength to provide this care and support. The sporadic availability and accessibility of anti-retroviral treatment in Zimbabwe often means that most patients are often in very poor health. In addition to the limited resources to treat those living with HIV, the care-givers also report lack of resources such as gloves, plastic sheets and bicycles. Despite the lack of such 'worldly resources' the women often remark, 'We cannot let these things let us down. When the left hand is sick the right hand works harder.' Indeed the women were working very hard to restore some form of normality to a community facing multiple deaths and illnesses.

Zimbabwean Gogos (grandmothers): the hands that cannot be sat on

HIV is reversing the norm of inter-generational contracts in care, in particular the expectation that parents will be looked after and buried by their children and their grandchildren – now the opposite is true. Gogo told me that she has six children that she looks after. Five of these are her grandchildren, children of her two late sons and a daughter. One is a great-grandchild, her late grand-daughter's child, who Gogo suspects died from *chirwere chemazuva ano* (AIDS). In her 'sitting room' there is a television, which belonged to one of the grandchildren's parents. When the children's parents died, the television 'went with the children' to Gogo's homestead. The television, according to Gogo, 'does nothing' as there is no electricity. They tried to use a car battery but there was no 'signal' and all efforts to watch what Gogo refers to as the 'teravision' were abandoned. Gogo suspects that the 'teravision' is one of her downfalls, as some people when they hear or indeed see that she owns one mistake her for someone 'with money' in a community where there are no, or very few, private televisions, thereby reducing some of the help she may get. Gogo tells me that the biggest challenges she faces are school fees, clothing, food and understanding if the children are actually doing their school work. She asks, 'How can I tell from these papers they bring me if they are doing anything at school? … Anyway my eyes are going.' Among Gogo's pillars of support are other local grandmothers, some of them members of her local MU. Home visits and information sharing is common among the grandmothers. Leaders within this women's group often instigate home visits, especially if a member has missed a number of meetings at the *China* (Thursday Mothers' Union meetings).

In addition to caring for the orphans in her own household, Gogo also visits children in the neighbouring child-headed households. Mothers' Union teaching, in particular on good 'Christian motherhood', has fused with local culture and evolving traditions regarding the 'African' or Zimbabwean sense of being a mother, that stretches beyond the biological link between a mother and her child. Social mothering of children whose parents have died of AIDS was also witnessed in the Church with women engaged in visiting child-headed households, offering guidance and support. In addition, Church leaders host weekly 'soup kitchens' at local parishes, where vulnerable children and grandparents are invited by Church leaders (predominantly younger MU members) for a meal. Women from the MU are vital leaders in food preparation, the food often donated by parish members and the Church. I was impressed by the spirit of resilience of the women and grandmothers, some of whom note that 'if they sit on their hands, the epidemic will sit on them and they will not be able to move'.

Nuns: hands in Wedu (our) orphaned households

Before AIDS became a national crisis, the death of a child's parents did not often mean that the child had to be removed from the family network and cared for by 'strangers'. The devastation brought by HIV to existing family networks has been unbearable, in particular for grandparents and widowed parents, straining these coping mechanisms. This strain has affected members of the congregation in various parishes. There are reports of children being abandoned by desperate parents and then handed over to the Church's children's homes. There are many boys and girls who have lost a parent or parents from AIDS in Zimbabwe. A joint report, *Children on the brink* (2004), estimates that of the 1.3 million orphaned children in Zimbabwe, most (78 per cent) were those who had lost a parent or parents from AIDS. Creative leadership that reflects the changes in children's lives is required, with nuns the 'helping hands' in the Church orphanages or children's homes.

At no other time has the leadership position of nuns in the care of children been so reflective of the contradictions that HIV presents to women and the Church. The vocation of nuns or sisters is purity in life, expressed in their public life as virtuous, single and celibate women. In our community in Manicaland, some people consider nuns to be the brides of Christ, who, by choice, have decided to remain childless. Such virtuousness should mean a minimum risk of being tainted by worldly vices, including the presence of HIV in their lives. A question often obliquely raised by 'faceless' women and men in Manicaland is 'why should women who have chosen celibacy be the "hands" in childcare?' The answer, I believe, is hidden in the Christian doctrine of caring for those who are vulnerable and the philosophy of *ubuntu-hunhu* that indicates that no one can afford to be untouched by the ripple effects of AIDS.

In their own ways, nuns or sisters strive to normalise children's lives by providing 'alternative families' for children who might otherwise have ended up as 'street kids'. To foster a common family identity, some children in one of the Church's orphanages have a common Shona surname of Wedu. The word *wedu* translates as 'ours', reminding the community that the children belong to everyone. One nun once remarked, 'Most of the children are Wedu; even on their birth certificate they are Wedu, and as such they have a sense of being brothers and sisters.'

As the 'hands' in the household orphanages, it remains unclear what the familial position of nuns in the Wedu family is. Are nuns, as the brides of Christ who died and later went to heaven, philosophically the 'widowed' mothers in the Wedu households or orphanages? Has the HIV epidemic obliquely and cunningly introduced motherhood to these virtuous women? The HIV epidemic is changing some family structures, with the concept of brotherhood or sisterhood no longer based on a common totem, but rather a common experience of abandonment and orphanhood. Within the Church a new family structure is emerging: one of children, unrelated by blood, totems or clan, forging new family identities. It remains less clear how children in the Wedu family make sense of this belonging and how they negotiate transition into adult life. Challenges, however, are also faced in such 'alternative' families, in particular access to resources to help children realise their full potential as they go through different phases of their childhoods. These resources include toys, books, computers, etc. However, as the girl in the opening paragraph illustrates, you need an empty container of Mazowe to play a game and indeed some of the boys, when I visited, were playing football from a ball of newspapers that they had bundled up. Why should they sit on their hands, waiting for someone to give them toys when they can make their own?

Parish members living with HIV: 'hidden hands' in HIV issues

The numbers of people living with HIV in the Anglican Diocese of Manicaland remains unknown, as some church members may not have been subjected to HIV anti-body tests. Given the sensitivities surrounding HIV research within the Church, Church leaders have used their work experiences to gauge the extent HIV is affecting their congregations. Various indirect statistics are used, such as the number of deaths, orphaned and vulnerable children, illnesses and, to a point, self-disclosures to the priests. Using these indirect measures, priests, working with a few people who have disclosed their HIV status, have created spaces within the Church for peer support. Support group members meet in church halls or other rooms within the church. In these spaces, they have developed ways of supporting one another and are often engaged in income-generating projects. When I visited these support groups, it emerged that the issue of disclosure within the Church still remained a challenge. Some members of the support group, when asked to say what they had told their families about their whereabouts when they were attending support group meetings, reported that they had told them that they were queuing for bread and sugar that were in short supply or that they had taken a stroll into town. None had openly disclosed to their family members that they were attending the diocesan support groups for people who are HIV positive. Although 'hiding' their leadership, people living with HIV are shaping the HIV agenda within the Church. For example, the Anglican Cathedral has a large red ribbon on the main door, with the inscription 'The Lord Cares, We care'. Attending the service, the priest and other ordained leaders never fail to bring the word 'HIV' into their sermons.

Conclusions

The Christian Church in Zimbabwe and the values of *ubuntu-hunhu* are a force behind the emergence of grassroots leadership formation. Women are critical 'hands' in this grassroots movement, and are shifting spaces within the Church for discussing matters that affect them. The women in the

Mothers' Union, grandmothers and nuns are all part and parcel of the hands that are shaping the Church's response to the epidemic.

It is often the case that community or grassroots leaders as those found in Manicaland, such as support group leadership in living with HIV and women's groups are often not taken seriously, as they are deemed to be 'doing God's work' which is often construed as requiring less recognition and financial commitment, but rather more spiritual devotion. It is time that women of faith are taken seriously at policy level, both nationally and internationally, as they are the group most affected by the epidemic and are also in the forefront of interventions. These women are very much part of the HIV solution and deserve more recognition by funding and policy-makers. Grassroots leaders are raising awareness of HIV and responding to the epidemic: this, as one grandmother, a member of the Mothers' Union, remarked, is done using our 'bare hands'. Further, the concept of *ubuntu-hunhu* is a tool that is well placed to facilitate the fight against the negative effects of HIV/AIDS, and it is up to Africans to 'get hold' of this tool and interrogate it for the benefit of answering some of Africa's problems.

Notes

Martha Chinouya and Eileen O'Keefe (2006), 'Zimbabwean Cultural Traditions in England: Ubuntu-Hunhu as a Human Rights Tool', in *Diversity in Health and Social Care: Vol. 3, No.2*, pp. 89–98.

CUNAIDS, UNICEF and USAID (2004), *Children on the Brink 2004: A joint report of new orphan estimates and a framework for action*.

Marc Epprechet, 'Domesticity and Piety in Colonial Lesotho – the private politics of Basotho women's pious associations', in *Journal of Southern African Studies*, Vol. 19, No 2 June 1993.

Geoff Foster (2005), *Bottlenecks and drip-feeds: Channelling resources to communities responding to orphans and vulnerable children in Southern Africa*. London, Save the Children.

Poverty Reduction Forum and United Nations Development Programme (2003), Zimbabwe Human Development Report, Harare Graphtec Communication.

Leadership and 'followership' in an African village

Onyekachi Wambu

The majority of Africans still live in rural communities. However, rapid urbanisation is just one of the most dramatic stories that has been quietly unfolding on the African continent over the last 50 years. Onyekachi Wambu looks at how his own small village has adapted to this phenomenon: what impact this change has had on village governance structures, and more importantly, how rapid urbanisation has transformed the community's very identity as a universe unto itself.

On a Saturday morning, the phone rang at my London house. It was one of my brothers. He had just spoken to a relative from our village. Usually one dreads these calls and the news they bring. It is always something serious, and there are two types of 'serious'. It may be a request for money you don't have, often to assist somebody who is seriously ill, needs school fees, or some other emergency expense, which you would be inhuman to refuse even though you can't afford it. On reflection, in many ways one prefers these calls because there is at least some room to act. The second type of 'serious' is infinitely worse and final: another person is dead!

Typically, the dead person would be older. Among those of my father's generation, every other month another of his peer group is called 'home'. When you hear that voice from the village hesitate before saying there's been a death, you always wonder who it will be. You don't want it to be the much-loved aunt or uncle who looked after you as a child; the old storyteller, the human library, who could tell you the history of your village from the beginning of the last century; or even more unusual and shocking, the smiling young cousin who has gone before their time, either through an accident or by contracting a terminal illness. Whoever it is, the death is always a 'double whammy': first there is the wet-eyed sadness at the loss of yet another individual to the earth; and then inevitably, the request for money to help with funeral and other ritual expenses. Sometimes in Africa, more money is spent ensuring the dignity of the dead than on the existence of the living.

Yet, this time the message from the village was neither of death nor a request for money: in many ways it registered a new level on the 'serious' scale. It was so jaw-droppingly shocking and unprecedented that I couldn't quite believe what I was hearing. A roving band of youths from the village had arrested several of our old men, physically detaining them. Nay, let's call it what it really was – *holding them hostage*, in the village school. The old men had been accused of practising '*Juju*', witchcraft, calling on dark forces to block the progress of others.

One of those arrested was a close relative. Stop. Let me rephrase that. *All* of the old men arrested were close relatives, given the kinship system that operates in our village. The village was established by six blood brothers, thus we were all literally blood brothers and cousins. In effect, what had taken place was that a group of youths had arrested their fathers, uncles, and grandfathers and detained them in the local school. My world was spinning. How could the young be so bold as to commit such a sacrilegious act? Overthrowing thousands of years of tradition and custom which venerated the generation before, their fathers and grandfathers, the possessors of wisdom, the sources of power, authority and legitimacy in the village? How could they arrest those who were indeed one generation closer to the venerated ancestors and to creation itself?

As we asked ourselves these questions, the phone calls went back and forth, across London, to Nigeria, to the US. The growth of mobile phone networks in Nigeria over the last ten years now means that we could follow developments blow by blow, and things were getting worse. We began to hear dark and even more unbelievable rumours from one cousin, rumours that were later confirmed as truth by those in authority. Not only had the old men been isolated in the school, away from their families, but some of them were now being beaten and tortured to coerce them to confess to practising the dark arts. How could this be? Then we heard the worst, one of the frail old men had died from a heart attack, probably induced by the stress he had suffered in detention.

Our world was spinning off its axis. The village seemed on the verge of a collective nervous breakdown. The invisible threads of understanding which held everything together seemed to be unravelling, fast. How had the order in the village collapsed so totally?

Begging a question?

I should have known that all was not well in the village. Going back over the years, especially since the World Bank-imposed structural adjustment of the economy in the 1980s, I had witnessed an ever-increasing deterioration in what was perhaps the very spirit of the village itself. Over the last few decades, every time I had returned, things had become more distressing. Underneath the sheen of obvious material progress, evidenced by the new brick houses, motorcycles, cars, mobile phones, water tanks, and other accoutrements of the modern world, one sensed that the human spirit was becoming more and more hopeless, even broken. The clearest manifestation of this, amidst all the surface progress, was the rise in begging.

More and more people in the village were begging. Do you have something for me? Things are really hard, I need money to start a business. I don't have money for medicine. I need money for school fees for the children. I need money to help bury my mother. I need money to get married. There seemed to be an insatiable number of desires, most of which remained unfulfilled, producing a deep malaise and lack of contentment.

The people begging now were not just the ne'er-do-wells I remembered from my childhood, some 30 years ago. Those had been the people who didn't want to work and were content to live off their hardworking wives' earnings. Yet in preferring to drink and while away the time, they had also suffered the opprobrium and contempt of being dismissed as lazy. They were inactive people who could not look after themselves and their families, people who created no value and just were, in a culture that denigrates people who simply exist.

The culture was one that, at its core, celebrated agency, activity and material advancement. It ritualised these through title taking. Titles were conferred for real accomplishments to those who, in the first place, must have worked hard through their lives to be able to afford the expensive ceremonies involved in taking the title. For those who didn't take titles there were other ways in which their achievements were celebrated and honoured. In this largely agricultural community, where the principal crop was yam, those who harvested the most were given the honorific '*eze ji*' – Yam King. These were people who had turned the potential blessing of *Ala*, the land deity, into a real product. This process of turning potential into reality, of creating value, the process, in other words, of *doing*, was considered so important that it had its own recognised deity – *Ikenga*. This represented the 'force' of the right arm, and was depicted by the double-horned ram.

On my recent visits to the village – given the rise in begging, this force seemed to be waning at all levels. Now everybody seemed to be begging. That proud, dignified old man, who I had always imagined as a giant, was now a shrivelled supplicant with his hands outstretched.

This beseeching that took place at the village level was also happening higher up the social strata, at the state, national and pan-African levels. Africa had become recast into the begging continent. However, like most ordinary Africans, particularly in the last 20 years, I had given up worrying about what was happening beyond my own level of existence. I had retreated to a place that I felt offered security, where one's individual voice was recognised, and which offered a means of accountability. This could obviously not be the pan-African level with a population of more than 750 million people. Nor indeed could it be at the Nigerian state level with its population of 140 million; or in fact at the regional (Igbo language/ethnic group) level of 30–35 million. The level of my state in the Nigerian federation 4–5 million and even the level of the Local Government Area at 200,000 – 500,000, would also prove to be impossible. It had to be at the level of the autonomous, sovereign community of 1,000–1,500 people, which was the village. Many of us in Africa had retreated once more to this village level, because most of the time it is here that we are truly offered safety and recognition. Things function. It works.

So when the phone started ringing in London, and the *Juju* madness started to flow down the line, I was alarmed. As with the quiet unease over the begging, there had been earlier premonitions of this impending chaos.

An earlier crisis

The last time I had been in the village was a few months before the phone call. I had gone to do some research on the village itself. I wanted to understand where leadership and power now lay; and if it had moved to a new locus, why this had happened. Inevitably the research was side-tracked. If you arrive in a place where everybody is related, you are invariably sucked into family business and disputes, which await your arrival for resolution. Also, in a village where land is owned communally, many of these disputes are about land. And my family was involved in a big dispute. Being the second youngest of my mother's children, I had no authority to make any decisions. I was merely there to listen to what was being said and to convey decisions my eldest brother had agreed with the rest of the family following our own discussions.

So, having arrived in the village, I tried to find out the different attitudes and opinions in this latest land dispute. I started in my father's compound, currently occupied by his deceased brother's wife and her son. I then navigated outward from this core, following the threads that linked relationships in the village. I went first to my father's surviving brothers and their families, the Wambus, then to the Wambus' closest relatives, those descended from Udo, our common ancestor from the six brothers who founded the village. *Udo* means peace, so, as Umu Udo, we are literally the 'children of peace'.

The land dispute involved common Udo land, so there was no need to engage the wider village, the families of the descendants of the other five brothers who had established the village.

Like the rest of the village, the Udo family had produced many successful professionals – doctors, lawyers, engineers, artists. But many of them lived outside where their jobs were – in Aba, the nearest town, in Port Harcourt, Nigeria's oil city, in Lagos, the commercial capital or abroad, in Europe and America. Those left in the village were frequently the old, and families that had not benefited from formal education or those who had remained farmers. In many ways those left in the village are those who are most challenged by the task of dealing with change and transformation.

I went around the compounds of the Udo family members. After greeting the oldest living males, I engaged with their wives, my peers, and then the younger members. Finally I was introduced to the newest members who had been born since my last visit. I listened intently to different generations, getting their unique take on events and hearing the different causes behind the land dispute. In time a broad picture of what was going on emerged, including who was responsible, and strategies for dealing with it. Wherever I went and whoever I spoke to, I was also reminded that the Udo family meeting taking place on Thursday evening was the appropriate place to resolve the issue, when all voting members of the family were gathered in one place. My visits were also important to assess who might be on our side in the dispute, as well as which way the meeting was likely to go.

Aba

Since it was still only Monday I decided I would get back to my formal research about governance in the village. I ventured further out from the Udo kin, visiting the descendants of some of the other five brothers: Umu Adiele, Umu Okereke, Umu Agwu; Umu Ajiagwa; Umu Adarba. Even though they had no immediate jurisdiction, it was important to hear what others thought was going on among the 'children of peace'. Away from the compounds of Udo, it was also an opportunity to say hello, catch up with news, pass on messages from London and talk about developments in the country more broadly.

Nobody mentioned it directly, but Aba, the big city about five miles away was the subject of much of the discussion. Some people, like my father's surviving brother – who loved silence, and the oasis of calm, cleanliness and order that was the village – were angry about the volume of traffic now going through the village, as people headed to Aba. Others now do most of their shopping at Aba and were constantly talking about having to cut short our conversation so they could go into town for something or other, instead of using the twice-weekly market that took place in one of the village squares. For many younger people Aba is the solution to their problems of unemployment.

Although Aba is a noisy, dusty, dirty, chaotic eyesore, it is an important city in Nigeria. A major manufacturing centre, Nigerians have dubbed it their Taiwan of the east. Traders come from all over the country, and indeed, the wider West African region, to buy its well-made shoes, bags and other leather goods, as well as car spare parts. The city is beginning to explode at an exponential rate and our village will soon become one of its suburbs.

The village has always had a strange relationship with Aba. Once, even as recently as my childhood when there were very few cars and people had to walk everywhere, those five miles seemed so far away. Now the cheap and efficient transport system of car taxis, *okadas* (motorbike taxis) and bicycles, has shrunk the distance, bringing this strange place ever closer. Whereas our village was built by us, Aba has developed into its present size as a colonial construct. Part of the name of our village was derived from this colonial encounter. Many Igbo people play a pun on our name, calling us *Ohuru – Umu-Ekwensu*, as though we were the children of *Ekwensu*, the deity of chaos, whereas the actual name is *Ekweasu*, 'either we agree or we fight'. We acquired the name when the first European arrived, riding a bicycle in the area at the start of the 20th century. As the imperial project unfolded, villages were being destroyed and annexed as the British crown sought to impose a trading monopoly through political control. Representatives from a wider group of 13 villages in the area had come together, ambushed the stranger and killed him. In retaliation, the colonial authority in Aba sent in armed soldiers who unleashed violence on the villages, as well as demanding that they bring out their shrines and ritual objects to be burnt. Twelve of the villages buckled under the pressure, but not Ohuru. Facing the threat of collective punishment from the British, the other 12 villages put enormous pressure on our village, but the people of Ohuru insisted that since they didn't agree, they would fight. Their stubbornness was rewarded with a new identity. And even today they wear the badge with pride.

Despite their unwillingness to change, the conflict with the British did eventually lead to profound changes. Having initially resisted the British, they then embraced aspects of the coloniser's culture that they thought would produce progress. In 1915 a patch of land was given to the Catholics to build the first church, which still stands in the centre of the village, and gradually people became Christians. Then their mission school, St Anthony's, was added. Soon other denominations moved in. So Aba had been the source of the alien insertion into our culture, and it had continued to be the place members of the village went for most things that were not available locally, such as a secondary school, the general hospital, etc.

Now it was threatening to eat into the village, and soon the village would simply be a suburb of this expanding metropolis. Pretty quickly it became apparent that it was actually the continuing geographical encroachment of Aba that was creating the tensions and increased anxiety around land ownership. This was leading to more and more disputes. Land was being commoditised. People were land grabbing, increasingly registering and selling what was communal land.

Sons of the soil

Interestingly, as I wandered around the village, the young men, *Nwa Afo* (sons of the soil), I spoke to seemed to welcome the advent of Aba. I thought I could detect a yearning. Perhaps Aba meant a space where they could make a living, earn fast money, buy their own property and escape the age-based hierarchal structure that was in our village? Power was generational in the village and many of these young people would not see power or make law for perhaps 30 years. They were frustrated that those older men who had it were not responsive to their needs. Land was commonly held, but once the old men had given you your portion to farm, you were expected to add value to it. Many of the young were no longer interested in farming, they had lots of other business ideas that they wanted capital and support for.

One entrepreneurial cousin was already producing handbags and sandals in Aba and needed capital to scale up his operations. Help for him was being co-ordinated at the family level, but resources were limited. There was no broader vision on how the village could itself support any of these activities, or plug into the other industrial activities happening in the dynamic centre of Aba. So once given the common land, for which they were supposed to be merely custodians, many of the young people were illegally selling it to generate liquid funds. Gradually, people outside the village who were not related to the six founding brothers were now buying land and therefore acquiring a presence in the village. This was a risky strategy. Some families were now down to the piece of land on which they lived. One could soon see a generation of landless people looming on the horizon. The land ownership structure in the village had ensured that everybody had land to farm and there were no destitute people, just people who had not added value to their land.

When I asked what the young men actually *did* in terms of governance in the village, two replied, 'not a lot, really'. But they had in the past acted as secretaries for the council of elders, and attended the meetings as observers where '*Omenala*' (law prescribing conduct and land use) was interpreted from the oral tradition. Observing all this, they learnt the ropes in preparation for when they would take over, and themselves preside over the *Omenala*. A young man in his mid-30s described the calibre of the men on the council a few years earlier when he was secretary. He had been spellbound by their oratory, the poetry of their proverbs, as they recalled what their own fathers had said in the dim mists of time and the precedents that allowed them to argue for whatever position they wanted to impose. What of now? He seemed wistful, sighing the disappointment of those who think all golden ages are always in the past. But he agreed that even now the council continued to be important, particularly in its most traditional function: principally resolving disputes that could not be sorted out at family or clan level, or which were village-wide in dimension.

Nigerian law still allows this customary resolution of conflicts, although people can always ignore its ruling and enter the Nigerian legal system if they want further appeal. Most people choose not to do that. Here, at this local level, the dispute is handled by people you know, within cultural rules that you accept, in a language all parties understand and speak. (Nigerian court business is conducted in English, a language many people do not speak or understand properly.) Locally, costs can be kept to a level that people can afford (usually giving the council some alcoholic beverages and livestock, depending on the nature of the case) and within a timeframe that works for them. Often, the Nigerian legal system is so slow that it is not unknown for people to have been held on remand in jail for ten years because they cannot afford lawyers.

Another young man I spoke to added that, beyond their secretarial duties on the council, the young men also continued to perform their most important collective traditional governance function, which was to police or defend the village on the orders of the council of elders, as well as music-making and other cultural activities during ceremonial events.

Daughters of the soil

For the young women Aba, and even further afield, Lagos or London, also offered escape and potentially full political and land rights. The village discriminates between two categories of women, *Nwa Ada* (daughters of the soil) and *Nwanyi Alurualu* (married-in wives). Neither have land rights independently of male relatives. The original reasons for this gender discrimination made sense in terms of the organising structure of the village. Due to the fact that village members are related through blood, through the founding six brothers, an incest-taboo is in place, which precludes village members marrying each other. They can only marry women from outside, usually from approved neighbouring villages. Wives coming into the village arrive with a set of rights that are applicable within and outside the village. Given that marriage is not just between individuals but also between families, there are also rights bestowed on offspring in the mother's village. In Chinua Achebe's classic book, *Things Fall Apart*, the hero is banished to his mother's village after a particular transgression in his own village. Here, as the son of his mother, he is accepted and given a house to live in and a plot to farm, but has no formal land or political rights – in order words, he is not considered a full man.

Within the village, the children of a marriage are treated differently. Both boy and girl children enjoy rights in the village in most areas – but in some critical areas, over land and political rights, these are gendered. The wives and their daughters can contribute to the political consensus as part of the various assembly meetings, but on the whole do not enjoy legislative or executive power. This is limited to the older men in the village because political power is linked to land, and those who guarantee it for the next generation, that is, the sons/men who inherit the stewardship. Land was not given to daughters because they were expected to marry out of the village, given the incest taboo. Unmarried daughters (which is rare and not encouraged, given the premium on reproducing the community) or divorced daughters who have returned to the village, are entitled to live on their father's land – but have no voting rights.

While the reasons for denying women rights might have made sense when the village was the universe, and most people lived and died within five miles of it, and land was owned by the descendants of the six founders, it is a total anachronism today, given the way the village has transformed over the last 100 years. Speaking to one young girl, I discovered the one thing she would like above all else was to own land, both for her livelihood and for the intrinsic political rights that would accrue to her.

When I asked about the power that women were supposed to exercise through the bedroom, in the married women's assemblies, and in the daughters of the soil meetings, she listened intently. In theory, in most Igbo communities the people who were the final moral arbiters – those who could pull the community back from madness if it was teetering on the brink, were not the men or the wives, but the 'daughters of the soil', including those who were married out. Perhaps this was because it was felt that they might be the only truly impartial voice, without an interest to defend.

She replied that that was all theory. In practice, the 'daughters of the soil' were not organised. The only public functions they did together as daughters, or their mothers did together as wives, were either ritual ceremonies around births, marriage and deaths, or community duties like keeping the village clean. They could not decide in which direction the village should go, and their voice did not matter in discussions over these big issues or changing law in the village.

But it hadn't always been merely theoretical. In 1929, women from villages like ours had shaken the British colonial authority when they had revolted against tax rises in the Aba Women's Riot. The men had been reticent and cautious, following their military defeat a generation earlier. It was the women who had organised in their groups and acted independently, unleashing the fury of the community. Through their mobilisation they had turned the potential space allowed by convention into a real site of engagement and transformation.

An older married woman I spoke to in the village had retained some of that fire and independent spirit. She had played a different game altogether from the young women, spending a lot of time and effort to take a title, which acknowledged her contributions to the village. Having the title had guaranteed her a place at the table in meetings and she was able to put her points across, to the annoyance of one of two of the men who had been against her acquiring the title.

Visiting Aba

The Umu Udo meeting was fast approaching. It was the following day. But first I decided to go to Aba myself to rent a few 'Nollywood' DVD films and to visit another cousin, a doctor in his late 50s, who had his own private hospital there and kept one house in the city and another in the village. He was arguably the most successful member of Umu Udo and, being nearby in Aba, was always the first source of help for people who needed it in the village. In London, we both admired and felt sorry for him. When I met him he confirmed much of what we suspected. He was personally supporting about 20 children in the village through school, and the demands for free healthcare were endless. Nonetheless, he seemed to bear it all with his usual calmness, formed by his sense of duty. We talked about the land dispute and he apologised that he would not be able to make the meeting the next day. He was very busy and village affairs were taking up more and more of his time.

He had become involved in the politics of the selection of the new village chief, who was traditionally the first among equals on the council of elders. The chieftaincy was for life, but on the death of each chief, it was rotated to a descendant drawn from one of the six brothers. The last chief, Ohuru's first doctor, had died at a ripe old age. It was now the turn of Umu Udo to produce the next chief, and given that my doctor cousin was the most successful son of the clan who lived anywhere near the village, he had been asked to assume the chieftaincy. He had refused, knowing how much would be involved – in court hearings, receiving people, representing the village at external functions such as funerals and chieftaincy gatherings. In addition, not to mention the intrigues of Nigerian politics: chiefs are expected to interact with local government officials, state assembly representatives and the state governor, all of whom are locked into national party politics that is frequently marred by lethal rivalries. Each party seeks to mobilise the traditional structures as a means of securing votes to support their national monopoly of power and control of the army, police, treasury, and oil.

Umu Udo received the refusal of the chieftaincy by my doctor cousin with huge disappointment. Some of the old men wanted the position, but could not afford the large expense that would be needed for the customary duties and hospitality, in what was in effect a voluntary position. My doctor cousin had been asked again. He refused again, but decided that he would instead become kingmaker, paying the expenses and other costs of the nominee Umu Udo eventually put forward for the chieftaincy. Playing the politics within the wider village to secure this choice was eating up enormous time and resources. An appeal had even come to us in London for extra resources, which we had foolishly ignored, and which would later have serious consequences.

My doctor cousin was also frustrated at the slowness of change in the village. With many of the old men in their 70s, 80s and 90s, this meant that he was still quite a while away from power. Whether it was deliberate or not is a moot point, but he and a few of his peers had formed themselves into a new group, centred on the village school. The St Anthony's Alumni Group had been established, attracting much interest from the younger people in the village who saw them as more forward-looking. They were beginning to refer all ideas for village development to the group. Most of the members of the alumni group were professional people like my doctor cousin. However, that also meant that most of them lived outside the village, in Aba, Port Harcourt, Lagos or even overseas. The group's impact on the ground had therefore been quite limited. What some of them had been successful in doing was spearheading new Christian evangelising in the village. Most of them, having come through the school, were Christians and part of the great 'born again' phenomenon sweeping through Nigeria since the 1980s. A religious response to the despair felt by many following the collapse of the economy and the World Bank-imposed structural adjustment which had devalued the currency, destroying the middle class. In 1980 one pound sterling had been worth two *naira*: the figure was now 250 *naira*. And in the gap real trouble and misery had been brewing in the land.

I rang London and told my brothers what was going on and, with this information, together we explored the best way to approach the Umu Udo meeting. In broad terms my advice was accepted but my eldest brother, the family representative, added his own ideas, which I was to convey to the village.

Meeting of Umu Udo

The night was very dark, but was alive with crickets scratching and cracking loudly. There were so many of them that it was difficult to hear the individual scratching of each insect. There was just one long drone. The village had been without electricity for a month. The meeting was being held in the compound of the oldest male of the 'children of peace'. He did not have a generator, so we sat with a small hurricane lamp, which emitted very little light. In the darkness beyond, we could hear noises of domesticity, as his family and children in the kitchen area washed up after the evening meal. There was a sufficient amount of light, however, to see that there were about 20 people who had made it to the meeting. All but one of them were married men with children from Umu Udo, the normal voting electorate. The exception was a lone woman, a married-out daughter of the soil. The chair of the meeting was a younger man, who worked with another young man who was keeping minutes.

The order of business began. Dues were outstanding for some customary issue that was to have been handled on a collective basis. The guilty were reminded and embarrassed. Other discussions took place on matters carried over from previous meetings and one dispute was referred to a future meeting because there wouldn't be time tonight to tackle it. We had a full agenda. There was dissatisfaction about this from the aggrieved party but the ruling was accepted. The sole woman then spoke. There was some tension between her husband's village and our village over a marriage issue. The meeting agreed to send a delegation to her village to resolve the matter. One or two volunteered for the delegation.

Then it came to my business. I rose to speak. I welcomed everyone in the Igbo language, reaffirmed the kinship bonds holding us together, and wished the community well and a long life, in the traditional way. I wanted the message I was going to convey to be precise: a lot was riding on it and I didn't want people to misunderstand. In a meeting like this where decisions were final and where you could lose votes by saying the wrong thing, I wanted to make sure I was saying what I meant. I therefore said to the assembled meeting that I would like to convey my brother's and my family's message in English, as I knew my Igbo would be rusty from lack of use and I would not be able to use the proverbs and poetry that win arguments.

There was mild consternation at this. Some of the old men, particularly those who had very little English, were put out. Somebody would have to translate what I said. A younger man said that this was an Igbo meeting and I should speak the language. A row was about to ensue when the chair ruled in my favour. I said my piece. The meeting received it in silence. When I finished the chair asked the oldest man to respond. He defused the situation by saying there was no issue. The land in question was ours to manage, nobody was trying to take it back from us, and people just wanted us to develop it. If, however, the land was not developed, it would be taken back into common ownership, as custom demanded since adding value was important part of the *Omenala*. I should convey that to my brother and family. Speaker after speaker then said the same thing. In strict terms they had reiterated the values of the community and the importance of agency. It was a fair judgement, develop it or return it to others who were hungry for land.

I said I would convey the message to my family and come back the following week to relay our response. I sat down and listened to the rest of the meeting. Much of it was taken up with arranging delegations to go to neighbouring villages to represent in-laws at funerals and other ceremonies. I enjoyed the meeting, the speeches and sense of solidarity that was there. But later as I returned home in the dark to my father's compound I began to worry about the things that had not been discussed at the meeting. Nothing about the issues the young men were talking about – jobs, capital, their lack of power or voice; there was no mention of what the women were saying about their frustration at the land situation and their desire for greater equality in the village; nothing about Aba and its encroachment.

In my mind I felt the main challenge the village would have to tackle, sooner rather than later, was how it integrates into Aba. Will it do so in a planned way, where it controls the chaos and filth of Aba, or will it be absorbed into that chaos and madness? Will it decide that by controlling the chaos it can become a special neighbourhood within Aba, or does it simply see itself as yet another slum of that expanding city? I believed that, with proper planning, it could become an upmarket part of the city, the Knightsbridge of Aba, or a 'quarter' specialising in whatever it wished – arts, crafts, etc.

The village has diffuse layers of leadership: among the young people, among the women's groups, among the church-based St Anthony's alumni, at the Umu Udo and other fraternal councils, and in the main village council. In spite of all this, the most significant threat facing its future was not being discussed in a co-ordinated way by any of these groups, separately or together. Instead, frustrations were raised in isolation without recognising the need for better co-ordination and perhaps general reform of the entire system.

The Umu Udo council's focus on ceremonial events was an interesting indication that something profound was already happening. Usually the less power there is in an institution, the more that institution retreats into ritual, symbolism and ceremony: contrast the pomp and circumstance of the British Queen and the 'average guy' image of the Prime Minister. In my village as power shifted away from traditional spaces, in terms of the council, the old men were increasingly retreating more and more into ceremony. The currency of their power had been allocating the land over which they were custodians. Through it they sat as heads of the council, they spoke first, they were revered and, yes, feared. As land was now being commoditised, privatised and sold, this power was disappearing fast. Increasingly, they were now just old men, pensioners, without the money, education or other assets that were driving the new economy.

Lying in my bed that night, I was overcome by a profound sadness. I thought again about the discussion in the meeting over my speaking English and the brief consternation it had caused. There was no excuse for my poor Igbo, but there were people in the village who were nevertheless pretending that they had not been conquered, that it was still 1850, when the village still truly had its independence and revolved around its own axis of power. The reality is that they are a part of the Nigerian state, for better or worse, and the working language of that Nigerian state is English. If any of those men wanted to talk to the president of their country, unless the president was Igbo, which, since the fall-out from the Biafran war, is still extremely unlikely, it is more or less certain that they would need to speak in English. Now, as leaders of our village, how can they negotiate effectively with the centre on our behalf, if they cannot speak English? They are living in a new world that is not just bilingual, but is multilingual, and they had chosen to remain monolingual.

But it was even worse than that. All around the village – in the school, in the various churches, in every public space with authority and links to the outside world, they conceded to this multilingualism. The language of transaction in all these institutions is English. Even the minutes of the meeting in which some people wanted me to speak in Igbo were being taken in English. The horse had already bolted and the attempts to close the stable doors were no more than pitiful. People who loved their language, were proud of their culture, its insights and profound understanding of the human condition, had done very little to invest in it or protect it. As time passes Igbo has merely become the language of ceremony, of a closed and contracting world, where the frightened old and the frustrated young, tightly hug each other in an increasingly fatal embrace. The language has not been evolved to handle new scientific thought. If any of us want to do this we switch to English. The further it retreats from a link to the forces shaping the world the quicker it will eventually die. The village was preoccupied with keeping the customs alive in a literal sense, while ignoring the economic underpinnings which truly nourish cultures.

In many ways their forefathers, within living memory, had handled the coming of the British with more assurance. They had recognised that they needed to domesticate the tools that would allow them to navigate this new world. They had brought in the church and the school. Later they had campaigned and fought for the British to go and won that victory. Now there was less assurance about how to fit into the new world that they had created, so like many of us they had retreated once more to the closed world of the village, shutting out Nigeria.

I had seen some of this when I had been in Aba and gone to the small national museum of colonial history which was located in the town. One saw the wider context of the arrival of imperial powers, slavery, palm oil, conquest and then withdrawal. The museum had stopped there, with time frozen at the point of withdrawal. But I wish it had continued. There should have been another museum nearby telling the story of the development of Aba since the imperialist withdrawal. It might have offered some ideas about what had been happening during the intervening years, giving people a map of the new world that was being created, and how to fit into it economically.

I realised that beyond the issue of language lay the frustrating and ultimately brutal quagmire of economic desperation. Earlier that week I had been told a frightening story, which came out of nowhere. I had not processed it properly until that meeting. A young man from the village had led other young armed men into the village to rob three households. They had beaten people quite savagely and taken their belongings. This was the first time an armed robbery had taken place in the village. Usually this is what happens out there in Nigeria, not in our village. For that armed robbery to be led by a person from the village, whose constitutional role was to protect the village, was unnerving in the extreme. I guess Nigeria was finally coming into the village.

That night was a long and difficult one for me. Something I loved seemed to be slowly dying.

A trip to Abuja

After a sleepless night, I set out the next day on the road to travel to my country's capital city, Abuja. I usually fly everywhere in Nigeria but on this occasion I decided to see the country. I hired a driver and asked my closest cousin, the son of my favourite uncle, to accompany us. He had never been to Abuja, but had heard so much about this glittering city in the middle of the country that he wanted to see it.

My village is located in the lush forest belt that lies east of the great River Niger. The river, after it passes us, fans out in the oil-rich delta, as it moves towards the Bight of Bonny. Before it reaches us, however it has completed a long journey through most of West Africa. Now we travelled north, going through the Igbo-speaking area. This is now divided into a number of states, populated by between 30 and 35 million people. As we drove, everything was familiar.

Igbo culture and civilisation, though it is village-based, nevertheless covers a huge area. Igbo civilisation was agricultural and based on the yam complex. By 950 AD, as revealed by the Igbo Ukwu excavations, the main planks of the civilisation were in place. A network of thousands of politically independent villages were linked by language, markets, marriage networks and a sophisticated culture which treasured art, music and proverbs. These thousands of independent villages were made up of equally proud and independent people who believed in direct democracy and evolved a scale of living (villages) which allowed them to represent themselves at meetings. Some of these villages had formed closer unions, producing towns, and more powerful 'kings', but on the whole they were not linked into big units or a state.

Soon we passed nearby to Nri, the old spiritual capital. Nri had been a centralising force among the Igbo, like modern Roman Catholics vis-à-vis the Pope, many Igbos recognised the religious authority of the priest king, *Eze Nri*, whose family had first brought agriculture to the region. Although the villages were autonomously run and enjoyed their own sovereignty, only the *Eze Nri* had the authority to declare *Igu-Aro* (a festival where the New Year was proclaimed after 13 lunar months). Through his representatives, seed yams were distributed to the people, to begin the planting season. Within a four-day week, and certainly no longer than three weeks from this festival, the first rains would fall. The *Eze Nri* would also send out the blacksmiths from Awka, who made the agricultural tools needed for farming, and the healers, *debia ugwu*, who would provide protection from spiritual and physical ailments.

Religion was the organising principle of these independent villages that I passed in my car journey. It was a religion that was structured around agriculture and the elements that were needed to make it work successfully. The most important deity was the land or earth goddess, *Ala*. Indeed, Igbo morality, or *Omenala*, is an aspect of *Ala*, literally translating as 'conduct and the land'. The most serious transgressions were against the land and had to be appeased. The worst abomination against the land involved the shedding of the blood of kin.

As we began to leave the Igbo language area the vegetation changed, becoming thinner and thinner, more savannah grassland. The people were also changing. Soon we left the Igbo language area altogether and since none of us spoke the neighbouring Idoma language, we would not be able to communicate with people if they did not speak pidgin English. As we drove along, I remembered one night in the 1970s, when the capital was Lagos, the brash and energetic Yoruba coastal city of 15 million people. I had been in a car with my favourite uncle, a soldier, and as we drove along a Lagos street, there was a man sitting in the middle of the road, alongside a child. We realised pretty quickly that he was one of the blind beggars from the north of the country, who would be led by a child while they completed their rounds. For some reason he had sat down and decided to stay put in the middle of the road. We flashed our headlights, but neither he nor the child moved. We tooted our horn. Nothing. My uncle decided he would get out of the car and use his authority as an army officer to move the man along. He spoke to the man in pidgin, but the man did not understand. He spoke Yoruba, the market language spoken by most people in Lagos. Nothing. My uncle did not speak Hausa and it suddenly occurred to me that it was possible to be in your own country and not understand your fellow countrymen.

But these people had never been strangers to each other. We had all lived in this part of West Africa for thousands of years, and we had traded and shared our cultures. Occasionally we had also fought. Our most recent battles had been in the 1960s within the framework of the Nigerian state. During the 20th century the Igbo suffered two massive defeats. First, when the British conquered their territory at the beginning of the century, and the *Eze Nri* was made to come out and denounce all the taboos and principles underlying the religion. The second defeat, during the mid-1960s, they lost their bid for independence during the Biafran or Nigerian civil war. Each of these events would change the Igbo profoundly and, at a lower level, change my village fundamentally. The first defeat would lead to incorporation of the Igbo into the Nigerian state and the second would be their attempt to escape from that state.

As the car hurtled along and the landscape changed, people's clothes as well as their languages were changing. In the centre of most of the villages we now passed, there stood a mosque alongside the churches. Every few miles, we were stopped by police. As the driver did not have one of his documents, we had already lost quite a bit of money bribing the police to let us continue. The bribes had been small, one pound here, two pounds there, but the transactions were usually quick, and usually exchanged with a great deal of humour, given that the main highway to Abuja was a busy road, and the police worked on the basis of volume. It was like paying a personal toll.

This continued until the road deteriorated significantly, and my driver decided he would take another road, which he remembered was in good condition. He came off the main road onto a deserted road but that proved to be in even worse condition than the one we had just left. We soldiered on until we saw a police checkpoint in the distance and our hearts sank. As we approached, the sitting policemen got up gingerly. They had been seated for a long time, which meant they had not had any customers. We knew we would have to make up for all their lost trade. One policeman held a semi-automatic rifle and waved us down with his gun, while his colleague watched. Frayed posters of the anti-armed robbery campaign, 'fire for fire', hung on the wall of a hut next to the road. They asked for our 'particulars' and of course soon discovered the missing registration document. We were asked to leave our car and return home in order to bring the missing document. This was the opening gambit for negotiation. So we asked what we could do for him. He asked for the *naira* equivalent of £25, a huge amount of money. We laughed and dismissed him too casually and then he got annoyed, raising his voice and the gun. I looked around; we were on a deserted road, surrounded by bush with nobody in sight. If he shot us nothing would happen. My cousin joined the driver to try and calm things down. The soldier ordered us to the station. The price had just gone up: we would now have to accommodate every officer in the station, including the sergeant. On the way to the station, the haggling and appeals began. It was too late: there was no turning back.

We were lucky, the sergeant was a nice man. You could negotiate with him. He explained how badly they were paid – £75 a month. They kept us for about an hour until we agreed on the equivalent of £35 as our 'toll'. The fear, the terror, the frustration soon turned to laughter and relief and jokes at the expense of the stupid police. But to be robbed at gunpoint by police in your own country is certainly a chastening experience. 'Fire for fire' indeed.

We crossed the great Niger River at Lokoja and traffic doubled. We had joined the main road coming up from the south-west, Benin City and Lagos. As we moved along we now saw many more licence plates from the different states reflecting their aspirations and the position they occupied in the nation: 'treasure base of the nation', 'centre of excellence', 'breadbasket of the nation', etc. The roads became two lanes, the traffic was getting fuller and faster, everyone was rushing to the centre. We were coming from the south, and equal numbers were coming down from the north; I suddenly realised the genius of locating the capital in the middle. We were all making the journey towards the centre of our own being, truly understanding the diversity of our country as we made our way towards its heart. Somebody once said that when the 1993 election was annulled by the military dictator, Ibrahim Babangida, after being won by the local champion M.K.O Abiola, the country would have descended into civil war had the capital still been in Lagos. As the nation's commercial capital, Lagos became the centre of the battles for democracy; while political horse-trading continued in the bubble that was Abuja, hundreds of miles away, and in a region where the surrounding ethnic groups were small minorities.

My cousin was amazed by Abuja, the city of steel and glass. He loved the scale, the cleanliness, and the order. He kept wondering why Aba was not like this. He kept wondering whether he was still in Nigeria. My cousin's reaction recalled an apocryphal story that is told about the late Sani Abacha, the ruthless military dictator who had replaced Babangida during the crisis of the failed political transition in 1993.

Abacha had jailed his opponents, and entrenched himself in power. After executing the Ogoni activist Ken Saro Wiwa, he launched a bid to have himself elected as a civilian head of state. He did this by manipulating the five political parties, which he had allowed to elect him as their sole candidate, then he bussed hundreds of thousands of 'area boys', or jobless youths, to sing his praises. Many of these boys were bussed in from the Niger Delta, and came from villages where there is no portable water, no electricity, where their environment is polluted, despite contributing over $250 billion to the nation's coffers through the oil that is drilled on their land. These boys arrived in Abuja and could not believe they were in Nigeria. Our money built this? 'Na Lie!' they said. Many are said to have returned home and unleashed the armed struggle that is currently raging in the Delta region with the kidnappings and killings of foreign workers.

Yes their money did build it. The city is a deal town, full of politicians and businessmen haggling over contracts. It produces nothing but deals and policies, and is sucking the life and productive output out of dirty cities like Lagos, Aba, or the Delta region that are producing the real wealth of the nation. The year I passed through Abuja, about $70 billion had come out of the ground from the Delta alone and what some of the cleverest minds in the nation were doing in this town was working out how to steal this money.

It was distressing on one level, this Babylon we had allowed to be created, yet most people said things were improving, slowly.

My most interesting moment was meeting one of the better-known traditional rulers from the Igbo-speaking region. He was in town to see the President. He was a modern man, had worked for a massive global company as a senior manager, and like my cousin doctor had been asked to become king. Unlike my cousin, his realm was a big city, and he had relished the challenge of coming home, and trying to transform these traditional institutions to deal with the modern world. His big talk was of harnessing science and planning the industrialisation of the city. Our conversation recalled another I had had recently in London with another intellectual, a cultural activist and peer of Wole Soyinka. This man had been asked to become a chief in his own south-west community, near Lagos. He said he had initially dismissed the call, but when he had gone back to the community and seen the needs for jobs, water and basic amenities, he thought that perhaps his generation had got it wrong by focusing on the Nigerian nation, perhaps they should have reinforced the local communities. But then the nation had been so fragile, and the villages so strong. People had streamed out of those villages to the bigger space, which they felt, had greater need. Now looking back they can see that they neglected the roots, and the whole edifice was threatening to collapse unless these roots were reinforced.

There is a powerful image from my village that vividly illustrates this. My grandmother, an extraordinary woman who could neither read or write, raised my father and his brothers after the death of her husband. She put him through school and sent him abroad as a diplomat for the new entity (i.e. Nigeria). Sixty years ago, he was able to build her a house in the village. His six children have been better educated, and I am sure have earned thousands more but not one of them has added to that house. My grandmother would weep.

When people lose faith in themselves, they turn to God

They turn to God indeed, as the old proverb goes. So I return to the 'witch finder' hysteria that gripped my village. This was not unexpected, given our neglect of all our villages. In fact the 'witch finder' hysteria had not been restricted to my village alone. Like a fire it spread from neighbouring village to neighbouring village across our region. What had happened was that a local practitioner of the dark arts, who had clients that came to him for charms and so on, had become 'born again'. He had begun to betray alleged clients after his transfiguration. He had identified the old men in the village as people who had come to see him. He had also given the police names of alleged armed robbers who had come to him for charms to protect them during their robberies. The police, having got what they wanted, were happy for the witchcraft allegations to be handled at a customary level.

The accused had been detained and tortured into confessions. As we sat in London and the US, it was difficult to have an influence over events or to shape them. Village traditions insist on due process, where the accused can be represented and guilt proven. But with the witchcraft charges, guilt is difficult to prove. It is the *intention* of those who want to perpetrate wickedness and the *perception* their victims have of being harmed, that counts. Confessions are therefore at a premium, and orderly resolution of this issue was therefore difficult. When my brothers and I had declined to help our doctor cousin to bankroll the installation of the new chief, it meant there was even less leverage for us in the unfolding crisis.

In any case the chief didn't seem to have much control over events, and neither did his council. The young men were driving the process, and getting the council, as required by *Omenala*, to endorse their decisions. Some of them were blinded with rage and frustration because relatives of theirs had died under inexplicable circumstances. They suspected witchcraft by some of the accused.

My eldest brother became heavily involved. Speaking on the phone to various people, it became obvious that there was a lot of scepticism about the charges, but people were afraid to defend the accused in the open village assemblies, lest they themselves be accused of being in league with the witches. The only person who seemed to have had much influence on the ground was another cousin, a high-ranking official in the Vatican, who was fortunately at home overseeing a huge Catholic seminary he was building to train a new generation of priests. He was able to have some influence, but the hysteria continued to mount. The village needed to be cleansed and purified, thus confessions were eventually extracted.

Once the confessions came, the legal process took its course and the guilty were sentenced, most being banished from the precincts of the village for 10 to 15 years, depending on their crimes. In effect they have been ejected from the story of the village, into the story of Nigeria. It may well be that as with its young, who have chosen voluntary exile, many of the condemned may indeed find a new liberation outside the village, in Aba and other parts of Nigeria.

Six months later

Following the verdicts, there has been a huge exhaling of breath, as though something evil has been purged. On the surface, village life has returned to normal, but underneath, the seeds of future conflict have been sown. You can't brutalise your uncles, fathers, grandfathers and imagine that this will not have a negative long-term impact. Also the underlying problems in the village – lack of jobs, power relations, and the encroachment of Aba – continue to demand action.

The crisis has, however, had a strange upside. It has led us to become much more intimately involved in the affairs of the village, not just through sending money, but in beginning to carry out our role as citizens. Initially, such was the anger that some of us wanted to break the umbilical cord with the village, because we felt we no longer understood this strange place, which had thrown out its own rules, and ceased to be a place of safety. What did it mean to be the 'children of peace' in a place where those closest to you were tortured? But eventually we calmed down. How could we not when our physical umbilical cords are buried under trees in the village! Anyway, where would we run to? To countries that have not been compromised by foolishness? Where were they? We were quite content to continue living in countries which, driven by a similar hysteria, had recently indulged in the folly of an invasion that had led directly to the deaths of thousands of innocents. The shock of the *Juju* crisis notwithstanding, we realised we had to try to get some meaning out of what had happened, and move forward, with the village.

After all, in the days when the village had existed in its own universe, goodness and evil had always lived side by side in this closed community. The world devised by my great ancestor Udo and his five brothers had its faults, like all social experiments. The interests of male inheritance meant that the system recognised rights for women only through their male kith and kin; attitudes to multiple births and a whole host of other practices were cruel and absurd. For all this, the village had been, and remains, an incredibly *humane* space. The social structure had ensured that the village did not have destitute people, as everybody had access to land. Ninety per cent of the time it was a place of incredible solidarity, and affirmed the lives of its members. For years it was a space that had been etched in my mind as the byword for democracy, accountability, security and harmonious living.

The current cruelties and idiocy surrounding the *Juju* crisis are fuelled by fear. As the Igbo writer, Obinkaram Echewa said in his novel *The Land's*

Lord: 'Our fears are older than our beliefs. When our fears die down, our beliefs change' (African Writers Series, 1976, p.63).

And this pragmatism and belief in change is what ultimately I love about the village. The people change, they abandon old gods that no longer work and embrace the new. As Igbo, they never dealt with gods in the abstract, their gods were the personification of specific functions of the universe. They were practical. When they ceased to be useful, when their energising potential was exhausted, they were discarded. As part of this they have always understood how to contain and transcend evil.

In their cosmology, beyond *Ala*, the earth deity, there were a host of other deities, which dominated their world. Some reflected elemental forces, some of which were physical (rivers, thunder, etc.), and others were metaphysical (*Ikenga* – agency, *Ofo* – truth and legitimacy, and perhaps the most important for our purposes here, Ekwensu, the trickster figure and author of chaos and disorder). 'In most towns on the western side of the river', wrote G. T. Basden, a British visitor to the area in the 1920s, 'three days in the year are set apart for Ekwensu's Day, for the express purpose of extolling the devil and all his works. During the festival the people indulge freely in all kinds of excess without the imposition of any restraint.' (Basden, *Among The Ibos*, 1920, p.221).

Ekwensu was given a privileged position by the Igbo, not because it is the 'devil' in the simplistic terms of some Christian missionaries, but because, as in the beginning, order emerges usually from disorder. What the Igbo understood through the figure of Ekwensu is that the force of chaos has a role. Ekwensu is the agent at the crossroads, the catalyst of choice and change, the bridge you walk over to a new understanding or space.

The new understanding the *Juju* disorder had unleashed is the importance of the role we play in saving our villages. In mine, fear of Aba and the wider world has produced crises among the community, leadership and the led, and we need to face these fears head-on and overcome them.

It is inevitable that in 50 years' time my village will be a suburb of Aba. Hopefully Aba will be a major manufacturing and hi-tech city in the West African neighbourhood that will emerge around the great Niger river that snakes through our region all the way, from Fouta Jallon in Guinea to the Bight of Bonny. Abuja will be another important city in this Niger area, as will Lagos, Accra, Abidjan, Dakar, Bamako and Cotonou. Like the six brothers who created my world, all of us in West Africa are tasked with making real this emerging world, and building it brick by brick from the bottom up with a new story of rules, cultures and leadership.

But the citizenship of this big new world should be constructed on more fluid identities, not just blood and land.

Rebuilding Rwanda's human capital

Jean-Bosco Butera

Jean-Bosco Butera returned to Rwanda after the genocide of 1994. Over half a million people had been brutally killed in 100 days. The country was in chaos, its infrastructure destroyed. Butera joined the survivors as they tackled the job of reconstruction. At the age of 37, he found himself Vice Rector, in charge of academic affairs at the country's only university, tasked with developing the country's human capital. With very few resources and almost no staff, he and others set about rebuilding the university and creating institutions that would seek to understand the reasons for the conflict in Rwanda and build the foundations for lasting peace in the country.

Introduction

In its edition of December 2006, the pan-African magazine *New African* carried a special report on Rwanda with the title 'A nation on the march'.

Indeed Rwanda has shown impressive strides in its progress after the unspeakable tragedy of 1994. There is no doubt that the country still requires immense efforts on its road to development – and improved livelihood for all Rwandans – but it seems that the pace is set.

One of the major challenges in the aftermath of the genocide was the deprivation of the country in human resources. Scores of educated people had been killed and many others had been forced into exile. The country was left with very little capacity. While its need for rebuilding was formidable, the people to do so were scarce across all sectors of life, infrastructure, health, education, agriculture, social services and many more.

While there was a considerable international response, it was also clear that this would only provide a stop-gap, rapid response, not the required sustained efforts for reconstruction. It was against this background that the government took the decision to reopen the National University of Rwanda, the only government tertiary education institution at that time, to resume training for the much-needed human resources for the country.

In the next few pages, I am going to talk about the role of the National University in the efforts to rebuild the human resources of the country and look at the impact that the university has had. From the outset, I would like to submit that I will not be talking about statistics but rather giving a personal, empirical point of view as the person who was put in charge of academic affairs at the reopening of the university, almost immediately after the genocide. I worked there for a total of ten years (1995–2005).

Getting involved

In its history as a Belgian colony, Rwanda witnessed the movement of many of her people for a number of reasons, mostly economic. Rwandans were taken across the border to work in the mines of Katanga in the Congo, while others migrated to the territory of North Kivu to work on the tea plantations that were being developed by the colonial power. Others, who were cattle owners, went in search of land to graze their herds. My family migrated to the Congo (Bwito, Rutshuru) in the 1940s, as part of the latter category of migrants.

Born in Bwito, I grew up in the town of Goma, adjacent to Gisenyi on the Rwandan side. All my primary, secondary and university education took place in the Congo (then Zaire). After graduating from the Faculty of Veterinary Medicine (Lubumbashi) in 1981, I went to work in Goma as an Animal Health Officer in the Ministry of Agriculture as part of a Food and Agriculture Organization (FAO) project.

During these formative years, we grew up with a sense of being Congolese. Goma was by and large inhabited by Banyarwanda and most parents talked to their children in Kinyarwanda. But as children our language of communication was mostly Kiswahili. This was the lingua franca among children outside and within families. There was no patent discrimination in school and promotion was on equal merit. As a young person, one did not therefore feel excluded.

However, there were periods of great insecurity for Banyarwanda in the 1960s, with the unfolding political turmoil of the Congo, and in particular in what was called the Kanyarwanda war in 1963–64. As far as I can remember, that is when the Banyarwanda were first castigated as foreigners by other ethnic groups. With many others, my father was jailed and we had to take refuge in the local Catholic diocese for protection. I recall an incident when I was seven years old when policemen raided our home looking for my father. My younger brother, who was four, and I ran to hide behind the fridge. One of the policemen tried to hit us with his stick. Another policeman told him that we were just kids. And the first policeman said: 'Today they are boys, tomorrow they will be fighting us.' There were other instances where we were labelled foreigners. One of the most vivid for me remains the time when I was in the first year of secondary school (1969–70), a missionary boarding school. One of the priests went through the classes registering non-Zairians. Nobody identified himself as a foreigner until he finally turned to me and asked: 'And you, aren't you Rwandan?' My response was a sharp 'no'. He was a Belgian priest.

Though blatant, these cases did not erode the sense of being Congolese. It is not until the late 1980s that my attachment to the Congo started to fade. It was all triggered when I met my wife in Nairobi in 1996 while doing my doctoral research at the International Laboratory for Animal Diseases (ILRAD). She was born in Burundi and her family kept their Rwandan refugee status despite the fact that her father was working for the government of Burundi and thus had the possibility of being naturalised as a Burundi citizen. Burundi maintained a discriminatory approach towards refugee children in schools and this raised their awareness of being foreigners from a tender age, unlike children growing up in Congolese towns.

The discourse on going back to Rwanda gained momentum in the Rwanda diaspora at the instigation of the Rwanda Patriotic Front (RPF). I soon joined the debate, becoming a member of the Front in 1989. At first, my own discourse concentrated mostly on the role of the Congolese of Rwandan origin in the struggle to a rightful home for Rwandan refugees. It was still more of a solidarity approach rather than a real engagement. Indeed, in early 1990, when the Mobutu regime opened up the debate on democratisation in Zaire, I was among the Congolese living in Nairobi who used to meet at the Zairian Embassy to discuss what we wanted from the process. My heart was still with the Congo.

The beginning of the war in Rwanda in October 1990 demanded a greater engagement with the Rwandan cause. More time was dedicated to mobilising international support for the struggle, sensitising people, raising funds, etc. The balance had started to tilt more towards the Rwanda side. After presenting my thesis in February 1991, I went to Goma and found Zaire in the middle of what was called the 'Conférence Nationale Souveraine' (Independent National Conference). The conference was anything but national. It excluded nationals of Rwandan origin from the debate. This apparent exclusion was later, in my opinion, the origin of the Banyamulenge revolt, which was to shake the Congo at the end of the 20th century. For me, it was the catalyst for my final choice. I went back to Nairobi and after a short post-doctoral stint at ILRAD, I became a full-time RPF cadre. The journey back to Rwanda had started.

Back to Rwanda

Soon after becoming a full-time cadre, I travelled to the small area controlled by RPF inside Rwanda in 1992. I was assigned to the commission for international relations and started travelling in a number of African countries and pan-African summits and conferences to explain the struggle and mobilise support for RPF. One of the memorable moments in these encounters, though not the most fruitful, was when I accompanied Tito Rutaremera, a senior RPF Commissioner, to Gbadolite to meet the late President Mobutu, my unsuspecting former Head of State. He had taken power in the Congo when I was eight years and I had danced to the tune of patriotic mobilising songs praising him as the greatest African leader. Our meeting took place in 1993 when he was trying to salvage the government of his friend, the late Habyarimana. I was later to be part of delegations that met him again in Gbadolite and in Tunis, on the margins of a summit of the then Organization of African Unity (OAU) in 1994.

After the defeat of the genocide forces in July 1994, the RPF set up a Government of National Unity with political parties that had not taken part in the genocide. I was appointed to the Ministry of Transport and Communications to second the Minister as Chief of Staff. In 1995, there was a government reshuffle. In October 1995, I was appointed Vice Rector (Deputy Vice Chancellor) for Academic Affairs at the National University of Rwanda (NUR) in Butare, a post I held until February 2003.

Though the university buildings had not been heavily damaged during the war like many other institutions, a large number of its teaching staff had been lost, either killed or fled. Though I had little experience in the management of tertiary education, I was given the challenge of organising the academic structure of the university and finding ways to teach the newly registered students.

According to records that we found at the university, NUR had had less than 3,000 students on the eve of the 1994 tragedy. These students were located at two campuses, the main one at Butare and another one in Ruhengeri. Beside the two campuses, the university also had the Faculty of Law, located at Mburabuturo in Kigali.

When the university reopened, about 3,200 students registered and were all installed on the only viable campus in Butare. The teaching staff records indicated that the university had 275 teaching staff before the war. When we reopened in 1995, there were barely 50. Laboratories had been vandalised and computers stolen.

Before the war, the medium of instruction at the university was French. With the return of Rwandan nationals from English-speaking neighbouring countries, teaching had to be provided in both English and French, in separate classes. This meant the duplication of classes, in particular in the faculties of Medicine, Economics, Social Sciences and Management, Law, Technology, Education and Agriculture. This compounded the issue of shortage of lecturers.

Search for solutions

In view of the numerous challenges facing the university, the search for solutions meant the adoption of a multi-layered approach that aimed at focusing on the following issues:

i)   recruitment of regional and expatriate lecturers for either short-term or longer periods

ii)   staff development programmes

iii) reform of the curriculum

iv)   organisation of the academic management structure

v)   initiating co-operation with regional and international universities

vi)   putting the university on a solid financial basis.

(i)   **Recruitment of lecturers:** If any of us in Butare was wondering what south–south co-operation meant, by the second year of operation we no longer needed any explanation. Indeed, faced with such a shortage in teaching staff, the university depended on a large number of visiting professors to provide the teaching. For the first two years the majority of them came from the neighbouring countries of Burundi, Uganda and Congo. This was a quite remarkable show of solidarity, especially from the lecturers from Burundi, who came almost instantly when the university reopened. Indeed, by 1995 the University of Burundi and the National University of Rwanda had already established a co-operation agreement to allow a flow of lecturers. Though the agreement talked of exchange of staff, it was by and large a one-way route from Bujumbura to Butare. The agreement with Makerere in Uganda was signed in 1998. The recruitment of visiting professors was supported by the Trust Fund managed by the United Nations Development Programme (UNDP). From 1997, apart from the visiting professors, the university started to recruit regional and international staff, mostly from developing countries, under a scheme that was funded by the Netherlands through the Trust Fund managed by the UNDP. This programme allowed us to invite visiting professors from other countries like Cameroon and Ethiopia, and to recruit professors and lecturers on a more permanent contract of two years and more. With the UNDP project, we received professors from Burundi, Uganda, DR Congo, Bangladesh, Burkina Faso, Cameroon,

Ethiopia, India, Nigeria and Kazakhstan. The university also recruited visiting professors from within Rwanda and allowed its own lecturers and professors to take on additional workloads that were paid by the UNDP project. The project had a budget of about $1 million per year for a period of five years, the majority of which went on the lecturers who had been recruited as United Nations Volunteers (UNVs), particularly to respond to the necessity to teach separate classes in English and French. In some instances, additional support was mobilised to respond to specific challenges in some faculties such as the Faculty of Law. The judicial system of Rwanda at that time was mostly based on French civil law while visiting anglophone professors were coming from a common law background. It became necessary to find people who could use the existing system while teaching in English. One project funded by USAID recruited visiting professors from Canada and another, supported by the Danish Centre for Human Rights, allowed the posting of two permanent lecturers.

It was thanks to this flow of visiting and permanent professors and lecturers from diverse countries that the university was able to sustain itself and its courses. As one might expect, academic delivery occasionally suffered because of the availability of the visiting professors. Their time was often limited and they could not continue to assist the students once they had left the campus. Bringing in professors with contracts for longer periods was the solution to alleviating some of these problems but it was obvious that it could not be sustained for a long period. As the university graduated students, it started to recruit junior lecturers for further training.

(ii) **Staff development:** As already indicated, when the university resumed in 1995 it had less than 50 teaching staff, compared to the 275 who were in post before 1994. The shortfall was immense. While the regional and international professors provided an interim response to the urgent need for teachers, the university embarked on the recruitment of junior lecturers to be trained further and provide the university with a more permanent teaching staff. Funds were sought through development partners and the government dedicated resources for training through the Ministry of Education Scholarship Commission of which I was deputy chair. By 1996, the university started negotiating with the Belgian-based consortium of francophone universities (CIUF). Co-operation with CIUF was also built along the lines of providing visiting professors while preparing junior lecturers. Starting at a modest 600,000 Belgian francs in 1997, it reached an amount of about 20,000,000 Belgian francs after four years. At one point, it provided NUR with the second-largest component of training after the government programme, through the Ministry of Education. Later, other development partners included a sizeable portion of their support for staff development, like USAID and the Swedish development agency, SIDA. Junior lecturers have been sent for their postgraduate studies to various countries for training, including South Africa, Belgium, France, Germany, USA, Uganda, Kenya, Netherlands, Sweden and elsewhere. The combined efforts have had a remarkable impact on the quality of teaching personnel at the university. While the majority of national staff were first degree holders until 1998–99, all of them now have a Master's degree and many have completed or are completing their PhD. By the time I left the Vice Rector's office in 2003, we had about 315 teaching staff. Though this number indicated a real improvement compared to the situation in 1995, the increase in the number of students was still compounding the shortage of lecturers. Indeed, the approach to education in our society following the genocide was rapidly changing the student population at the university. A broad-based and well-educated workforce was now seen as a key plank of the country's development. Starting with some 3,200 students in 1995, NUR had close to 8,000 students in 2003.

(iii) **Reform of the curriculum:** The National University of Rwanda is the only comprehensive public university in Rwanda. It produces graduates in various fields: Agriculture, Law, Medicine, Science, Technology, Economics and Management, Social Sciences, Education, Arts and Humanities. It is imperative for the university to reassess its courses and their relevance to the needs of the country on a regular basis. The syllabus taught at the university when it reopened was the result of a 1978 reform. In 1997, the university convened a stakeholders' conference comprising students, professors, government officials, the private sector and faith communities to discuss the needs to which the university had to respond and how to adapt the curriculum. It was a wide consultation which guided the different faculties and the university in general on reforms to be undertaken. Some of the cross-cutting outcomes demonstrated the necessity to engage all students in reflections about the society and the humanism that deserted the country during the genocide, to the extent that university professors, students and administrators killed or incited others to kill their own colleagues and students. As a result, the university introduced a general introductory course on Philosophy and Rwandan Ethics in all departments. Also strongly expressed was the need to expose students to the information and communication technologies that were transforming the world. Here again, the university introduced a compulsory basic ICT course for all first-year students. This course is normally followed by a second, to strengthen the ICT knowledge of students with specific reference to the content of their training. Faculties undertook various changes in their curriculum as a result of these consultations and continued to do so in subsequent years. A consequence of these continued discussions appeared later in the concern about the stark imbalance between the number of students registered in social sciences/humanities versus the science block. At one graduation ceremony, we had more than 200 students graduating in the Faculty of Economics, Management and Social Sciences alone, while the whole Faculty of Science with five departments had fewer than ten students. With the aim of promoting science and technology, the orientation process of government-sponsored students was reviewed under the guidance of the National Examination Council and a few years later, the Faculty of Science, which was lagging behind all the other faculties in terms of number of students, had partially recovered, ranking third position in terms of numbers.

(iv) **Organising the academic structure:** The management of the university was very centralised with decisions often taken at the level of the higher administration of the university. The restructuring process aimed to give more responsibility to departments so that they could better manage the academic problems arising within each department, and strengthen accountability of both the teaching staff and the students. Indeed it was not uncommon to have a professor request permission from a Dean to be absent without informing the head of department, who was in charge of running classes. The approach was gradually to make departments take charge of the various academic and administrative issues that needed a quick response, especially in view of the ever growing number of students. Faculties' administration was overstretched and overburdened with issues. At the level of the office of the Academic Vice Rector, commissions were created to deal with the crucial components of research and pedagogy. The two commissions allowed the teaching staff a more transparent and participatory approach towards the research agenda and pedagogical issues, drawing membership from elected representatives from all the faculties. This contributed more to the governance of the university, enabling the teaching staff and students to participate in all the decision organs: the University Council, the Academic Board and the Administrative Board. One aspect that was still hampering changes by the time I left the office of Vice Rector was the law governing the university, which dated back to 1981. Proposals had been made to change it as early as 1998, but the text remained in place, with minor adjustments, waiting for the enactment of a new higher education law that was to give way to more reforms.

(v) **Co-operation with regional and international universities:** from the indications given earlier in the text on the visiting professors, it is clear that the National University of Rwanda could not have managed to pursue teaching without the co-operation of various other universities. One of the major tasks of the office was to develop the co-operation and to sustain working relationships with sister universities. Site visits were conducted in Burundi, Uganda, Kenya, Ethiopia, Cameroon, Côte d'Ivoire, Senegal, South Africa, India and Belgium. The partner universities were also sought out for their support in the implementation of the exit strategy of training NUR junior staff who would gradually replace the contract external professors.

(vi) **Placing the university on a solid financial basis:** The visiting professors schemes, the UNVs, the staff development programme and the curriculum reform all required substantial financial resources. The university was supported in this by both the government and the development partners. The government of Rwanda provided the running budget for the university and funded a good number of scholarships. The office of the Vice Rector entailed maintaining high-delivery performance and sound relationships with development partners for them to continue their support to the university.

The account above is not exhaustive in identifying the various aspects that were needed to be worked on in the effort to rebuild the National University of Rwanda. The big lesson I learned is that undertaking an institutional change requires the committed engagement of the people who are involved in the exercise. This engagement can only be driven and maintained through committed and focused leadership. Such leadership builds a strong working spirit through participation, transparency, discipline, humility and consistency in respect of a rules-based order.

Beyond academia

Besides being an academic entity, a university is also a community where students meet people with whom they share common interests in non-academic activities. This results in the creation of various associations, groups, forums, etc. I believe that it is important for university authorities to support and encourage such initiatives since they often also serve as a peer-grooming environment where older students will invite younger ones and thus facilitate their adaptation to university life. While at the university, I supported a number of such youth organisations and felt that it always gave the students more confidence in their work. It was also part of building their capacity and sense of engagement in social endeavours. I was the Patron of the university band called SALUS. Its name derived from the university motto *'Illuminatio et Salus Populi* – light and salvation of the people'. With Professor Simon Munzu, who was then representing the United Nations Commissioner for Human Rights in Rwanda, I participated in the launch, and became Patron of, an association called *Association des Jeunes pour les Droits de l'Homme et le Développement* – *AJPRODHO–JIJUKIRWA* – Youth Association for Human Rights and Development. It was quite amazing to see how university students were organising advocacy discussions on human rights in secondary schools and going to help rural communities to write project proposals to develop various aspects of their life. Originally composed of university students, former members continued to be active after completing their studies. This brought a new dimension to the association, which has in turn become a sizeable, local, non-government organisation, enriching the country's civil society. Other university student groups that I supported included the university chapter of the Pan-African Movement, the University Women Students Association (UWSA), the Association of Student Survivors of Genocide (AERG) and the association of young writers (La Muse).

My involvement with the youth organisations continued after my tenure as Vice Rector. In 2004, for the commemoration of the tenth anniversary of the genocide in Rwanda, I worked with the Ministry of Youth, Sports and Culture to organise nationwide youth participation in the commemoration through drama, poetry and sports events. The event was sponsored by the British government's Department for International Development (DFID) and managed through CARE Rwanda. The Ministry's partners in the organisation were the AERG and the Rwanda Chapter of 'Never Again', an international youth organisation constituted with the vision to uphold the promise that genocide will never happen again. They organise activities with the aim of sensitising and mobilising youth and society in various parts of the world against exclusion, intolerance and human rights abuses. At present I am the Patron of 'Never Again Rwanda'.

The support for 'Never Again' builds on my earlier participation in the creation of a Centre for Conflict Management at the National University of Rwanda in 1999. The Centre was created as part of the university's efforts to contribute to the understanding, through research, of the root causes of the conflict in Rwanda. It was established with four principal areas of analysis, the origin and consequences of genocide, the psycho-social impact of the genocide, justice and reconciliation and the socio-economic aspects of the conflict.

My involvement with the Centre for Conflict Management was the stimulus for my current work with the Africa Programme of the University for Peace (UPEACE). Indeed, in 2002, a UPEACE mission headed by Professor Mary King visited the National University of Rwanda on a tour of ten African countries. They interacted with African scholars, policy-makers and civil society organisations with the view to establishing an Africa programme that responded fully to the need for peace and conflict resolution expressed by Africans. As National Director of the Centre for Conflict Management, I had the opportunity to meet the delegation and to understand the work of UPEACE. Though the programme was run from Geneva at that time, there was a clear aim to establish an office in Africa. It was decided to locate it in Addis Ababa. After an interview I was selected and joined UPEACE in April 2005, taking leave of absence from the National University of Rwanda, where I was then teaching, having served as Vice Rector for close to eight years.

The mission of the UPEACE Africa Programme is to stimulate and strengthen the capacities of African institutions, particularly tertiary education institutions, in the areas of peace and conflict studies. It is essentially a capacity-building programme that gives me an opportunity to pursue the efforts to contribute to building human capital at a continental level in an area of paramount importance for Africa. The underlying basis for the programme is that education provides the best channel for entrenching a culture of peace on our continent and hence create the conditions for sustainable development. Working with local partners in various regions of Africa, the Programme aims to reach out and mobilise wider segments of society to contribute to peace at all levels of our communities. I am convinced that such an approach will contribute to the realisation of the 'Never Again' promise.

Conclusion

The theme of a conference convened in Tunis in November 2006 by the organisation LEAD Africa was 'Making Africa a land of opportunity'. It was basically looking at ways to move from an Africa plagued by wars, disease, misery and human rights abuses to an Africa on the road to progress. The conference stressed that an essential factor for the transformation of Africa is its leadership. Indeed, Africa's burdens are, in my opinion, the total responsibility of our leaders. While external forces have and will continue to interfere in the affairs of Africa for their own interests, they only succeed when they find an accomplice in internal leadership. The most dramatic illustration of Africa's failed leaders is the genocide in Rwanda. It happened because the leaders of the day planned it and led the masses into perpetrating it. If Rwanda's efforts are being acclaimed today, governance is at the core of the transformation of the country. After the genocide, Rwanda could have plunged into a period of revenge killings and the destruction of whoever or whatever were perceived as the perpetrators. Such senseless killings would have just exacerbated sentiments of resentment and thoughts of more killings. Rwanda did not go that way but rather chose the path of justice and reconciliation, thanks to its leadership. The choice was not an accidental one but more the continuation of the commitment to rebuilding the country shown already by numerous people who first joined the struggle to fight the injustice of being deprived of their nation. The mobilisation of the Rwandan diaspora was remarkable in the years of the struggle. This mobilisation resulted in the spontaneous return to Rwanda of many people after July 1994. I believe it is that commitment, developed over the years, that created the path for reconstruction. It is the same commitment to delivery that has guided the reforms undertaken in Rwanda in a continuous search for improved systems.

A vital component in any reform agenda is the aspect of human resources. The human capital of Rwanda was devastated by the genocide. The National University played, and continues to play, a major role in the provision of the much-needed human resources in various sectors. Today, a large number of the staff in the newly restructured local government consists of graduates of Butare. The same applies to the judiciary, various government offices, non-governmental organisations and others. It was proposed at one point to create an employment observatory to follow up on the insertion of graduates in the workplace. I believe that this will help in clearly determining the impact of the university. As in many discussions in Africa on the quality of education, at times one hears debate on the quality of graduates. And, as in many situations in higher education in Africa, the means put at the disposal of the tertiary institutions are very often very meagre. The request for high quality is legitimate and should be pursued as a constant quest for accountability on the part of the education institutions.

High-quality education is indeed crucial to development. Nevertheless, the quest should be accompanied by appropriate means that allow the tertiary institutions to develop fully the three fundamental areas of their mission and leadership for their societies: to provide relevant teaching; conduct high-quality research; and render service to their communities.

Speaking truth to power
Eva Dadrian

Eva Dadrian is an Egyptian journalist, broadcaster and cultural activist who has worked extensively across North, East and Southern Africa. She currently works as a reporter for the BBC World Service, covering the North Africa region from her base in Cairo. Courageously, she considers the frustrations media practitioners experience as they endeavour to hold rulers to account and empower citizens with the information that will allow them to understand what is going on in their own societies.

There is a saying in Egypt: 'If your mother tells you she loves you, check it out before you start believing her'. This may not apply to every mother-daughter relationship, but I believe that it should apply to every single journalist in the world. In 2006, together with hundreds of media professionals, gender activists, human rights groups, grassroots communication organisations, academics and students of communication from all over the world, I attended the first-ever Three Weeks of Global Action on Gender and the Media held in Canada. The title of this unique gathering was 'Who Makes the News?' During the few days I spent there I realised how challenging, influential and at the same time how vulnerable, the profession of a journalist has become. It was there also that someone said that the first challenge for journalists is to make 'scepticism' their profession and this made me reflect on the old Egyptian proverb.

Reporting Africa
As a reporter for the written and broadcasting media, I was never short of stories to talk or write about. From Morocco to Egypt, from Chad to Eritrea, I had plenty of opportunities. These were presented to me on a silver tray by officials as well as by the man in the street. However, the difficulty lay in getting to the 'heart of the matter' and while witnesses were generally ready

to reveal the hidden truth behind an incident or talk without any reservations about a problem, officials on the other hand were reluctant to do so. If discipline and a curious mind helped me throughout my career, I have to admit though that I benefited also from two excellent editors, both South African exiles, who patiently and diligently showed me the secrets of the profession. From them I have learned how to reveal deception, discern misinformation and expose lies, how to pursue a story to the end and foremost how to be objective and not allow my own opinion to come through my writing.

But, doing stories from Egypt, Sudan, Morocco, Ethiopia or Chad made me more aware of these challenges. I came to realise that while stories have been out there all the time for me to probe, ask, question, and verify, often this kind of journalism becomes a costly affair. The number of journalists and reporters being killed, beaten, arrested, imprisoned or harassed has dramatically increased. A recent report by the Media Foundation for West Africa (MFWA), highlighted 168 cases of press freedom violations in the region and an increase in attacks on journalists and media outlets in 2006. The situation is not very different in North Africa where violations of press freedom were also on the increase. Reporting the facts, in an honest way, is a very dangerous affair, says my Algerian colleague, Hefnaoui Ghoul. Correspondent for the daily *El-Yum* in Djelfa and a human rights activist, Ghoul was imprisoned for six months in 2004 for supposed libel. But Ghoul's sincere and frank statement can easily be heard in Egypt, Tunisia, Morocco or Libya.

The media in North Africa have always been dominated by the state. A small margin of independence existed here and there but as military dictators and civilian autocrats took power after the independences, free media soon disappeared.[1] So, one could say that from the mid-1950s and throughout the next four decades the role of the media in North Africa was confined to 'glorify the rulers and legitimise their regimes'. Media became not only a propaganda tool in the hands of the rulers, but also it fell victim to the totalitarian regimes of that age.

Today, as the Cold War is over, the Berlin Wall brought down and the Soviet bloc dismembered, bilateral and multilateral donors feel free to put conditions to their aid to development. Criticised by many and labelled as 'new strings attached to aid', these conditions however are helping, somehow, the democratisation of the political systems in many parts of the world by bringing about concepts until then unknown such as press freedom, freedom of expression, freedom of information and respect for human rights. Yet, it is mind-boggling to see that the more the concept of human rights is brought to the fore and calls for freedom of speech are made, the more violations are perpetrated and restrictions put in place.

In our continent, the Committee to Protect Journalists has spelt out more than once the often-desperate situation in which African journalists operate, and if fewer journalists were killed or imprisoned in Africa than in some other regions, 'the problems they face are insidious and ongoing' says the Committee. The African Charter of Human and Peoples' Rights, adopted in 1981 and in force since 1986, gives every African citizen the right to receive information and to freedom of expression. This is also clearly stated in the 1991 Windhoek Declaration on Promoting an Independent and Pluralistic African Press and in the 2001 African Broadcasting Charter. Considered as the fundamental components of the African Union's policies to develop democracy and pluralism, the aims of all the agreements were fully adopted in 2002 by the African Commission for Human and Peoples' Rights in its Declaration of Principles on Freedom of Expression in Africa. In addition to enjoying the rights given by these African charters, North African journalists secured the Sana'a Declaration in 1996.

The Sana'a Declaration, which as a matter of fact not all the Arab regimes in North Africa and the Middle East region endorsed, was the key for independent media to flourish, particularly in Egypt and in Morocco.[2] In both countries, newspapers enjoy a relatively good level of independence, but radio and television remain state monopolies. Keeping broadcasting media under state control is not a haphazard decision by the authorities in power. On the contrary, it is a conscious, calculated and deliberate choice due to the fact that a sizeable portion of the population in these countries is illiterate and television and radio transmissions are the only means to reach them, therefore, to be kept under state control.

If, as claimed, an informed civil society is the basis of democracy, whom do we trust to tell us the truth? Should the journalist depend on the government official version of events and pass it straight on to the public? Should the public believe the national media, the independent media, the government or now the ever-growing number of foreign, satellite, 24-hour news channels? My profession means that I have to reveal secrets, uncover lies and deceptions, elucidate the truth, expose corruption and bring the powerful and mighty of this world to account. In Egypt for example, from where I have been working for the past four years, it often happens that daily news items are presented in *Al Ahram* or *Al Goumhoureya* or *Al Akhbar* – the three main state-controlled dailies in the country – from a different angle, not informative enough and not revealing every aspect of the event or incident. On the other hand, the same news item published in the independent press provides more details and features finer points on the item. But who is telling the truth about what is going on? Is it the journalist, or it is the government official? Should people trust the media or the official source of information? And which media should they trust, the independent one, the opposition's or the state-controlled media?

Media is a double-edged sword. It can be used to reveal the truth or it can become an antagonistic propaganda tool to instigate conflict and spread hatred. This kind of media is not new, it has been around and part of, for example, the American political and religious landscape, domestically and overseas. Throughout the Cold War, Radio Free Europe/Radio Liberty, today based in Prague, Czech Republic, was the main US propaganda tool against the Soviet bloc. In Africa, the Rwandan genocide in 1994 is a clear example of this dual role played by the media. The private radio station Radio Television Libre des Mille Collines, known also as the 'Hate Radio', incited the mass killings during the 1994 genocide.

We are living in a world in which the media increasingly provide what communications experts call the 'common ground' of information and ideas and when media persistently represent information and ideas in particular ways these representations become accepted as the norm. The public becomes so brainwashed that it hardly accepts what the opposition or independent media say. The media also has the power to influence ideas and shape behaviour that transcends national boundaries and affects public policy as well as individual behaviour. This was the case of *Sawt al Arab* (The Voice of the Arabs) in the 1950s and 60s, during Gamal Abdel Nasser's era. With a specific nationalistic mission, *Sawt al Arab* was calling for a unified Arab nation 'from the Atlantic to the Gulf' and also for the destruction of Israel and the establishment of a Palestinian state from the 'Sea to Jordan'.

George Orwell's novel *Nineteen Eighty-Four* confirms this staggering truth. In my country, many journalists suffer from that 'naïve nationalism' and 'blind loyalty' Orwell talks about. In the name of patriotism that sometimes echoes jingoism, my peers rather ignore the realities on the ground and beat the drums of chewed and re-chewed information. In Sudan, the people have been so badly misinformed by official state media for many years that they use the expression 'oh, this is newspaper jargon' when they want to say that someone has been lying or telling fibs, or '*Kalam Saket*' (meaningless words) when they talk about the promises made by politicians. For me, the combination of the two sentences giving the same idea is rather significant, because indeed when the credibility of politics declines, so does that of journalism if and when it fails to resolve issues that don't make sense. The credibility of the media depends on asking the questions again and again, till we get an answer, whatever the cost.

In his book *The Illusion of Progress in the Arab Word*, Galal Amin, the renowned Egyptian professor of economics, writes that the last and real victory for totalitarian governments is not to 'root out opposition members and to throw them in prison' as often happens in North Africa, but rather lies in 'changing the thoughts that run around inside their heads' and in 'replacing them with more suitable ones'.

Recently a photograph published in one of the genuinely independent

Egyptian dailies showed a young veiled woman standing behind a news-stand and selling newspapers and magazines. Just next to the news-stand sits a policeman from the state security. Not only does the picture reveal a painful truth, but so too does the caption under the picture, which reads 'Media under state scrutiny'.

While governments worldwide as well as non-governmental organisations are working to secure a free press, according to reports on the state of the media in North Africa, countries in the region 'move backwards', with journalists being jailed, murdered, censored or kept under control. Repression by the authorities in Tunisia and Morocco, violence exercised by security forces against media in Egypt or by armed groups in Algeria in the 1990s, all contributed to curtailment of freedom of the press.

Debates between journalists

Throughout the past ten years major changes have taken place in the media in Africa. The two most important factors have been training and capacity-building activities that have contributed to the development of the media. Today, with the exception of Libya, a relatively substantial degree of freedom of expression is present in the North African region. It is true that 'direct censorship' is no more practised by the state, but indirect censorship is still operational in some countries. In Tunisia and in Egypt, for example, the state continues to indirectly manipulate the print media by financing 'independent' newspapers, whose main function is 'to rein in and discredit the really independent journalists and newspapers'. Some of my Egyptian colleagues reckon that the increase in the number of publications should not be seen as a 'healthy sign of pluralism' but a clear indication of 'internal political manipulation of the media' by the authorities. Another tool used by the authorities to limit the growth of a free press is the state's (or big business's) monopoly of newsprint and the printing industry.

The large majority of journalists I meet and talk to, especially editors-in-chief, be it in Algeria, Egypt, Libya, Morocco or Tunisia, have been trained in a totalitarian environment and under totalitarian regimes and are unable to think and write in the spirit of diversity and plurality. But as a new generation of journalists, more open and more daring, conscious and committed to the profession, are coming to the fore, the media community in those countries is experiencing a definite improvement, a kind of renaissance fuelled by the breaking away from state patronage.

Often, journalists from the state-controlled media shift responsibility for government crackdown on the free press, to their colleagues from the independent press. They often blame the free press for being too 'fault-finding' and 'hostile' to the government. Some even go as far as saying 'they deserve it' when state security harass or arrest journalists. Sitting one evening on the terrace of the Press Syndicate in Cairo, I had a heated discussion with an Egyptian colleague working for the financial daily *Al Alam Al Youm*, which is one of few independent dailies in the country. Yet, this particular journalist was in favour of a 'state-controlled' media in Egypt. He objected also to having 'foreign' reporters in any given country. 'Every reporter should write about issues related to his or her country', he said, adding that journalists' loyalty is to their government and to their country and not to their profession, or the public.

It is not surprising then that some African leaders hold journalists in total contempt and in line with their hatred of the profession these leaders have imposed harsh and severe laws to regulate media and limit the activities of journalists and editors. Incidentally, their wrath is more specifically focused on the analytical or investigative journalists who reveal corruption and scandals within government circles or who act as watchdogs of governments' own performance.

In Egypt, the three-year-old *Al Masry Al Youm* (The Daily Egyptian) has gained enormous popularity because its journalists and columnists act as watchdogs and bring to the attention of the public issues that the state-run media often ignores or dismisses as fictional. Yet, the investigative journalism *Al Masry Al Youm* manages to produce is also evidence for any thesis they press forward. The recent scandal of contaminated blood sold to hospitals, and in which a member of parliament is deeply involved, would not have been revealed to the public if the journalists at *Al Masry Al Youm* had not published the story, backing their argument with official documents they had secured through a 'mole'.

Watching, listening and reading news in Egypt shows that politics plays a major role in the country. It influences thinking, shapes attitudes and forms opinions. Although this pattern of politics-dominated news is repeated throughout the region, yet efforts are being made to bring in non-political issues: gender issues, arts, culture, social affairs and education.[3] Egyptian national television has a variety of channels airing these issues. This requires professional, technical and financial capability, which neither the state nor the independent media currently enjoys.

On various occasions while discussing with Egyptian journalists and media analysts, I discovered that after many years of having a mainstream media that provided information influenced by ideological and political bias, Egypt now has a business bias media. In fact big business has joined in and, in favouring the interests of advertisers, it is holding hostage both the independent as well as the state media. Furthermore, with the liberalised economic policies being pursued by the government, big business has established a strong relationship with the regimes and has infiltrated state as well as independent media, shaping the coverage of corruption, of presidential or parliamentary elections, economic as well as social issues.

During the presidential elections in 2005, there was a blatant contradiction between the publicised popularity of the Egyptian president and Egypt's worsening economic situation. This could only be explained by misinformation or biased coverage by the mainstream media outlets and their influence on a national scale. The same misinformation was repeated again and again during the parliamentary elections in 2005. While covering these elections, I came across polling stations around Cairo where voters, holding up their legal voting cards, were protesting because they were being turned away by undercover special units of state security. Later, when votes were counted, these particular constituencies all went to the ruling NDP members and with some of the highest recorded number of votes. While opposition and independent media took up this scandalous vote-rigging, very few journalists from the state media wrote about it, and if ever some of them did, the accusations and criticism were very subdued and insignificant.

Back in 2005, I remember that on World Press Freedom Day, the International Federation of Journalists, the world's largest journalists' group, released a report detailing how media and independent journalism were not immune to a 'pervasive atmosphere of paranoia' and how increased police powers and data collection and surveillance 'on an unprecedented and global scale' have granted 'extensive new powers to the state.' That same report also threw light on how dissent inside and outside the media was being restricted and how governments were working together to 'circumvent national resistance to attacks on civil liberties'. It is clear that journalists globally, not only in Africa, north, south, east or west, now have to cope with new and more insidious threats to their independence. The report points to an enormous transfer of power to the 'security state' in order to combat a largely exaggerated threat under the name of terrorism.

Since the events of 11 September 2001, attacks on press freedom have indeed increased everywhere in the world. In North Africa governments have been using the fight against terrorism as an excuse to step up repression, muzzle political activists calling for democratic reforms and repress all opposition activity. In Egypt, a state of emergency has been in place since 1982. Furthermore, the government spends most of its time focusing the attention of Egyptians on non-Egyptian issues, such as the Israeli–Palestinian conflict, in the hope that the people will forget about major internal problems such as poverty, corruption and the repression of minorities.

With globalisation and the introduction of large numbers of television channels into numerous countries, the power of the media to shape public opinion and influence ideas and behaviour at all levels of society has increased significantly. New outlets have emerged and although still struggling to find their place under the sun, they are reshaping the image of the media in North Africa. On an assignment in Algeria throughout that troubled period, I've noticed that Algerians turned off the state-run media to watch foreign stations via satellite. Even news aired by neighbouring Tunisia and Morocco was more credible than the news aired by the Algerian state television channel. Visiting Algeria a few years later, I noticed that the practice was still continuing, but to a much lesser extent.[4]

Hopes on the horizon

In fact, big changes are paving the way to democracy and a return to stability and normality in Algeria.[5] In terms of media, although the 1990 press law that allowed the rise of an independent press has been tightened and it is now harder to set up new publications, the 'reading committees' that were established to censor the private press, after the creation of the independent press in 1990, have now been abolished for almost a decade. Since the re-election of President Bouteflika (2004) who won on a platform of 'national reconciliation,' promising peace and prosperity after a grim decade of Islamist violence and state counter violence, democratic improvements are noticeable and a 'new era' in press freedom for reporters is under way. At the end of 2006, the Algerian Communication Minister, Hachemi Djiar, announced an ambitious programme to upgrade the state media (radio and television), launch several thematic television channels, a new international multilingual radio station and a number of regional stations. There are also plans for training journalists in reporting ethics and management techniques. These ambitious projects are a big step forward for a country where some 60 journalists were murdered between 1993 and 1996.

Even Libya, long a world pariah, is now moving towards democratic reforms, albeit slowly, say human rights activists. The information and press systems are still controlled by the Libyan state, and there is only the national television broadcast medium – privately owned televisions stations are prohibited. Despite this, a few recent measures to liberate the press and media are shaping up and it could be that the reintegration of the country into the world community and the globalisation of media will play a major role in the liberalisation of the sector. A few years ago, according to the World Press Freedom Review, the government agreed with the French government on a 'programme to assist employees in the media sector that will allow Libya to benefit from cutting edge media and telecommunication technology'.

In Morocco, the young King Mohammed VI had promised to strengthen press freedom, safeguard plurality of information and guarantee the modernisation of a sector. Contrary to the description 'weapons of mass destruction' given by President Bouteflika for radio and television, the Moroccan king describes the media as 'one of the pillars of our plan for a modernised, democratic society.'

Violations of press freedom have continued, but here again, there's some light at the end of the dark tunnel through which Moroccan journalists have to travel. In 2002, the new press law adopted by the parliament included some improvements. Prison terms for journalists were reduced, the procedures to launch a new newspaper were simplified and the need to justify seizures of newspapers was added. Surprisingly, one article reinstated the government's right to ban Moroccan or foreign newspapers 'if the publications in question tend to threaten Islam, the institution of the monarchy, territorial integrity or public order'.

Where there has been limited progress in Algeria, Libya and Morocco, there has been overwhelming disappointment in Tunisia. Projecting to the outside world the image of a liberal and democratic country, Tunisia is however under the tight control of President Zine el Abdine Ben Ali's regime. Despite pressure from numerous international institutions and human rights organisations, the authorities have not relinquished their harassment of journalists. In my journeys through the region, I came to know that President Ben Ali's nickname is 'Ben-à-Vie' or 'Ben-for-Life'. President Ben Ali is one of few remaining African leaders who holds journalists in total contempt and scorns their rights to freedom of expression.

The abuse is so widespread that for the first time in many years, the pro-government Tunisian Journalists' Association (AJT) denounced the gagging of the media on one occasion in 2004. Since then, the authorities have silenced opponents, and like elsewhere in the region, paid Arab newspapers to write virulent attacks against dissident journalists.

Overall, in reality, the media establishment in North Africa still lacks credibility first and foremost because they are owned directly or indirectly by governments.[6] This may not be the case in other parts of the continent where independent media have a wider presence.

Currently, our continent is facing a multitude of problems. HIV/AIDS has a devastating impact on the lives of millions of Africans, adults as well as children. Maternal and child mortality are among the highest in the world. Violent conflicts, hunger, famine, desertification and food security are still widespread. But bringing an end to Africa's problems is as important as recognising the rights of its citizens. Fostering stronger media in Africa is an indispensable part of tackling poverty, improving development and enabling Africa to attain its development goals. But could private media operators replace state-controlled media? And what would be the advantages of replacing state-controlled media by big-business-controlled media? It is still difficult to establish new media outlets in North Africa where rules and press laws are restrictive to such an extent that it takes years for a newspaper to get off the ground. For broadcasting services, radio in particular, it is even harder to get permits and licences. But we have seen that, despite the restrictive regulations, things are moving and reforms are shaping up. Despite unfavourable media legislation and strong government stances on media content, the newspaper and television market has grown across the continent. In addition, rights activists have succeeded in establishing a broad range of national and regional organisations and institutions throughout the continent. Supporting broadcasting reform, monitoring media output and a range of related activities, these homegrown and grassroots institutions are working towards the repeal of repressive legislation. Since the beginning of the new millennium, a number of independent newspapers are in circulation in Egypt, in Algeria and in Morocco. The quality is still mediocre and their readership limited, but they are at least contributing to raising awareness among citizens and are helping to 'diversify the media landscape'.

What if Africa has a pan-African satellite television channel that airs the unabashed voice of the African street, and is a source of information about African public opinion, an opinion which may not be reflected in African politicians' policies at any given time?

What if a powerful media institution fulfils Africans' need for the genuine truth about political and economic events in their continent and around the world? What if a pan-African satellite channel that presents the wisdom of the African society that supports it is set up and provides a valuable service to Africans at home as well as to the diaspora, in the five official languages of the continent and even with services in local and regional languages, such as Hausa – or isiZulu?

What if it was based on the model of Al Jazeera – private in management style and strategic intention but not in actual ownership – a pan-African television channel that will have a geographic breakdown with a cohesive pan-African broadcasting system that takes into account the specificities of regional cultural differences? Is this a far-fetched wish, a nebulous dream in the world of utopia, or can civil society in African bring it about and make it real?

Notes

1   A free media existed in Egypt under British colonial rule and some of its most celebrated columnists were the likes of Mustafa Kamel and Mohamed Abdou and Kassem Amin, initiators of social and political reforms. Publishing blossomed during and after the Second World War, and *Al Ahram* daily, which was established in 1875, was to be joined by *Masr al Fata, Al Watani, Rosa el Youssef, Le Journal d'Egypte, Le Progrès Egyptien, The Egyptian Gazette*, to name just a few. A few years after the 1952 revolution, some of these disappeared completely while the rest were put under state control. *Akhbar Al Youm* (News of the Day), privately owned by brothers Mustafa and Ali Amin, was the most popular daily until 1960 when it was nationalised and the Amins arrested. In the Maghreb, especially in Algeria and in Tunisia, press and publishing were the monopoly of the French and the colonial authorities held the power to censor and print at their discretion. However, the vast majority of the Arab-Berber population 'was illiterate and could not read either the French or the Arabic newspaper editions' (Jonathan Keith Gosnell, in *The Politics of Frenchness in Colonial Algeria, 1930–1954*, Routledge, New York, 2002).

2   Indeed Al Jazeera TV was launched in 1996, a few months after the Sana'a Declaration. But the idea for an 'open media' emerged much earlier in the region. The new powers of the media worldwide, the performance of the foreign media, in regard to the region and to the Middle East conflict and particularly the Western-centric vision of events in Palestine contributed towards the transformation of the media environment in the region, where journalists and editors were spurred on to show 'the other face of the coin'. As for Al Jazeera TV, often acclaimed as the beacon of 'open media' in the Arab world, it should be noted that Al Jazeera is based in Qatar and sponsored by many Qatari state-owned enterprises, and therefore never produces any political, economic or social news about Qatar, with the exception of programmes paying tribute to 'international events', i.e. sport, festivals, UN conferences, etc., held on the island.

3   There is no overt political debate on these issues. The debate occurs only and when such issues become crises. The absence of effective political parties further stifles the real political debate on these issues. Furthermore, politics in the region continues to be a field mainly dominated by men and social affairs, education, arts and culture remain 'female issues'.

4   The private media, which has gone through deep introspection and change since its inception in the mid 1990s, is increasingly contributing towards democratic governance and accountability on the part of state officials. Although there are still some troubling concerns, the private media is increasingly influencing people and opening new means of communication, such as private websites, online news and more recently blogs on the internet. Becoming more informed and more aware of the issues relevant to their needs and problems of their daily life – the economy, education, health, public services – Africans are becoming increasingly involved in the democratic process not only in their country but also in their continent. Recently, during the World Social Forum held in Nairobi (January 2007), media practitioners recommended engaging African governments in media best practices. Opening such a dialogue with governments would assist national, regional and continental African media operators to invest in producing culturally relevant content, countering the Western-centric content of media absorbed, to date, by Africans.

5   Restoring the credibility of its institutions, heavily damaged by almost ten years of domestic conflict, and involving young people in political life remain daunting challenges for the Algerian government. To gain political legitimacy, the new government had first to distance itself from the army generals, allegedly implicated in the 150,000 dead and more than 10,000 disappearances, and promise national reconciliation. Yet, the draft Charter for Peace and National Reconciliation, put to a public referendum (September 2005), asked Algerians to give the government a blank cheque to bring about reconciliation as it sees fit. Furthermore, it could not wipe out the psychological scars left by the internal bloody conflict.

6   There is no attempt even to put in place a kind of BBC-style independent public service organisation which is open to its staff and could be considered private in management style and strategic intention but not in actual ownership.

Translating Africa and leadership: what is Africa to me?[1]

Wangui wa Goro

Wangui wa Goro is a UK-based Kenyan intellectual, academic, writer, translator, and cultural promoter. She has been engaged in promoting literary practice in Europe, Africa and the USA and in the campaign for human rights in race, gender and democratisation over the last 20 years.

She is a pioneer in the translation of African literature and its promotion, and her translation of Ngugi wa Thiong'o's novel Matigari *from Gikuyu to English brought her global acclaim. She also translates groundbreaking and award-winning authors from French to English and Gikuyu, including Véronique Tadjo's* As the Crow Flies. *She is currently translating Fatou Keita's* Rebelle *from French to English and* The Decameron *from Italian to Gikuyu. Her research interests are in the field of human rights and translation, and the ethics and norms of translation theory and practice. In the essay below she argues for a new group of 'mediators' who can facilitate intercultural African dialogue.*

Introduction

In my work as a translator, I have been struck by how values are transmitted in everyday contexts through the powerful act of translation, mediation and intercultural dialogue.[2] It has made me revisit my thinking of the work of those translators and mediators who work throughout African communities, whether at local, global or international levels. Thinking about issues such as genocide, African unity, democracy, corruption, human rights, peace, truth and reconciliation and social justice and how these are negotiated and understood across cultures has enabled me to reflect more deeply about the leadership role that such mediators can and do play. This is particularly pertinent in relation to our own individual values, the values that we expect of others and the values that others hold for themselves and for us. These are contained in language and culture and conveyed through translation.

Many have spoken of universal human values that make the heart beat with hope and enable either acts of solidarity such as with South Africa during apartheid, or the disengagements we have witnessed with genocide such as those in Rwanda and Darfur. These two extremes demonstrate to me how easy it is for communities to understand or misunderstand each other based on mediations by translators. It also makes me wonder whether it is because translation was missing or because the translations went wrong or whether they were just bad translations in the first place. In any case, if any of the above scenarios are the case, who has the power to hold those mediators to account? In reflecting on this, I pay tribute to translators who uphold the values of justice, truth and fairness in their work given its importance to decision-making and leadership. Some have even sacrificed their lives in pursuit of principles of truth, for example Hitoshi Igarashi, the Japanese translator of Salman Rushdie's *Satanic Verses*.

By drawing attention to the importance of translation this article raises awareness of how translation produces ways for societies to understand the workings of communities other than their own. It can assist them in defining a shared framework for democracy and practical leadership in multilingual and multicultural (multi-'national') contexts. To highlight some of these issues, I look at a case study of the S.M. Otieno burial issue to demonstrate the losses and gains in translation and the importance of acknowledging translation in leadership within a rights framework, a code of ethics, public scrutiny and accountability.

Finally, I argue that for democracy, equality and diversity to work, accountability should be built into leadership. Such leadership should also articulate universal human values, taking into consideration nuances of these values that may be a result of diverse cultures at the pan-African, state, local and individual levels. Accurate translation and mediation is critical in understanding and negotiating these nuances.

Background

The knowledge of the power of language struck me from when we were children, playing a game called Chinese whispers. One child would whisper something and this message would be conveyed round the circled group in a whisper. It would be the job of the child sitting next to the one who first uttered the sentence to tell the group what the final message was. In most cases, the message that arrived at the end was distorted, although everyone in the game took great pains to reproduce, as faithfully as they could, what it was they thought they heard, or did they? What became clear to me (and you should try it if you like) is how distorted the message can sometimes become, to the point that it becomes the exact opposite of what was first said, or something far removed from the original message. We would then go round the circle and narrate what we had heard, tracing where the transmission had broken down and the way it had changed from one child to the other. This message was often transmitted in one language. Imagine, then, what would happen if the message was whispered in different languages and was expected to arrive back to the last speaker in the original language!

This game provides sharp relief as to what can happen in translation in general and specifically so in the African context, where for political, socio-economic and cultural reasons, information is often relayed in the fashion of the Chinese whisper. By the time it filters through the various cultural, geographical, language, religious, gender, age and class prisms it can be distorted to disastrous effect. Many have not recognised that these breakdowns can occur due to the manipulations or failures of the translation process or out of sheer error or lack of competence, even where individual translators mean well. This essay therefore urges that close attention is paid to translation-as-leadership and encourages responsibility for accurate and honest translation practice in order to deepen democracy, development, peace, social justice and equality. By honest translation, I mean that translation practice has to be based on a set of ethical and universally accepted values.

Context

At the beginning of any encounter between different cultures, translation/interpretation facilitates the initial exchange and is in fact the main pivot upon which the relationship hinges. Given its immense diversity, Africa's history has been marked by translation as its different cultures interacted. The more recent encounters with imperialism have produced additional linguistic and cultural manifestations that have shaped the context of translation. This recent presence is even marked with the birth of new languages of translation such as pidgin and Sheng'. On a wider scale, translation includes the rendition of sacred texts, translation of oral narratives and wisdom, other fictional and nonfictional literatures, subtitling and cinema into different languages, broadcast and intercultural dialogue and communication. It also includes a wide range of processes such as the practice of slavery and slave trade, colonialisation and other democratic processes such as the Truth and Reconciliation process, intercultural trade, political dialogue and diplomacy, and development and cultural dialogues among others.

When court decisions are made or if new laws are introduced, the majority of people will learn about them only through translation and the oral medium. This is partly because they are not conversant with the languages in which the laws or legislation are written (including formal and legal language), or because they do not or cannot read. Trade too, in many local contexts, takes place in translation as do many socio-political and cultural events and relationships. It can even be said that communication in general, even in one language, is about translation and interpretation owing to the various 'dialects' of language that exist in any culture or cultures, as will become evident below.

An exploration of translation, its processes and power allows us to interrogate leadership and its impact on individuals and society. Dealt with in a transparent way, it allows such leaders to genuinely subject themselves to scrutiny. Do they understand the other cultures in their society? Has their own internal self-identification had an impact on their identification or lack of identification with others? This is because translation affects identity and intercultural issues which in turn significantly affect our diverse communities.

It enables people to see themselves and others through the prism of language. It determines the decision-making processes of leadership at state and local levels based on insights developed in this way. Many Africans are aware of the diverse sensibilities of their varied populations and negotiate these on a daily basis, given the complexity of the nation state and its multicultural make-up. For instance, most countries operate both national and 'common law' statutes. So, the question of how common law works, for instance, in relation to equality, given the diversity of values in any one nation state is one that is often overlooked, as will become evident in the case studies below. Also political leadership is often associated with the nation state. However, when we fail to reflect on the impact of translation, power and power relations as well as geographical location of power, on the nation state, we take the nation state and its cultural structure for granted. The nation states on which most African states are modelled are 'monolingual'[3] societies such as those of the UK or France. This model is not the predominant model on the continent and even where we have monolingual state societies, other factors such as clan systems, social class, religion and gender cannot be overlooked.

It was not until 1884 that the nation states of Africa were formed, bringing diverse linguistic and cultural entities together, with some ranging from monolingual nation states such as Somalia, to others such as Nigeria with very large linguistic communities living within the same frontiers. As is the case of many communities, the demarcation of the state also meant that some communities were spread between different countries, although they shared a common history, religion, language and heritage links with people across the border. Here, I am thinking of communities such as the Somali communities living in three border states as well as in the diaspora with different value systems which impact heavily and in complex ways on translated identities. The same can be said for other border communities in other parts of Africa such as the Arabic-, Kiswahili-, Wolof-speaking, and Hausa communities at the macro level. At the micro level, this includes even dialects within one language and cultural grouping such as the Gikuyu, etc. Translation has also impacted heavily on nomadic communities, such as the Masaai or San communities, whose livelihood is not imagined in fixed borders and the laws that govern frontiers.[4] There are also borders of class, gender, disability and religion, a factor that is often overlooked in leadership.

The development of colonial education has meant that we have not had the proper space to learn about each other's cultures or the cultures of these border and nomadic communities. As a result ineffective translation or lack of translation can lead to serious consequences. For example the San community have been moved from their hunter-gathering lives and plonked in urban settings, without the benefit of understanding how they could adapt to urbanisation. A loss of identity has followed, with attendant social problems such as alcoholism. A whole community maybe facing threats to its future survival through a translation gesture.

Translating ourselves

June Jordan in *On Call* argues that: 'We would make our language conform to the truth of our many selves and we would make our language lead us into the equality of power that a democratic state must represent.'

Beyond our nation states and the former imperial powers, the encounters and experiences for most Africans with the Middle East and Asia, or with the super powers of the Soviet Union and the United States, have had a significant impact on the cultures, identities and societal formation. More often than not, these are not factored in discourses on identity, justice, governance, development and the dispensation of power through leadership in most cases. Some of these identities include the notions of 'Commonwealth' and 'Francophonie' or pro-East or Western ideologies, which are an acknowledgement of some of the wider modes of identification that have an impact on leadership models which continue to assert influence on what is considered to be a homogenous space of the local, national or African identity. Yet these are not scrutinised closely in terms of what they mean by power and leadership, in terms of African unity and in terms of democracy or individual or collective rights as understood through translation.

As my experience in the translation of Ngugi's and Véronique Tadjo's work[5] into English has demonstrated, the discrepancy of values of inequality and diversity can be exemplified by the kinds of images of Africa seen on European television screens, and the kinds of perceptions different ethnicities have of one another. In the European context, many have decried these images and narratives on the basis that they are far from how Africans see themselves, and are tilted to a specific bias, when ideally, they should represent a more objective view from which the viewers can make up their own minds. Drawing from this, one realises that the translation of words, values and culture requires a careful negotiation of terms of value between and across African and other cultures. The silent processes of translation choices are not often articulated in overt terms, nor accountability sought. I remember an impromptu invitation to interpret from French into English at a conference when I opted to invite the audience to engage in a public translation exercise where I would ask them whether my version of translation was accurate as we went along. Collaboratively and in public, we arrived at a consensus on most of the issues. Where the audience was happy with my translations, they would remain silent, but if a contentious issue arose, they would quickly intervene in the manner of the African oral tradition. It was an enjoyable and empowering experience, being held accountable on the spot. I also introduced playfulness in the translation process by occasionally translating 'I think' as 'He thinks' when I did not agree with the speaker. Where I agreed with him, I translated his speech as 'I think', thus drawing attention to the power that translators can hold. The audience understood this device and also demonstrated to me that translators should not be seen as powerless machines translating 'neutrally' but as people who are vested in power.

Other examples where this power of intervention can be seen in practice and where headway has been made can be found in interventions on words such as 'tribe', 'natives', 'nigger' and so on; words which have been interrogated over history by oppressed people and are now relegated to other locations. These acts of empowerment demonstrate the power of language and translation and its importance for leadership. Commenting on language, bell hooks identifies language as a place of struggle in what she calls 'the oppressor's language'.[6] This view is reflected in issues which arose from my own translation practice. For instance, in *Matigari*, I had to translate the term *kaburu*, which describes the brutish British settler colonist. There is no equivalent term for this in English and suggestions for Yankee or Nazi were made in its place, yet they do not address the specificity of the Kenyan/British encounter as they are located in events elsewhere. In the end, I left the term untranslated to emphasise its particularity to the Kenyan colonial context.

At another level, perceptions of culture sometimes tend to assume homogeneity and continue to reflect monolingual, 'pure' ethnicities such as Berbers, Egyptians, Namibians, Sipedi, Igbo, Twi, Tuareg, Kikuyu, Zulu, Tutsi, Hutu, Luo, Arabs, Batswana, Acholi, Turkana, etc. in relation to what traditional values are/were and what contemporary African culture is. I do not wish to be simplistic here about what culture is and how complex it is, but I believe that for society to exist in harmony, an articulated set of shared values has to be in play as a contract between the individual and the wider society. In contemporary society, such a contract should be based on notions of wider good and also the respect for the universal rights of individuals which are inviolable. At present, these exist for the nation states through contracts such as the constitution or Bill of Rights or in wider frameworks such as the ratification of African Union or United Nations declarations. Whether or not these are embedded in practice or domesticated is another matter.

Yet, the translation of these values determines everyday life, sometimes leading to co-operation and at others to hostility. Here too, distance, space, demographics and location as well as other factors such as ideology, gender, religion and class markers make even these tenets more complex. To implement a translation of values is even more complex, given the various dialects produced through language itself, politicisation, ideology, faith, education and culture but most importantly a lack of will in, or the manipulation of, translation.

The wars based on ideology, religion or ethnicity reflect some of the extreme excesses of hostility which can emerge where the translation of values fails or its importance is overlooked. What for one person is the fight for freedom constitutes terrorism for another as was perceived to be the case, for example, in the South African struggle at one point. This provides insight on the outcomes of perceptions or misconceptions which are created through an absence of wider translation accountability between leadership, peoples, languages and values. This is not only reflected in the wider global context but also at national, regional and local levels, including public and private spaces. Tensions and conflict arise when there is lack of harmony around the values of democracy, social justice and equality for all irrespective of gender, race, ethnicity, religion, class, disability and geography. This is often a question of translation of ideology.

More recently, visual, technological and audio culture, telecommunications (mobile phone technology in particular), travel, and migration have also meant that the local and global are ever more interdependent and that those lines of 'cultural purity' are more blurred by translation. This is because in some instances, global carriers of values (such as the BBC, CNN, Hollywood, Nollywood, Al Jazeera) project conflicting notions of justice and democracy through translation. The national and international mass media, popular culture and education systems play an unwitting translation role in determining the perceptions societies have of themselves and the meanings of leadership through this translated space.

With all these wider norms come ideas of leadership or lack of it, as in all these locations are nuanced and cultural modes of leadership: ideas about Didier Drogba, David Beckham, Serena Williams, Kipchoge Keino, Tony Blair, the Pope, George Bush, Nelson Mandela, the Queen, Barack Obama, Sojourner Truth, Winnie Mandela, Jacob Zuma, Wangari Mathai or Condoleezza Rice are woven into the imagination of what leadership is in cultural ways through the media, popular culture and education.

Further, the wider educational and cultural practices, such as I experienced growing up in Kenya, have tended to embrace the global realities whether through colonial curricula or through post-colonial educational policies. At the same time they have retained a hold on their constructed 'Kenyan' or specific nationality heritage, whether consciously or unconsciously. For instance, the unconscious translation culture produced through the teaching of literature begins at an early age. I was aware in a seamless way before my teenage years of Humpty Dumpty, Rabindranath Tagore, Jomo Kenyatta, Majorie Oludhe Macgoye, Mark Twain, Ngugi wa Thiong'o, Charles Dickens, Ayi Kwei Armah, Rebecca Njau, Asenath Odaga, Chinua Achebe and several other writers from across the world. Equally, in the oral tradition, I was aware of stories of Marimu, Djinni, Brer Rabbit, Abunwasi and Anansi and others. In addition to the Hollywood menu, we also watched many Indian films and identified with the likes of Mumtaz, Rajesh Khanna and Sharmila Tagore among others. I spent many a happy break time in primary school singing 'Dunia Me' with my friend Shaila or enacting scenes of *Nobody's boy* (a tale of a homeless boy in France)[7] with another friend, Anne.

We also sang many songs in Swahili such as '*Njugu karanga*' and '*Malaika*', we sang pop songs, 'Puppy Love', and 'Obladi Oblada' through similar peer connections (see Manthia Diawara's account of the musical influence of Rod Stewart on him in *We Will not Budge*) and grew up under the umbrella of Motown (this is of course all generational and class-loaded). We watched European and American cartoons on television. We also read *Beano* – the Bash Street Kids – and *Bunty* comics. We read Enid Blyton's Famous Five stories and later Mills and Boon, James Hadley Chase, Denise Robbins and Barbara Cartland among other 'popular' texts over and above the formal curriculum. We watched films such as *Herbie* and *Chitty Chitty Bang Bang* and *James Bond (007)*, *Sound of Music*, films of cowboys and the Wild West and numerous other movies which have long faded from memory but left their indelible mark. (We even met Sean Connery in our young lives in Kenya, bringing a part of that cinema magic to our personal cultural encounters.) Every person can narrate their own similar multicultural exposure, depending on location, gender, class, family, peer group through space and time to various degrees, and even in the 'remotest' of places, these translational influences continue to assert themselves, whether directly or indirectly, on judgements of leadership and the decision-making process.

After all, culture is not static but forever shifting.

In similar ways, the identification with reciprocal identification of Africans on the continent with Africans in the diaspora, displaced through slave trafficking, through travel and subsequent migrations has also brought new dimensions to perceptions of leadership and the importance of translation. The identifications of old and new African diasporaic identification with Africa maintained through translation leadership, through a complex global 'continuum' is evident in the Negritude movements, the Civil Rights movements and in works of writers such as those of Olaudah Equiano, Langston Hughes, Countee Cullen, Pushkin, Jomo Kenyatta, Kwame Nkrumah, Margaret Busby, Marcus Garvey, Maya Angelou, Bibi Bakare Yusuf, James Baldwin, Alice Walker, Caryl Philips, Ama Ata Aidoo, and so many others in a long continuous translation trajectory to the present day. Similar experiences have continued happening throughout African life through translation whether at home or away and each African has their own narrative to tell of 'what Africa is to me' that it is harder to talk about than that idealised spot of Africanness we sometimes carry about in a monochromatic way.

My own life, shared with several other Kenyans/Africans reflects this cultural and linguistic richness and diversity and the tensions arising from the ambivalence we have sometimes institutionalised as the prevalent translation norm. As will become evident below in the case of the burial of S. M. Otieno, the judicial ruling demonstrates the power of translation, thus setting a precedent which in fact challenges other overriding universal tenets of democracy, equality, justice and universal human rights.

These influences continue to affect our decision-making processes and our negotiation with power. We usually hide behind the institutionalised ambivalence we hold towards our translated selves, and do not articulate these values openly until we are confronted with a problem such as the case of the burial of S. M. Otieno in Kenya.

Case study 1: the burial of S.M. Otieno

The late S.M. Otieno was a prominent Kenyan/Luo from western Kenya who was married to Wambui Otieno from central Kenya, an equally significant Kenyan/Gikuyu woman. They married according to civil law and established their matrimonial home in Nairobi. S.M. passed away and then an enormous stalemate occurred as the Luo tradition was pitted against the values of the nation state and his birth family demanded that he was buried as is customary in the home where he was born in western Kenya. Wambui, his wife, wanted him to be buried in his matrimonial home in Nairobi. His body remained unburied for a considerable time while the matter of his burial place was resolved through litigation, making this one of Kenya's and

Africa's most significant legal cases related to translation. It was testing not only modernity versus tradition, but also gender power issues, the issues of the values of the nation state versus those of nationality and universal rights.[8] As it happens, tradition and patriarchy won, and S.M. Otieno was buried in his traditional home. Wambui's patriarchal culture had no claims on her once she was married and she in essence belonged to her husband's people. In their own turn, his paternal and maternal family had claim over S. M. Otieno and his wife under Luo tradition, and required that he be buried in his ancestral home. The legal ruling determined in favour of S.M. Otieno being buried in his ancestral home.

The challenges presented by this case and others demands that we examine the impact of socio-cultural linguistic diversity, equality and power through translation more closely.

In Kenya, as elsewhere, the complex linguistic and cultural norms are evident in the internal African language encounters of the region including what are termed Bantu, Nilotic, Nilo-Hamitic, Semitic and Hamitic languages, cultures and norms and their encounters with other external factors.[9] As an example, a language like Kiswahili, the lingua franca of East Africa has had to additionally contend with English, Arabic, Italian, Portuguese, German, Italian, Hindi and Punjabi, as have the other mother tongues over several centuries at different stages and with different intensity for a variety of reasons. Young children now in Mombasa ostensibly prefer to learn Italian and German than English (one of Kenya's national languages) owing to the tourist culture which is dominated by Italians and Germans. Most of the children already speak Arabic because of old historical ties with the Middle East and because of religion and education. The choice of languages makes social and economic sense to their reality and is reflected in the changing translation space of language and socio-economic and cultural practice. The Kiswahili language itself, for instance is an ancient Sheng',[10] made up of Portuguese, African, Arabic, and Asian languages. For example, the term *meza* is derived from *mesa*, Portuguese for table; *hadithi* from *hadith*, the Arabic for story are just two of the many examples that we take for granted and that impact on everyday life. The Indian language Hindi has added words to Gikuyu such as *shavi* for key, which I understand also gave the Chubb lock its name in English. Traditionally there is no term for a lock in the Gikuyu language, which goes to show how the interactions with new cultures impact on not only language, but also cultural practice, as doors and locks are introduced into the culture. In the culturally expressed life, in Kenya as in other parts of the world, curry, chapati and pilau rice have become national dishes. In other spheres, Victorian values also continue to have an effect on many communities, as does the love of European football, which runs deep into the fabric of cultural make-up of many African men. The Islamic culture also has an extensive influence on the regional cultures given the importance of mother-tongue Kiswahili culture which is predominantly Muslim. Kiswahili is now the national language in a predominant Christian country.

The case of S.M. Otieno did not seem to reflect this incredibly complex mix of translated values and translated selves.

Case study 2: the story of David Sandera Munyekai, the Kenyan whistle blower

Another case in point is the fascinating real life complex identity of the Kenyan David Sandera Munyekai who blew the whistle against corruption. He lived an extraordinary and complex life as a Maasai/Kikuyu, English- and Kiswahili-speaking, modern urban worker, Christian/Muslim, living an urban/rural and coastal life all at once among other identities (see *Kwani?*, 2005). For a long time for instance, he lived as a Muslim with his wife's family and they did not know that he had another identity as a Gikuyu/Maasai and a national banker. From the account, he was a 'good' husband and Muslim. However, at a national level, he felt he should perform his duty as a Kenyan, by exposing grand corruption and he sought to expose it. Elsewhere, he was the dutiful Gikuyu/Maasai son of a rural family. He, like most Africans, was faced by several dilemmas at personal, local, national and international levels as he tried to balance his own complex identity 'truthfully' with the wider values of the nation state and universal human rights. His case best exemplifies translation as an embodied practice and the challenges and conflicts it can cause. (In his case, as a result of the breakdown in democracy and the rule of law.) Like Wambui Otieno,[11] he was choosing wider universal values of human rights and justice along which to pitch his ethical values and concerns while not compromising his own individual rights and freedoms.

Case study 3: John Githongo and corruption in Kenya

This case above is similar and closely tied to the case of John Githongo. He took a stance in relation to corruption, where he has placed the welfare of the state above his own rights yet sought exile to protect his own human rights against a state system which failed to guarantee universal rights enshrined in the law. His case is even more exemplary as he was employed as the Permanent Secretary in the Office of the President to safeguard ethics and governance and thus uphold the law.

In all three cases, the question is posed as if there is a conflict between individual, family and 'community' as well as Kenyan rights. The three are being taken to task over loyalty to personal rights, family and various 'traditional' cultural and considerations against those of the nation state and universal norms as though these are incompatible.

These cases only go to demonstrate the lengths to which people are stretched by translation of values of rights, particularly in contexts that demand that they ascribe to values that are too restrictive and which neglect the translational nature of our societies and the wider tenets of universal rights which underscore these. They also expose the fact that through a democratic translation process, the rights of the individual are compatible with the universal civil rights in a democracy. They demonstrate the abnormality of operating dual legal systems in multicultural societies as well as the failure of the state in relation to corruption, upholding the rule of law and universal rights.

It is reflections such as these concerning the seeming coming together or clash of values, of evolving cultures that have made me ponder on the implications of translation and mediation in general and the ethics around these in relation to leadership. Most importantly, I am raising the question of what can be done to harness translation/mediation as a positive force for democratisation.

As demonstrated in the examples above, the role and impact of translation leadership and accountability and transparency in translation is critical within a rights framework. National, regional and organisational policy should acknowledge and articulate translation, spell out what the ethical norms of translation are, as well as share translation outcomes. Issues such as corruption, equality, human rights violations, truth and reconciliation and social justice for instance, need to be spelt out clearly in relation to local, national and international cultures. Further, there needs to be clarity on the kinds of value systems which would be used to determine the outcomes of such translations and I would strongly suggest that the universal rights model is an appropriate starting point.

Lessons can also be learnt from the processes and outcomes of the Truth and Reconciliation commission in South Africa or Rwanda and their linguistic and cultural uptake. For instance, what are the specific data of those who used the systems, or what were the outcomes in relation to gender or location? When the Truth and Conciliation process was being constructed, I was struck by how important the question of translation of values would be to the process including status, gender, culturalisation, education, location, etc. I wondered which values would be applied, given the various backgrounds from which people giving evidence in the Truth and Reconciliation hearings derived. I was struck by the fact that many Bantu people take the truth and reconciliation mode as norm as it is derived from their heritage cultures. I wondered how the three systems of codes would be reconciled including the apartheid laws which had been breeched and beyond that the incompatibility of apartheid with the wider universal laws.

The dilemmas for translation seemed to be many and evaluations of the usefulness of this method are still under way. It made me aware of how wide the gap is between the understanding of universal norms of justice and a rapist who feels it is appropriate to sexually abuse a child or 'HIV widows' to cleanse himself from HIV/AIDS. It raises the question of how the wider value systems are communicated and how compatible these are with traditional or popular cultural practices. It raises the question of how universal values for the wider good can be translated and domesticated to society as a whole. It raises the question of the role of translation in how cultures of impunity can be held to account and justice is seen to be done in the instances of the genocides and other atrocities such as apartheid and the genocides in Darfur, Liberia, Rwanda and Sierra Leone. Did Truth and Reconciliation in South Africa only happen for the Bantus given that this operated within their norms? Should the apartheid abusers of human rights have been tried by the universal norms of the day?

Recommendations

First, I believe that for translation-as-leadership to be effective, it has to be open and transparent about the system of values it is using even if it is a mixture of values as was the case in the post-apartheid South Africa, where some of the cases were referred for judicial review in the state legal system and others were dealt with through the Truth and Conciliation and Amnesty systems.

Second, the inequalities in translation and mediations have to be spelt out in clear terms for all parties in a language that they not only understand, but also accept. What does justice mean to a woman, black person, disabled person and through which cultural mode is this expressed: local, traditional, African, or universal?

Third, institutions which address the seriousness of translation to policy, both linguistic and cultural, need to be established and this should feed into the formal legislative, policy, executive and legal processes of the state, but more importantly, into the practical norms of everyday living through work, play, religion, society, the economy, politics and culture. For instance, South Africa is one of the few countries with a national language and translation policy.

Fourth, translators and cultural mediators should be trained within a broad domestic and international framework, bearing in mind the historical and located inequalities as discussed above. As we have seen, despite clarity as to whether civil law overrides common law as in the S. M Otieno case, a translation framework would have assisted in clarifying the issues to all concerned by drawing on the specific and general norms for all cultures of Kenya. The universal framework provides a useful basis for a discussion that would evolve equal law for all Kenyans and raises sharp questions of citizenship rights within the diverse framework. This case has implications not only in Kenya but beyond. Further, the work of translators should be open to scrutiny through revisers or other peer mechanisms and professionalisation of both community, national and international translation and mediation processes.

Fifth, translators and policy-makers should be held accountable, through making it possible to justify their translation choices within a wider democratic framework. It is therefore important to establish institutions, standards, codes of practice and codes of conduct for the various kinds of translations necessitated by the local, national and global contexts as in other professions.

Finally, the education and cultural systems should take translation as an important tool for learning, research and teaching and therefore invest in a multicultural curriculum, media practice and public communication systems which enable society to interrogate and engage with the various norms and values which shape democratic society. We should not gloss over the complexity of the multicultural, global, national and local cultures which shape our societies. There is a 'translation moment', when the hand is not revealed, when the translator can choose what to translate, when the translator as the person in the middle can con both sides, the person they are translating for and the person they are translating from. Or sometimes even themselves. It is important that we are transparent, accurate and honest.

Conclusion

I have tried to demonstrate the issues of power at play in translation and in the role of translators and mediators. I believe that the more people have linguistic and cultural competence of each other's worlds, the greater the possibility of peace, justice and equality based on real knowledge rather than on unequal and unfair systems of knowledge and perceptions.

The training of translators should acknowledge the issues of power and their impact on leadership and shaping society. Translators too should be accountable to a code of best practice which upholds the universal values of equal rights for each person.

The article has demonstrated the importance and creativity of translation for justice and democracy. It has also demonstrated that society and translators are important social mediators for politics, law, order, socio-economic interaction, social justice, development, communication and cultural and educational transmission in all areas of life.

I have demonstrated how power through translation makes it possible to hear the 'good' and 'bad' things that happen in our own and in each other's cultures that may challenge us not only to an understanding, but to defining and acceptance of who we really are. Some of the most enjoyable games emerging on the internet and SMS are the translation-related jokes which parody the translation space and each other's cultures. These have provided me with the greatest amusement over the last year. I am also acutely aware of how this same force can be manipulated to disastrous effect and prejudice. The paper has also drawn attention to how the power of translation, its manipulation or abuse can lead to misunderstanding and conflict. Therefore, the articulation and training of translators in relation to ethics, values and their transmission of what Africa, the nation state and the local community is, has to be a central question in our understanding and engagement with leadership. It is through this kind of understanding that equal justice, democracy and development for Africa and Africans' engagement with power can genuinely emerge. It will call for revealing those practices which are in conflict with the wider tenets of the universal framework for human rights whether they represent 'traditional' or national culture such as female genital mutilation or corruption.

In conclusion, for leadership to metamorphose and improve not only in Africa but globally an acknowledged democratic translation norm has to be accepted and promoted vigorously. Taking from lessons gleaned from history and from translation practice, through reversal of oppressive misconceptions, it may be possible to undo some of the worst excesses of actions based on false or distorted perceptions which run counter to the aspirations of the universal will to justice and democracy. How far society can move is exemplified in French, through the shift in translation of the meaning of the word *homme* which alludes to human beings, even though historically it alluded to 'man' because of the prevalent patriarchal societal order. This may not look like a big step forward, but its cultural impact is immense in its inclusions. Today, thanks to gendered discourse awareness, we now know that by translating *homme* as 'people' we can begin to redress a social and linguistic injustice by explaining.

My belief is that if translational competence for all 'mediators' is applied in the context of democracy based on principles of social justice, democracy and equality and a genuine desire for human development and peace. These will usher in an exciting project of pluralising democracy in ways that enhance African life. The Truth and Reconciliation model in South Africa may have begun to do just that and other models can be sought. In this way, the African identity will be revealed for its rich tapestry of values through new kinds of leadership which will enable us to live at greater ease with our selves and others through knowledge rather than perception and misconception which I believe continue to hold us back.

Notes

1. The title is drawn from the first line of Countee Cullen's poem 'Heritage' in the *Norton Anthology: African American Literature*, Henry Louis Gates Jr and Nelly Y. McKay (eds.) (1997), Madison. Countee Cullen (1903–46) was a poet of the Harlem Renaissance.

2. In this paper, the term translation is used to encompass the wider sphere of translation, mediation, interpretation and the space of intercultural dialogue and communication, given the oral nature of our communities and developed cultural practice.

3. Monolingual here implies a standard national language such as English or French. It also acknowledges that these countries have regional languages, such as Welsh and Gaelic, as well as regional and local dialects.

4. See Robert K. Hitchcock: 'Background notes on the Central Kalahari game reserve and Ghanzi land and resource issues.' *www.kalaharipeoples.org/documents/ghanzi.htm*

5. Ngugi wa Thiong'o's *Matigari* (1989) and Véronique Tadjo's *As the Crow Flies* (2001), both translated by Wangui wa Goro, both published by Heinemann, London.

6. bell hooks, 'This is the oppressors language yet I need it to talk to you: Language as a place of struggle' in *Between Languages and Cultures*, Eds. Anuradha Dingwaney and Carol Maier (1998), University of Pittsburg Press, Pittsburg and London.

7. The English translation of *Sans Famille*, an 1878 French novel by Hector Malot.

8. Kenya has ratified several human rights declarations including the UN Declaration of Human Rights.

9. See Mahmood Mamdani's discussion on 'customary laws' and 'native authorities' in 'The History of Genocide' in *Kwani?* 2003, published Kwani Trust, Nairobi, Kenya.

10. Kenyan language derived from Kiswahili and English and a combination of the various Kenyan languages. It is prevalent in cosmopolitan areas, with Nairobi Sheng' being the dominant dialect.

11. Wanjiru Kariuki (2005). 'Keeping the Feminist War Real in Contemporary Kenya: The Case of Wambui Otieno,' *JENDA: A Journal of Culture and African Women Studies*: Issue 7.

4

African leadership: from the present to the future

Enquire about everything that you may understand it.

Onchsheshonqy (Ptolemaic period)

Creating the business leaders of tomorrow
Taddy Blecher

Taddy Blecher *attended Wits University in South Africa and was awarded the Liberty Life Gold Medal as the top actuarial science honours student in the country. He was involved in a number of entrepreneurial pursuits while at university. After graduation, he worked first as an actuary, and later for the international management consulting firm Monitor Company. He became a senior project leader and was voted consultant of the year in the firm three years in a row, and was rated in the top one per cent of the firm's consultants. Following the collapse of South Africa's apartheid regime, he left his high-flying job in order to create a unique kind of university – one that would respond to the acute shortage of entrepreneurial skills among the poor of South Africa, tackling the persistent high unemployment levels in a country still suffering from the legacy of apartheid. Here, he recounts how he came to create CIDA City Campus.*

Right now in downtown Johannesburg, South Africa, well over 1,000 students are working towards earning their undergraduate degree in Business Administration, and in total 3,000 are studying for programmes that are likely to have them in jobs in the short term. Millions like them are also studying around the world – but these are not your average students, and this is not your average university.

These students come from some of the most rural and poverty-stricken areas of southern Africa, and without the birth of CIDA City Campus in 2000, that is where they would still be now – with no prospects for furthering their education to become leaders and entrepreneurs.

I grew up in a family of achievers. As a white Jewish boy aged eight, I already had a stock portfolio, and my friends and I used to trade excitedly at the dinner table. I led a privileged life, with no black people in my school, my neighbourhood or on my list of friends. Growing up separately was totally normal, and I never questioned it.

When the time came to go to university, my father told me I could study to be an actuary or a doctor. I chose what appeared to be the lesser of two evils and went to Wits University to study actuarial science. I began my first job at a pensions company which I found dead boring and eventually decided that a job with Monitor Company as a management consultant would suit me better. I was soon earning R1.3 million a year.

It was 1994. The country was still reeling in the aftermath of apartheid, no one was sure what Mandela's government would bring, and there were so many people emigrating that a whole profession emerged of people who would organise your visa for any country in exchange for a small fortune. If you wanted to leave the country, you only had to take down some of the many details tacked to lamp-posts throughout Johannesburg advertising these services. My brother and I were the only two of my five siblings left in the country – the others had gone to America and Australia. I decided I might as well join them.

I paid one of the lamp-post guys R50,000 to organise my visa to the US, and off I went in search of a job. I soon found one, but, as you may know, actuaries are quite risk-averse. My training had left an impact, and I thought, 'What if this job doesn't work out and I have moved here leaving everything behind?' So I organised a back-up job and returned to South Africa to pack up my stuff. But then I began to think, 'What if America doesn't work out? What if I find I don't like it there?' So I paid another lamp-post professional another king's ransom to organise a visa to New Zealand, which seemed to be a very popular destination. I flew over, got a job in Auckland in an insurance company, and then I organised a back-up job at an insurance consulting firm just to be safe. But while I was over there, I thought, 'Hey, my brother and sister-in-law are in Australia; they would never forgive me if I didn't try to relocate there.' So I hopped over to Australia and organised a job – and a back-up job – there, too. Then I went home, resigned from my job at Monitor and continued packing my boxes. By now I had six jobs on three continents, and I was getting calls at all hours of the day and night from them, asking when I was coming. I would appease them as best I could, promising 'Don't worry, I'm on my way!' Soon after, I bought my ticket to the US and put 43 boxes in my mother's basement. I packed two suitcases that would come with me, figuring I would send for the rest later. I didn't know it then, but I would never retrieve or unpack those boxes.

The night arrived before I was to leave. I lay in bed staring at the sword of light that spilled in through the crack in the curtains and stretched across my bedroom ceiling. I couldn't get to sleep. I tossed and turned, got up and paced the room and was distraught with thoughts about my life and the decision I had taken. Was this really the right thing to do? What would the country become if I and others all ran away looking for selfish, greener pastures? Why I am I here? Why are we all here? Surely there has got to be magnificence in life, and a cause greater than any individuality?

Not long before dawn, the headline of a front-page news story I had seen in Australia came to mind: 'Ducks Escape from the Zoo'. I thought to myself, how could that possibly make front-page news? Is that truly the biggest problem facing their population? And I decided the same could be true for the US. Did I want to go somewhere that had no problems? If they have no problems, what would there be to do? By morning, I walked into my mother's room with a tear-stained face. 'I'm not going,' I told her.

A change of direction

A week later, I found myself in a township for the first time in my life. Shabby houses (the term 'house' applied generously) sprawled out before me for as far as my eye could see. Some kids ran around barefoot in the streets while the slightly luckier ones were in school. I was there as a director of a non-profit organisation, which focused on teaching self-development programmes such as Transcendental Meditation, something I had learned when I was ten years old. Our paramount focus was helping kids get through school.

I got there by asking a few friends of mine, who were running a charity called Community and Individual Development Association, or CIDA, if I could do anything for them in their work. They told me to come to see them and talk it over. I found the two of them at the address they had given me, and we chatted about their work in the townships. Then they asked me to wait on the other side of the room for a moment, and they conferred for about 30 seconds. Then one of them walked over to officially invite me to become a director of the charity. I realised at this point that it was somewhat easier to get a senior position at a charity than at a management consultancy.

Over the next four and a half years, we helped over 9,000 students get through matric, or secondary school. I remember in the beginning that, as someone used to making a lot of money, I would feel compelled to pull out my wallet when I saw a kid with no shoes or not enough to eat. But over the years, I saw something even more heartbreaking: I may have helped these students with an immediate, glaring problem, but it was actually irresponsible of me to do so. What does giving a man a fish accomplish? Only that his death from starvation is delayed. I looked at the kids we had helped. Although I felt an enormous glow for having given them hope, I also felt guilty. Had I given them false hope? These kids were leaving secondary school perhaps with more disappointment, as they had no prospects for anything more than menial labour, and that only if they were lucky. There was absolutely no chance they could go to university – they didn't have the money and they were not going to get a scholarship. Instead, they would languish in these townships, with no access to an opportunity to pull themselves out of poverty.

I was deeply determined to find a more practical way of helping these kids. Monitor Company, in its immense kindness, kept an office for me for the five years I worked in the townships (I still have the same office there today). And it was Monitor who agreed to help us set up a think tank with the aim of discovering the best way to fight poverty and give the youth of our country the opportunity to become self-sufficient providers for their families and themselves.

After three months of research by Monitor consultants and external participants, we uncovered some staggering indicators. The 1996 South African census showed that in sub-Saharan Africa, only three per cent of individuals over the age of 20 have a post-school educational qualification. The figure was six per cent in South Africa, but that did not make us feel any better. A 1998 World Bank study showed that there was an 89 per cent correlation between the level of education a nation's population had achieved and that nation's wealth. And just from personal experience, we all knew that there were more African skilled workers like scientists and engineers working abroad than in Africa.

Beyond that we discovered that for every hundred kids who started out in primary schools in South Africa, only one would complete university. The rest, who fell by the wayside, did not seem prepared for very much else. This traditional model seemed to us to represent a huge waste of resources and potential.

Our team emerged from this exercise with renewed determination, now focused on beginning a different kind of university – a university for the poor that would prepare them for the realities of South African life. One of those realities was that it was highly likely that they would have to provide their own jobs. We had no experience in academia, no money to found a university and encouragement from people only to *not* try to start a university for the poor. Still, after convincing each other that this was the cause to fight for, we went about figuring out how to start a university with nothing more than an overdraft.

We briefly considered the idea of a faculty for the disadvantaged at an established university, but dismissed this idea almost as quickly as those we spoke to did. We then spoke to the Ministry of Education, who eventually, and very reluctantly, handed over a list of 1,000 schools throughout South Africa. I then set to work: armed with the Monitor letterhead (I thought the logo made my letter look more official) and their fax machine, I sent a letter to every school on the list, proclaiming that if they could send us their five top students, we would grant them a scholarship to South Africa's first free university for the poor.

A bit of nervous thumb twiddling ensued for the next couple of days, as no reply came through. And then one day, as if by magic, Monitor's fax machine came to resemble more a popcorn machine, bubbling over with so many faxes that Monitor Company could not receive client faxes for hours each day. The response was incredible. We had 3,500 applications to a university that did not exist. We also had evidence of a well-known fact: Africans are nothing if not resourceful. Mothers had studied my fax and deciphered the logo to the extent that they linked it to an address. Security at Monitor was at its wits' end, arguing with hopeful parents of children who rejoiced outside the consultancy's offices: 'Oh, what a beautiful university! Please take my child!'

As it got harder to send these parents away, I thought I'd better set about finding premises. There were actually a lot of empty buildings in downtown Johannesburg in 1999, as the streets had not been very safe for many years, causing companies who had been headquartered there to flee north to suburbs like Rosebank and Sandton.

Success came when a friend of mine (who had lent me his call centre services to handle the deluge of inquires we were getting) mentioned that he had access to a building that he could lend us. The building had been deserted and had absolutely nothing in it. We went up the stairs, inspecting the ruins of each floor, and found, waiting for us like a gift from above, 400 plastic chairs on the fifth floor. I made an executive decision at that point to accept 350 students, so that if we got a few extras, at least everyone would have a chair.

The birth of a university

And so CIDA City Campus was born. On 7 February 2000, the five proud founders of CIDA City Campus opened its doors to 350 unsuspecting students. It was an incredibly joyous occasion, and we did everything we could to make them feel welcome.

Once they had taken their seats, the five of us stood before them and introduced ourselves as the founders of the university. We then took a step back, and after a short pause, I called everyone forward again so that I could introduce the students to the faculty. More than one brow furrowed. The students were a bit perplexed as to why the same five people were not only the founders and the faculty, but also the kitchen staff, the building maintenance, and everything else. In fact, some were so dubious that the next day, we lost 100 students. Apparently these students thought: 'We may be poor, but we're not stupid.'

The days went by, and we all began inventing the curriculum as we went along. I taught five or six subjects (some of which I had never taken), and we seemed to be getting by and slowly laying the foundations for our new university. We wanted the students to feel it was their university, so we gave them very important responsibilities. We had no books, but we had brooms and cleaning products, with which we furnished the students, along with the charge of tidying the halls of their university.

Some students began to voice their concerns. They asked us how they could be at university if there were no computers. I tried to appease these students by telling them that when they were ready, the computers would come, but they were positive they were ready. Feeling that I did not want to disappoint them, I somehow thought it might help to announce a date. The night before I had promised the arrival of computers, I sat at my Monitor office racking my brains for ideas about where to get some computers. A glance at my own computer keyboard became a fixed gaze that switched between that and the photocopier.

The next day, I announced the arrival of the computers. The students were beside themselves. They got up and danced and sang (as is not unusual in Africa), and this went on for several minutes. The celebration came to an abrupt halt, however, when they began to look at the pieces of paper I was handing out to each of them. On the paper was a photocopied image of a keyboard. Their faces dropped. 'Betrayed' was stamped across their foreheads.

One of them finally stated the obvious: 'But these are not real computers.' 'These are *better*!' I said. 'These are laptops and you can take them home with you. The other kind we wouldn't have let you.'

I quickly began to explain how we would learn. I would sing songs and they would work in pairs. While one person was learning to touch-type the words I sang, the partner would look at the paper keyboard to ensure the typist had transcribed the word correctly. And so we went for days, they typing, me singing 'Emancipate yourself from mental slavery, none but ourselves can free our minds...' – until one fine day, three months later, real (albeit second-hand Pentium 1) computers that had been donated arrived. Most of our students that we taught on paper keyboards had never touched a computer. From the moment they began to type on the real thing, they could do as many as 30 words a minute.

Having to start from scratch with very scarce resources made us – well, rather resourceful. To date, CIDA has implemented nearly 300 innovations to cut costs, bringing the budget of a university with around 2,000 students in at around £2.5 million a year.

After nine months in operation, we were blessed with the donation of our first and current premises: Investec Bank's old downtown headquarters, worth £9 million. I had been to see them and managed to hook them on our dream of creating the next generation of young previously disadvantaged business professionals and leaders. I could hardly believe that a bank would take the risk of putting their name to a university project that had no track record; if they had not believed in us at that early stage, in all likelihood we would not have been able to go further.

A world-renowned university

Today, some seven years later, I still have to pinch myself for a reminder that CIDA has become as real and as influential as it is today. CIDA is a world-renowned university that runs an accredited degree programme in Business Administration alongside several faculties and certificate programmes. There are now 900 BBA (Bachelor of Business Administration) students, 360 Foundation College students (a pre-BBA full-board bridging year programme), 120 students in the Life Skills programme (a pre-Foundation College basic development programme for AIDS orphans and at-risk youth) and 1,800 students in vocational training. The graduation ceremony in August 2006 added some 200 students to the 250 who have graduated from CIDA already and are now in the marketplace.

CIDA has worked very hard to structure its programmes in a way that provides relevant education for students to transform themselves from unemployed youngsters caught in the terrible cycle of poverty into economic actors. CIDA is not just a university; we want students to learn in a holistic environment that nurtures their personal development as much as it provides academic training. We do this by offering consciousness-based education and transcendental meditation, to help students manage stress levels and to develop and unfold their latent inner genius, along with a rich curriculum which includes components such as experiential learning, sports and activities, community outreach and self-management.

Recognising that its strategy to tap the potential of students from varying backgrounds means that many will need more attention than they would get at a regular university, CIDA has designed its programme to maximise learning and minimise the need for remedial studies. CIDA students spend up to triple the time in classes of a student taking a traditional degree in South Africa.

There's a test or an exam every week, and students can access all lectures on video, viewing them again to consolidate understanding. Action learning methods, used at top universities throughout the world (such as Cambridge) mean that students learn by doing, both in the knowledge component (case studies, conducting research) and the experiential learning component (starting small businesses, internships). Personal development skills are embedded into the curriculum to help students become more confident, proactive learners. And there are dozens of extramural activities, ranging from sports to choir and poetry clubs.

At CIDA we decided to start with the offer of only one degree – the Bachelor of Business Administration – because this was the most relevant degree we could offer to students who needed to start supporting themselves and their families straight out of university. We believed that by concentrating students on practical studies, with work experience and classes taught by leading professionals, they would be best placed to enter the labour market.

To ensure students learn relevant skills, CIDA has developed several specialist courses, partnering with leading companies in each industry. Students can specialise in HR (Human Resources), Finance, or Marketing. They can join the ICT (Information and Communications Technology) Academy, complete with free training from T-Systems, Oracle, SAP and Sun Microsystems, and study for a certificate in ICT alongside their degree. Students can also specialise in Entrepreneurship, joining the Branson School of Entrepreneurship at CIDA, which has incubator space and a seed fund to provide capital for students to start their own businesses.

CIDA is unique in that it partners with business so that students are learning from experts, and companies have the opportunity to take on CIDA students as interns and effectively 'try out' and even groom potential employees. Access to strong black talent is a fundamental need at South African corporations.

The business partnerships are also international. In 2006 the Branson School of Entrepreneurship began teaching students, and over 1,000 students benefited from its courses. Market days were a risky time to walk on campus with any money in your pockets, and many CIDA staff and visitors found it was certain that CIDA students peddling their wares would effortlessly rid you of any spare cash.

The School's renovated premises were launched by Sir Richard Branson and dignitaries in late 2006. Housed on the second floor of the Nelson Mandela FNB building on the corner of Harrison and Commissioner Streets, this is the building where Mandela had his first job as a legal clerk when he joined the ANC. The building was generously donated to CIDA by First National Bank. It is very fitting that this building is now owned by CIDA, a true representation of the 'long walk to freedom' from political redemption of South Africa to a totally new focus on the creation of economic freedom through entrepreneurship and business education.

In line with the values at the core of the university, CIDA believes that students should take ownership of the university and responsibility for their own education. While they are on 90 per cent scholarship, they are responsible for paying ten per cent of their education – R350 (£30) for the entire year at Foundation College, and R150 (£12) per month for the three years of the BBA degree. While our students still have difficulties paying these amounts, they are paying under ten per cent of the cost of other universities in South Africa. It also means that CIDA students do not develop an entitlement mentality, and learn the value of their own education by having invested in it.

There is an old African adage that goes, 'It takes a village to raise a child'. CIDA has turned that on its head; we think it takes a child to raise a village. Many CIDA students are the first in their family if not their entire village to go to university.

To encourage students to give back to their communities, it is compulsory for them to return during holiday time to their hometowns in order to teach some of what they have learned. This project, called CIDA on the Move, gives students the tools they need to go back to their former schools and teach basic business skills, as well as HIV/AIDS awareness. Students begin with a group of 30 students when they arrive at CIDA, and stick with them throughout their degree, forming a bond with them and becoming a mentor to some of them throughout their studies.

Every student is on a scholarship at CIDA, and each one knows that someone has contributed financially to make his or her education possible. CIDA encourages students to 'pay it forward' by committing within five years after graduation to funding another student from their hometown for the full duration of their degree.

Investment in people

I feel extremely blessed to have been able to play a small role in the future of my country. South Africa has so much wealth – in its land and its rivers, but most importantly, in its people. Investing in our people means changing the social and economic landscape of South Africa and ultimately the region. We have made a small start by sending a few hundred graduates into the marketplace, but there is a significant multiplier effect. Each graduate can now support a family of four or five people. Each of the hundreds of students that goes back to his or her community to teach reaches 30 more students. And working graduates generate millions of rand that goes directly into the hands of the poor.

I am admittedly an extreme optimist by nature, but I believe CIDA is on to something. My next challenge is to look beyond the Johannesburg campus, finding a practical way to replicate the model we have created. A replication feasibility study will spend 18 months analysing and creating a practical action plan towards strengthening the Johannesburg campus so that it can act as a hub for satellite campuses throughout the country and the region.

We also want to create a rural model for the campus, which incorporates self-sustaining practices related to the construction and maintenance of the campus itself, as well as to businesses relevant to rural areas, such as organic bio-dynamic farming. Already in 2007 at CIDA Park, where the Foundation

College is based, a Construction Academy has opened, teaching students valuable skills that some of them will use to build these rural campuses.

CIDA City Campus's Bachelor of Business Administration degree and vocational training programmes have already helped 2,800 young South Africans into a career and a new life, which combines to annual salary earnings of R120 million/£10 million. Given that most graduates are between 20 and 25 years old, and will work for 40 years, we would expect to see over R4 billion/£333 million being earned by these working graduates over their working lives – a meaningful achievement for all involved in CIDA.

But this is about more than just statistics; there are real lives involved here. Take Elihle Mguni, who is now Marketing Director at Honeywell. She sits on their Executive Committee and has travelled internationally on the company's behalf. She earns about £35,000 a year. From her humble beginnings in a single parent home in Soweto, she has now grown to be able to provide for her mother and family, and has bought a house and a car. On the side, she and her husband have found time to start a successful clothing label. Elihle is one of the very lucky ones who has been able to achieve her dreams through CIDA's scholarship opportunity.

I cannot begin to imagine what my life would be like now had I boarded that plane to America ten years ago. Would I now be oblivious to the potential of my country and the plight of my continent? Would I have felt regret at not being involved? Or would I be blissfully unaware, living in a high-rise in Manhattan? There is not much point in speculating. I prefer to look at our graduates instead, and marvel at how different their lives are.

2017: empowering and engendering the future

Susan and Juliet Kiguli

Susan and Juliet Kiguli are lecturers at Makerere University, Uganda. Susan lectures in the Literature Department and is a respected poet in her own right, while Juliet lectures in gender and public health in the Department of Health and Behavioural Sciences.

For social and cultural reasons girls and women continue to be marginalised in many African societies, with profound consequences. It has been observed that, for instance, if mothers are literate, their children generally are, so it is understood that one of the quickest ways to reduce the high rates of illiteracy in many African countries is through educating girls and women. Empowering and involving African girls and women much more centrally in governance, land ownership, and social and cultural spaces would have a dramatic impact on African societies. Looking forward to 2017, Susan and Juliet Kiguli tackle their own university, Makerere, as a site for action since a lot of changes and reform have been happening in this university since 1986. Makerere's motto is 'We build for the future'. It is an important institution in the East African region, and could itself strongly lead by example. Susan and Juliet Kiguli consider three future scenarios for empowering and involving women much more in the running of the university. The three imagined scenarios provide a road map for what needs to be done or avoided, in order to realise the positive future we want to see.

The oppressors maintain their position and evade responsibility for their own actions. There is a constant drain of energy which might be better used in redefining ourselves and devising realistic scenarios for altering the present and constructing the future.

AUDRE LORDE, *AGE, RACE, CLASS AND SEX*

The context

Makerere, Uganda's premier university and, for a long time, its only public university, began its life as a technical school in 1922. The university achieved its glorified status as one of Africa's most respected institutions of higher learning between the time it became the University of East Africa until the mid-1970s when Idi Amin's regime made it hard for the institution to operate normally as a place for intellectual vibrancy. As Musisi and Muwanga observe:

> Makerere University's strength lay in its reputation, its location in a vibrant and growing city, and its well established infrastructure. The quality of its staff, the highly selective quality of its student body, sound and innovative management and external linkages and support were a source of great pride.
>
> (MUSISI AND MUWANGA, 2003:8)

Makerere struggled through Amin's and subsequent regimes until Yoweri Museveni took power in 1986. The university then embarked on a period of extensive reform and recovery. The university's reform and recovery process is well documented in the work of Musisi and Muwanga, as well as the assessment of the history and current state of Makerere by Carol Sicherman.

One observation that has been strongly made is that even during the years of crisis and struggle, Makerere's reputation remained unshaken. Currently, it is viewed as a place that has spearheaded challenging reforms in higher education in the African region. A number of reasons have led to Makerere becoming a centre of focus in the review of higher education in Africa (see Musisi and Muwanga, 2003), but we will concentrate on one striking change pertinent to the major focus of this discussion.

Among the major academic reforms of the 1990s was the establishment of the Department of Women Studies which began its programmes in 1991 with 13 students (Sicherman, 2005:229). The introduction of the department now known as the Department of Gender and Women Studies has had an impact on the gender dynamics in Makerere as an institution that was all male at its inception. The department, right from the outset, aimed to create an impact by building a strong outreach programme in gender training. It has run a series of non-degree courses with the aim of promoting gender awareness in the country and at the university.

The Department of Gender and Women Studies has consistently endeavoured to be relevant both in and outside the university. As Sicherman notes, the department was active in addressing the issue of 'gender discrimination in hiring and promotion at Makerere' (Sicherman, 2005:235). The department held workshops to create awareness on equality and equity issues at the university. A number of tangible results are evident (see Sicherman 2005:234). The Gender and Women Studies Department has, in co-operation with other departments, planned, lobbied and pushed for the gender agenda to be on the tables of the university decision makers.

Today at the university, women are 40 per cent of the student population, 20 per cent of the teaching staff, and 15 per cent of the administrative staff. The highest position a woman occupies is that of First Deputy Vice Chancellor for Academic Affairs. With the policies of gender awareness and affirmative action introduced by the National Resistance Movement government, we would expect the percentages to be much higher than this.

It is against this background that we look forward to 2017, and imagine the kinds of policies that might truly transform gender relations at the university or retard them. Each of the scenarios will face their own champions or detractors, either a new cohort of newly enfranchised women impacting on their environment, or a set of entrenched attitudes and centres of power which will resist change. We propose them, nevertheless, as starting points for a discussion about the obstacles and challenges that prevent us creating the kind of future which can nurture and bring out the best in all of us.

Imagi(ni)ng Makerere University

Scenario 1:

The year 2017: the venue is Makerere University Main Building. We walk into the Vice Chancellor's office. A self-assured woman is behind the huge mahogany desk. She is at ease even amidst the all-male portraits of Vice Chancellors that have led this university for over a century. The leadership picture now is spectacularly different from the scenes of a hundred years back. The current mood is that progress is achieved through both women and men academicians appreciating their differences and relating on equal terms. The phenomenon of only three female professors in the whole university is a trend of the past. There are 90 female professors in the different faculties of the university. The intellectual participation of women is a given. We are products of the late 20th century and are keen to ask this professor and Vice Chancellor about female intellectual invisibility and issues of woman oppression. She, on the other hand, wants to discuss the progress of a genderless (though not sexless) society where one's position and opportunities in society are not determined by one's sex. She is part of a reality where the meeting of minds is far more important than the categorising of sexes. To this leader, the identification and ways of meeting the needs of both female and male employees in the university are the crucial issues on the agenda. She talks about ensuring channels of dialogue for members of staff and students. She is preoccupied with the importance of making a difference in various areas of expertise in academia. She explains to us that the entire staff on recruitment undergoes training courses to strengthen their skills in negotiation and conflict resolution and as a result the administration feels close to the academic staff. The equality in numbers and equity in opportunities for both female and male employees has also ensured balance in arguments for the welfare of both sexes. The qualities of empathy and understanding are actively encouraged by the system and the old cultural construct of these qualities as belonging exclusively to women has long been dead.

The woman behind the power desk is comfortable about the fact that difference does not mean subordination. She is flexible in her approach to decision making and is outstanding in her ability to do different tasks simultaneously. Because she has grown up in a community where gender differences do not determine one's welfare in society, she uses her strong qualities to do her work quickly and efficiently. She tells us that she has a team of administrators, both women and men, who make decision implementation prompt and smooth. The attitude here is not to win or feel powerful but to build a strong academic chain by listening and using different opinions. This woman is amazing, she leans back in her swivel chair and remarks, 'In leadership no one has all the answers. We work together across all units of this university to ensure that our quality is high.' We know for a fact that the leaders in the university are far more accessible now than they were in the late 20th century because the present Vice Chancellor believes in the sharing of ideas and the debating of improvements to the university's leadership and academic structures. The avenue for feedback from different departments of the university is a strong one. As a result the 2017 Makerere University knows no strikes because job expectations are well defined.

This is 2017, where technology has made it possible to accomplish tasks swiftly and competently. Identity cards, certificates and transcripts are available from the Academic Registrar's Department in time and forgeries are a myth in this environment of honesty and efficiency. Despite the machine culture, people are still valued and talent is respected. It is evident that there are some values from Ugandan traditional systems that have been retained for continuity and harmonious living. Every member is important to the university community and the university policy encourages healthy relationships between academicians, administrators and students. The presence of many female leaders at different levels of the university has promoted the quality of appreciation of achievement and hard work. The history of Makerere University has taught the new administration that appreciating employees encourages them to stay on. The administration has realised that the previous policies of affirmative action for women, particularly in the sciences, were good for the times they were instituted. They have reviewed them and now have a system where difference relates within equality. The quality of encouraging and motivating workers is not labelled a female characteristic. This is the era of emphasising cost-effective approaches and not dominance.

In this era of 2017, the percentage of women leaders increases markedly with each level of promotion in the academic hierarchy. More girls are joining the university because there are many female role models and many more mentors. The women are no longer assessed along gender terms but on the basis of their qualification and achievement.

As we leave the Vice Chancellor's office we remark to each other: 'If someone by some miracle walked out of the year 1922 and came back to this university now, he or she would not recognise this community where talent is drawn from a variety of sections of society without thinking of male and female categorisation.' This is indeed a different university, where equal partnership is valued, where it is acknowledged that half the population is female. This is a generation of policy makers that has outlawed favouritism and bias. Most crucially, this is a university where the increasing participation of women in the university management and the presence of a female Vice Chancellor has ensured a supportive environment for competent women and men to find their creativity and abilities in various departments.

Scenario 2:

Another kind of scenario. It is 2017 and at Makerere University there are some women in leadership positions. The numerous debates led by Ugandan female academics 25 years back provided a route for the examination of patriarchy and social inequalities in Uganda but they did not manage to ensure a tremendous increase in female participation and leadership in the university echelons. There are three female professors and one female dean in the entire university. One of the female professors manages the Gender Mainstreaming Department. This department guides the involvement of women in leadership positions. It is involved in organising gender training workshops to increase awareness of staff, especially among the men, about the importance of gender. It greatly advocates gender rights.

The university is receptive to new ideas, particularly those that guide gender awareness. Makerere University Institute of Public Health, for example, is implementing a leadership skills development programme within the Faculty of Medicine. They are training both female and male staff in leadership attributes and management.

In addition, the Department of Gender and Women Studies under the Faculty of Social Sciences trains both men and women to explore gender issues. It also campaigns for both men's and women's rights. It carries out research in gender-focused areas such as domestic violence, politics and many others. The department has ensured that gender issues are part of the curriculum. It is now common to find subjects such as gender and sexuality taught in the Sociology Department, the Faculty of Social Sciences, and Epidemiology Department, and the Institute of Public Health among others. There is an increased introduction of non-traditional modules such as these to add to the traditional ones such as Obstetrics and Gynaecology where ideas of femaleness and maleness are regarded as part of the gender question. There is a decisive shift away from the focus on what was implicitly coded as feminist and women issues to what is seen as gender studies.

Several World Women's Forums have been organised at Makerere University and spearheaded by the female head of department of Gender and Women Studies. These have played an important role in bringing women and some men from all over the world to debate gender issues together. Slogans such as 'Talking gender and walking gender' are now commonly heard at the university. These forums have focused the world's attention on Uganda as a gender-sensitive country.

In another heartening development, the science policy to promote girls' involvement in science education and scientific work has recently been emphasised by the government of Uganda. The development arm agency of a northern partner in the United States of America has been giving grants and scholarships to enhance the women numbers in science development. This has led to an increased number of women taking up science courses and featuring prominently in scientific discovery and innovations. This can be attributed to the positive attitude and affirmative action by the university policy makers. Such a scenario emphasises the fact that gender equity is pertinent to academia.

Scenario 3:

Yet another possible situation. It is 2017 and a new motto for Makerere has just been put up prominently at the main entrance to the university. It reads 'Make us all Men'. Women are excluded from the university decision-making bodies and where they feature they are definitely subordinates to the men. 'Male culture' flourishes and there is absolutely no debate about the obvious exclusion of women from the council, senate, central administration, faculty and departmental boards. All the administrators and academicians are content with the male-dominated leadership structure. The main argument presented to anyone who comments on the absence of female spaces in the university is that African women consider their natural role as wives and mothers paramount. Women benefit from education only in order to service their families. In fact the university has a body of research showing that most women prefer to put their education and careers aside to enable their husbands' careers to advance. Thus in the university leadership discourse, women are viewed as assistants who tidy up after major work is accomplished by men. There is no legislation in the University Act that provides space and recognition for women's struggle. The male administrators hold formal power over the University Employment Act. They do not see the need to allow for a debate on change in employment regulations since the existing structure works well for them. This is 2017 and the legal rights of women even at the university do not count. No one seems to regard the absence of women from the public sphere as a problem.

Conclusion

Speaking in 2007: evaluating all the drawn scenarios, we are led to believe that more increased female participation and respecting differences can lead to a situation where men and women are happily participating in leadership and female qualities are actively promoted at the same level as male ones. We feel that we need to devise ways of relating across our human differences as equals. (Lorde, 1998:631).

We are aware as we write that remarkable strides have been made in changing the face of Makerere University's leadership structure. This has enabled increased promotion of women in management positions (for instance the First Deputy Vice Chancellor for Academic Affairs is a woman). Such openness to change gives a good foundation to build on and introduce more radical measures.

Positive action is already evident. Due to consideration of gender equity in academia, admissions have greatly incorporated vulnerable groups. Disabled females have been admitted as students and this has enabled some of them to occupy specific positions of leadership. Musisi and Muwanga (2003:32–3) say that female admission increased by 25 per cent over the period 1993–2000. They go on to say it was a credible and positive trend. Therefore, we are of the opinion that such increments have led to changes in female enrolment and promotion of women in new leadership positions.

Female academic staff account for only 20 per cent of the total number of staff at the university on university payroll. This poses the question of gender disparity in terms of staffing. Much as the females lag behind the males in employment, a significant change has been registered where currently the curriculum development programme at the university ensures female participation. Nevertheless, the picture demands more action in order to ensure significant female presence in leadership.

Ultimately we must emphasise that for a better future, we must all examine ways in which gender equality and equity can be achieved. We must not allow ourselves to fall into the trap where existent structures are glossed

2017: empowering and engendering the future

over and not critically appraised in terms of the historical, political and cultural distinctions and contexts. Further, we need to look at our major hindrances, such as the fact the school drop-out rate is still very high, and deal with them with compelling urgency. At Makerere University in particular we need to overhaul the outdated centralised organisational structure with only male leaders at the top and galvanise ourselves into a structure that greatly supports a wide variety of achievers. There is need to find ways of improving our current financial base so that the structures can stop promoting the already privileged categories. The university needs funding to support the groups of its employees that fill the bottom layer. Most women occupy the lowest ranks and need further training and support to rise up in the ranks. We also have to remember that Ugandan society has been plagued by war and oppressive regimes for a very long time and the women have been a very vulnerable group in these situations therefore extra support and a realistic analysis of their circumstances may go a long way in ensuring their visibility at for example the higher institutions of learning such as Makerere University.

We need to campaign for the appointment of more women on the main policy committees, editorial boards and all important networks. It will also be advisable to introduce training sessions on cultural change in order to promote systems that cater for the needs of a more diverse group of people.

As African women (we hazard a generalisation), we should make a deliberate effort to acknowledge our full identity and fight for the full liberation and accommodation of the various parts of our identity and being. We should constantly encourage the psychological liberation of women.

Speaking from Makerere University in 2007, the men are still a dominant group although once in a while they feel a need to step into the role of liberals and offer token attention to women. We think that the direction to pursue is equal participation in addressing the gaps and identifying where we could share responsibility in order to make female participation in leadership a balanced reality. There is need for collaboration, common vision and the personal commitment of those in places of responsibility to see to change in the socio-cultural conditioning that prevails in this dominantly patriarchal setting.

References

Audre Lorde, 'Age, Race, Class and Sex: Women Redefining Difference' in *Literary Theory: An Anthology*, Julie Rivkin and Michael Ryan (eds.), 1998, pp. 630–636.

Nakanyike B. Musisi and Nansozi K. Muwanga, *Makerere University in Transition 1993–2000: opportunities and challenges*, James Currey and Fountain Publishers, Oxford Press/Fountain Publishers, 2003.

Lynne Pearce and Sara Mills, 'Marxist Feminism' in: *Feminist Readings/Feminists Reading*, Pearce et al. (eds.) 1996, pp. 185–224.

Carol Sicherman, *Becoming an African University: Makerere 1922–2000*, Africa World Press, Trenton and Asmara, 2005.

Tongues on fire –
the Sheng' generation

Parselelo Kantai

Parselelo Kantai is a Kenyan writer and investigative journalist. He edited Ecoforum, *an environmental magazine. His features focused on the politics of conservation and the experiences of people living away from mainstream Kenyan life. Seen as one of a new generation of accomplished Kenyan writers who have emerged in the last ten years, his work has been critically well received. His short story 'Comrade Lemma and the Black Jerusalem Boys Band' was shortlisted for the the Caine Prize in 2004.*

Many of Kantai's generation of new writers have gathered around Kwani?, *the Kenyan literary journal.* Kwani? *appeared as a haven, offering an open forum for discussion and reflection as the period of authoritarian rule under President Daniel arap Moi came to an end. Here Kantai explains how the Sheng' generation was born.*

> 'When the madness of an entire nation disturbs a solitary mind, it is not enough to say the man is mad.'
>
> FRANCIS IMBUGA, *BETRAYAL IN THE CITY* (1976).

At a book launch in Nairobi in April 2006, Kenya's most famous historian, Professor Bethwel A. Ogot stood up and declared that Project Kenya was dead. The ideals that the nationalists had stood for were bankrupt. Kenya, he said, had never been more distant an idea than it was now, at the beginning of the 21st century. Nationhood no longer existed. It had been replaced by sub-nationalism: the different ethnic groups, in effect, had eaten up the country. These declarations were a terrible indictment on leadership in Kenya, especially since they were coming from a man who had devoted over 50 years of his life to writing Kenya into being, to defending – at a time when the study of African history was considered primarily to be the study of Europeans in Africa – the notion that the 43 African communities that fell within the colonial construction that was Kenya Colony were people, distinct nations. They had heritages and aspirations, traditions and worldviews. Later, Ogot was instrumental in giving life to what was little more than a rickety idea: by textualising a national identity he and others poured an Afrocentric history into what had previously been a space colonised by whites. People crept out of the darkness of their imagined savageries. We, Ogot had long postulated, had not been invented; we *were*.

That such an obvious statement could be so transformative is difficult for me and people of my generation to fully appreciate. People were validated, and at the euphoric moment of their validation – as the Union Jack fell and the Kenyan flag went up – were made to enter into a new enterprise: Kenya. It was a huge undertaking. And now, one of its principal architects was announcing its failure.

We who were born under the Kenyan flag had listened to the propaganda of nationalism for so long, we internalised its cadences and often missed its import: that nations were built, were projects, ideas. We were its building blocks, constructing in the very enterprise of our construction; we were, as we so often heard, the leaders of tomorrow. We were raised on a diet of free primary education, mandatory mid-morning primary school milk and personal rule: whatever His Excellency, through the Voice of Kenya and/or his domestic representatives (the parents), said was good for us. The Party was good but *Playboy*, for instance, was clearly not. So *Playboy* was banned and new Party offices opened and those who sought out *Playboy* were bad and those who sang at the opening of the new KANU branch were good. I am simplifying of course, but living within the ubiquity of power made it impossible to imagine that your existence was in itself an experiment.

All around us, the experiment was going wrong. When I was 13, the Prisons Band – at the time His Excellency the President's favourite – sang:

> We are a loving nation
> United and free
> We are! We are!
> We gonna tell it all again
>
> Ethiopians!
> Welcome to the land of Kenya
> People are happy and are living in peace
> Ugandans!
> Welcome to the land of Kenya
> People are happy and are living in peace

Moi, Son of God
Moi, President of Kenya
People are happy and are living in peace.

The soloist of the Prisons Band was Kalenjin, from His Excellency's ethnic group, an ever-smiling man with a gap in his front teeth wider than mine. He sang with a heavy accent that mangled English and caused us city kids much superior laughter. But His Excellency liked the band and the song was played over and over. We noted the accent and therefore registered the words as nonsensical. Only later did I recognise their self-congratulatory import. His Excellency would often remind us that 'Kenya is an island of peace in a sea of chaos'.

For the longest time, I had pronounced chaos as CHA-OS, had no idea what it meant. My mother is from Uganda and we always knew, in the way that you know a beat on a distant drum, that there was trouble there. Once a year, my *Jaja*, my grandmother, would appear at our doorstep, unannounced and thin and wearing a silk *busuti* beneath a faded blue sweater. Once she had settled down and mother and daughter had exchanged greetings, she would tell us about Kampala. When she started making her annual visits to Nairobi, she would tell us about Nyerere's guns that boomed so deeply they could break your heart. But they had also chased away Amin. And then on later trips, she would tell us about Obote's soldiers who every evening drove in huge lorries into Kampala's neighbourhoods announcing in Kiswahili (which every Ugandan disdained as army language): *Ombeni Mungu wenu!* Pray to your God! It was a cue to switch off your lights and run into the bush.

My uncle Miro Kasozzi, who taught us to play chess and had two degrees from the Soviet Union, arrived one day from that bush. The soldiers had come to his house and he had run out through the back, hid in the bush for two days and, when it was safe, caught a bus to Busia on the Kenya–Uganda border. All he had was the shirt he was wearing, his trousers and his certificates in an old brown briefcase.

These were stories from visitors who occupied a storybook reality. They smiled as they told us these stories, smiled that Kampala smile that insisted above all else that dignity must be retained even in the direst of circumstances. In lessening the blow for us, they banished us from that reality, gently pushed it over into an impossible realm. So we listened patiently and then politely enquired whether they liked *Football Made in Germany*, dragged whoever it was to our bedroom, my brother's and mine, to show them the giant Fuji poster of Karlheinz Rummenigge. CHA-OS to a nine-year-old boy obsessed with football could be defined as being deprived of the right to watch the Bayern Munich–Borussia Munchengladbach game because a new relative had suddenly appeared and the adults were talking in the sitting-room where the television was.

I marvel at the ingenuity that it took to keep the experiment alive. The codes unconsciously communicated across the landscape of our earnest faces that prevented the visitor from dragging us to the edge of the abyss from which he had only just emerged; the elaborate infrastructure of adult secrecy that ensured that in ignorance lay our childhood bliss. The nation was being built inside us. We were its unconscious laboratory. We needed to be protected at all costs. But it was also the age: His Excellency was the Father of the Nation. We were all his children. The Prisons Band sang 'Welcome to the land of Kenya' bowed, boarded the green Prisons bus and went back to the office to torture some dissidents, misguided university lecturers who were being paid by foreign elements out to destabilise His Excellency's government.

Like our other successful experiments of the time – tea and coffee – we were rooted locally but designed for export. We, the sons and daughters of the nationalist elite, sat behind dark and heavy wooden desks wounded with the insignia of those other children – the white kids of colonial bureaucrats. 'JT was here' carved out of the wood with the tip of a compass point. We spoke only when spoken to and bowed and curtsied and said properly by skipping over the superfluous 'er' or else got a rap on the knuckles from Mr Gerson Fonseca. We disdained Kiswahili and crammed facts about places we would never visit so that we could pass exams and slip behind other desks in national schools that were extensions of our primary schools, schools named Lenana and Nairobi that had not long ago been Duke of York and Prince of Wales. The prize at the end was the White Collar, a job behind another desk, a car in the secured parking lot, 2.8 kids in a primary school much like the ones we were in. So, repeat: wheat was grown in Regina, cattle ranched in the Pampas, the Bantu came from the Cameroon Forest and the Maasai thought they had come down from heaven on the skin of a cow.

This was our real heritage, despite Professor Ogot: ritualised incantation with no meaning save for the inner logic of developing collective obedience. We were signs that signified themselves, and we were rooted in contradiction. Sons and daughters of the victors of anti-colonial struggle, the only reliable precedent for our ongoing invention was the colonial elite our parents had replaced. And that was the problem. That at the age of ten, some 20 years after independence, I was sitting behind a desk that had been marked years before by a settler boy; the disused inkwell probably still contained ink samples from his fountain pen. We had failed to produce new realities for ourselves. Along the way, the new African elite, so young and transcendent when they came to power, were now older and fatter, had lost their hunger. They were the Firsts: the first large cadre of Western-trained university graduates which, in the heady days of independence, filled the gap left by the departing colonial administrative bureaucracy. By the age of 30, many of them were sitting at the head of public corporations, running government departments, taking over senior management positions in multinational corporations. Doctors, engineers, administrators, others: they gave muscle to the rhetorical idea of Black Rule. Their extended stay in the West, their return trip with a rolled-up degree certificate and a graduation photograph, had given them Promethean reputations in their home villages. They were called *mzee* (old man) before they were 40. When they stood up to speak at local gatherings, entire locations fell silent; people cocked their ears and stared at their bare feet and tried to decipher every nuance and cadence in the great man's voice. The great men lived in Nairobi and did important things. They did not visit often. They were building the nation.

And yet a scene in Ayi Kwei Armah's unflinching account of corruption in early independent Ghana, *The Beautyful Ones Are Not Yet Born*, comes to mind: it is the early years of independence and The Man, the main character, is walking through a former white neighbourhood in Accra. All around him the houses are now occupied by the new African elite. It is the names by the entrances to the mansions within that begin to disturb him. Everybody has changed their name to fit their uplifted circumstances. People who only a few years ago had been called Joe Amoako and Peter Kuffour are now A. Joseph and K. Peters: 'Perhaps it was not hate that drove us but love: love for the white man's things, his life,' observes The Man. Or words to that effect.

In Kenya, the heroes of the independence struggle had been deftly replaced post-*uhuru* by the traitors of the struggle, the sons of the colonial-era chiefs who had collaborated with the colonial government during the Mau Mau insurgency. Once in power, President Kenyatta, a Gikuyu and Mau Mau's inspirational figure, had surrounded himself with the chiefs' sons. Further betrayals had taken place after independence. His most powerful supporter during the struggle, Jaramogi Oginga Odinga, a Luo from Nyanza, was shunted aside as the government took on an increasingly Gikuyu character. One of the catch-phrases of those early days: *kula matunda ya uhuru*, eat the fruits of independence, became the code-word for elite accumulation generally and Gikuyu patronage specifically.

On national days, we dutifully remembered the names of the original heroes. Cardboard characters who had lived heroically and died tragically at some point in a misty past, we only knew them as blank spaces for the end of term exam: Field Marshall Dedan Kimathi Waciuri was the ... of Mau Mau. Mau Mau was the ...of independence. History was one of several subjects to be conquered over three days of examinations. It had nothing to do with present reality. Words substituted meaning, and the past, with its betrayals and accommodations, remained in the shadows.

So the past was out of bounds. And for good reason: who were our parents within the context of these huge betrayals? As benign and apolitical as, say, the pursuit of engineering or medicine was, what had they done to achieve what they had? They had worked hard, they explained. And so we lived under a code of hard work. The pursuit of educational glory became our defining objective. Such arid values combined with the secrets of our parents' previous lives produced in my generation not curiosity, but a vast need to conform. Instinctively, we knew the consequences of unconventional thought. So we feared unbeaten paths, ideas that had not been endorsed by authority. When we were older and unable to find meaning anywhere else, we excavated the already hollow words of our education and, judging them to be valuable, the best of us laid them down as a foundation on which to live. That, ultimately, is the meaning of the story I am about to tell you.

My friend Bee was found hanging in her ground floor apartment in Nairobi's Kilimani area on a Thursday morning in March 2005. She lived alone and left no suicide note. Fanatically neat and notoriously absent-minded, her farewell gesture was to leave her curtains partially open. It was a plea that whoever should discover her corpse would do so before it began to putrefy. So they found her and took her away. And then the phone calls and text messages and e-mails – the whole ritualised jumble that follows a death in middle-class Nairobi – all of it was set in motion. If anybody, a newcomer late to arrive into the circle gathered on an evening in a designated house where the funeral arrangements were being made, asked what had happened, it is quite possible that they received an honest answer. It is also quite possible that they did not – did not dare ask for fear of provoking that embarrassment always so present during such occasions. And if one of the mourners in a moment of weakness and honesty broke down and asked 'Why?' it would have been to a reception of equally confounded faces.

I was not there. I was in faraway Oxford being paid a nice scholarship stipend to ruminate on the Kenyan state. The last time I had seen Bee was on my daughter's birthday the previous December. Bee was Santayian's godmother. I received the news of her death from Santayian's mother, Bee's closest friend, Jane, my ex. She and Jane had known each other since their university days. I knew Bee differently. We had gone to the same primary school. Her brother was my classmate. We had lived for a time in the same neighbourhood. There had been many hours spent drinking and talking in what seemed to be several Nairobi incarnations: in our early 20s as students at the police canteen that was our neighbourhood local; as salaried folk, bumping into each other in bars and clubs downtown, a coincidence that on one occasion led me to Jane; even later, swapping invitations to parties at each other's houses. There were memories of shared holidays and lazy

Sunday afternoons. Oddly fixed in my mind is a photograph, vintage Bee, taken of Santayian, one-tooth old and in a yellow sweater knitted by one of her grandmothers, scrambling across the carpet towards the camera, screeching, her eyes sparkling with mischief.

I remembered other things: the funeral of another mutual friend, Betty, who, finally accepting her HIV-positive status and deciding to go public with it, had died a few years earlier. Her funeral service had been held at the church in which I had grown up. I remember another friend, the playwright G, Bee's and Jane's year-mate at the University of Nairobi, who, refusing to accept that he was positive, had died prematurely; going on anti-retrovirals would have been an admission to himself of his condition. Bee had worked with G's brother. G and a cousin of mine were a couple until his death. And in the vines of our tangled relationships but cut off from the confines of Nairobi, that village of four million where such questions were not openly broached, something in me arrived at a tentative conclusion. We used to joke that even when you *did* die in a car accident, it was probably still HIV-related. A suicide was so much easier to deduce; the act itself only confirmed lingering suspicions. AIDS was the silent guest at every death.

'Was she positive?' I finally had the courage to ask. 'No,' Jane was emphatic. 'She would have told me.' 'Then what was it? Why did she do it?'

Jane told me an implausible story. Bee was depressed. Depressed because she was in debt.

'Why didn't she come to you if things were so bad?' I asked. 'She had. She already owed me quite a bit.' 'But still...' 'I offered but she refused,' Jane explained. 'She said borrowing would just depress her some more.'

Bee owed all her friends money.

She had gone quiet soon after Christmas, the last time I had seen her. Eventually, when Jane had sought her out she had rolled up her sleeves and revealed a set of slash-marks across her wrists, barely healed. That last conversation, those slashed wrists, they agreed, would be their secret. They would never discuss that foolishness again. Thinking about it now, it seems to me that even as she promised to desist from the foolishness, Bee had already retreated to a place from which there was no return.

Her father was inconsolable at her funeral. When Jane told him what she thought – when she gave him an answer to 'Why' – he asked, broken, why Bee hadn't gone to him. But who can explain how far away, how impossible to reach everybody is when you are down that black hole?

Beyond our grief and her despair – beyond our private Whys – Bee's suicide seemed to suggest a larger failure. If, as Stalin had once infamously remarked, one man's death is a tragedy and one million a statistic, what drama had my friend been involved in? On what canvas was her death painted? What was her 'tragic arc'?

Let us pull out from the close-up image on that grim Thursday morning. In March 2005, the sunlight glinted off the dozens of brand new cars parked in Bee's large apartment complex where US$ 500 a month secured you a prime piece of Nairobi upper middle-class real estate, with uniformed guards at the gate, electric fencing and ayahs taking out the trash and walking the baby.

Beyond the high stone walls that protect this brahminic existence lie the questions – the street with its statistics, its faceless many, the potholes, the honking *matatus*, the rat-race for rat-holes – questions we must answer in order to understand the state this enterprise called Project Kenya finds itself at the beginning of 21st century.

But not so fast. You need first to understand how and where Bee fitted on that canvas.

Bee was 36 years old, single and postgraduate, at the top end of that growing 'demographic' that Nairobi's advertisers and copywriters pulverised with 'disposable lifestyle' – cars, clothes, credit cards and cosmetics. She had in the 1990s accumulated a vast number of postgraduate certificates in addition to her degrees (a Bachelor of Science in Botany and a postgraduate degree in Journalism). She had a diploma in management, the mandatory certificates proving computer literacy, a certificate in disaster management, another as a human rights trainer. Like so many young Kenyans negotiating their way through the 1990s, Bee used certificates as a shield to ward off the evil spirits of those uncertain days. You never could tell when the next wave of retrenchments would come, and who it would carry away.

All around her, the old certainties were disappearing. Her parents had retired to their farm in Nyanza – they were Luo – after quietly distinguished careers in the civil service in Nairobi. They had managed to buy a house in Woodley, the same house in which Bee had grown up. But the ownership of the house was now disputed. Somebody with links that through a series of intricate paths eventually ended up at State House, somebody 'connected' had obtained a duplicate title deed on the property and was trying to sell it. So there was a court case or, more accurately, the dispute over the property was now in judicial quicksand. Unless Bee or her siblings or her ageing parents knew someone at the High Court, the case would not be heard for years. The file would be lost. Or else, because they were dealing with somebody 'connected', there was every chance that they would one day be surprised to find the furniture from their childhood sitting on the sidewalk, and a strange woman, mistress of Mr Connected, inside the house, supervising the movers, waving a copy of a court order.

In the 1990s, His Excellency fell out of favour with his Western backers, and the privileges of an entitled elite two generations deep began to be shaken. The inalienable rights of the Firsts, the undoubted pedigree of their sons and daughters, their collective rights to the spoils of the post-colony (rural land, urban real estate, corporate jobs, resultant from years of cultivating the right accent); all that, as well as the old boy networks that secured those privileges, was profaned. The First Network, that of His Excellency and his tribesmen, was desperate for cash. Frozen out of the Paris Club – some dubious charge of trampling on human rights – and other Western donor clubs, this network turned inwards and began cannibalising itself. It liquidated everything it could lay its hands on: rivers and road reserves were privatised; forest and wildlife parks turned into 'plots' for its beneficiaries; public toilets and government houses disappeared, became shanty towns and apartment complexes, all property of mysterious new men with names that had no pedigree. Unprotected sex and AIDS became a metaphor for free-fall – for the unsheathing of the privileges of the independence elite and, as always, the victimisation of the citizenry in whose name this public shafting was conducted.

Certificates were condoms. But one also needed to know Who – more than How – could guarantee protection. Bee was prepared to sleep with no one, both literally and figuratively. She drew a line at that point. She had not been brought up that way. She had faith in merit. And so she drifted from job to job, assuming that she was not rising up the career ladder because she was restless, searching for that elusive 'right' path. She moved from the aid industry to the corporate sector, and back and forth and went to school at night. She was careful with her money and talented enough to ensure that there was always enough for rent and a little extra. Many of her friends left for the US and the UK. They left, or they died in alcohol and HIV.

In December 2002, a Gallup global poll declared Kenyans the most optimistic people in the world. Moi was leaving and a new coalition government, NARC, led by his old deputy Mwai Kibaki, was taking over. Over a million people gathered at Uhuru Park in Nairobi to witness Kibaki's inauguration on 30 December 2002, numbers as many if not more than those that had turned up at midnight on 12 December 1963 to watch the Kenya flag rise for the first time. This was the Second Liberation. The new president sat in a wheelchair, recovering from a car accident, and pledged a renewal of Kenyan values – hard work, decency and honesty – and an end to corruption.

A decade of accumulated certificates suddenly had real value.

Even as the propaganda of renewal, the busy-ness of cleaning up and sorting out, sounded from State House, the old politics of betrayal returned. Kibaki suffered a stroke. His old friends, a group of businessmen, retired technocrats and politicos – the Firsts, in their mid-dotage – fenced off the Presidency and locked out the NARC coalition partners, including its chief architect, Raila Odinga, son of Jaramogi Oginga Odinga.

Like the nationalism of the 1960s, the idea of renewal became farcical.

An anti-corruption czar was appointed and run out of town as soon as he uncovered evidence of new corruption. Cabinet ministers gave television interviews in the basement gymnasia of their new mansions as the press revealed fresh information on the latest corruption scam. As a sign of the new openness, the Mayor of Nairobi gave out his mobile phone number during a live FM appeal – he was appealing for patience at the height of a crippling water shortage.

Farce and cosmetics. Nairobi yielded to a beautification campaign. Streets were closed off for days. City Council workers in new luminous green jackets were repainting street signs. People joked that the paint was probably supplied by a good friend of a council strongman. A blacklisted company was contracted to redo a major city road at four times the advertised cost and twice the time. Hawkers and kiosks were cleared out of the city centre and the middle-class neighbourhoods west of Uhuru Highway, usually at night. Somebody wrote a Letter to the Editor, saying it was all very well to eject the hawkers from the city centre ('they are a menace') but there was absolutely no justification for Council *askaris* to use machetes in the process. A 50-year council estate was demolished. Its occupants were given 24 hours to pack up and leave. A few days later, the President laid the foundation stone for a new market at the site. Poverty was being eradicated. Street kids were sent to rehabilitation centres and arrested if they returned to the city centre. Even AIDS disappeared. Anti-retrovirals were made widely available. You no longer saw the ashy faces and falling hair and emaciated figures of full-blown AIDS sufferers, and the statistics proved that infection rates were falling.

There was money everywhere and nowhere. Banks offered personal loans for the salaried as taxi drivers complained that even during the worst of the Moi times, there had been more business than there was now. New appointments in both the government and the corporate sector were heavily lopsided in favour of the President's ethnic group, the Gikuyu. Mortgage finance companies put the customer first and apartments rose like hosannas across middle-class Nairobi. The stock exchange was booming and corporate Kenya launched wave after wave of IPOs, all ridiculously over-subscribed. It was a festival of Tiger Economy capitalism. Still, the UN's Human Development Index report in 2004 said that standards of living in Kenya had fallen to their worst levels ever. But the economy was growing at five per cent and there were day-long traffic jams to prove it.

Bee had an epiphany, quit her job, sold her car and went to Durban for six weeks. When she returned, she had another certificate. She was a certified mountain-climbing guide, one of a handful in Kenya. She had decided that she was going to start her own business, 'Under Open Skies', a safari company that would specialise in walking tours. Its target market was the new middle class, people like herself who loved to get away at the weekend. She registered the company, got her brother to design a website and started printing posters and leaflets and brochures. Like everything she did, she wanted to do it right.

Some months before she died, Bee was featured in *Eve Magazine* as 'young, independent, female and entrepreneurial', the embodiment of the new woman that was the magazine's target audience. Still the business did not pick up. Somehow it wasn't working. I met her less frequently now that I was no longer with Jane. But when we met, the usual Nairobi question of 'how is *biashara*?', how is business? yielded a little too often, the response of the dark 1990s: it was slow, it wasn't picking up, it would take time. It did not occur to Bee – it never would have – that who you knew still mattered more than what you knew. She borrowed some more and sank deeper into her hole, a smile on her face.

Bee killed herself because, even after everything had changed, nothing had changed. After democracy and renewal and anti-corruption drives, after the privatisation of public services and collective dreams and the repackaging of tribalism as the victory of decency over *grabiosis*, nothing had changed. She had bought into the highest ideals of a sham project where public good was code for private accumulation and the acquisition of papers could never protect you if you were from the wrong tribe. Bee, a Kenyan, had not been designed to speak in ethnic code, had not been designed to 'deal'.

Modern Kenya was not built by conquest or by mutual agreement; it was the product of negotiated settlement, Lancaster House where the Firsts haggled over the fine print of a constitution drawn up by the departing colonials. There was no referendum at independence to decide whether the wholesale adoption of the colonial constitution was a good idea. The project existed in name only. It had been abandoned in favour of private accumulation based on the fiction of collective ethnic advancement: our people deserve to 'eat' because we suffered. In other words Kenyan identity was something attained through the experience of the Kenyan state: how had Kenya arrived at your doorstep? As a friend or an occupying force? How had you survived the experience?

In November 2005 a truth about Kenya was uttered. During a referendum on the draft constitution – in which the country was divided into two — Bananas (Yes to the new constitution) and Oranges (No) – people voted overwhelmingly against the government's draft. Kibaki and his Gikuyu community, having voted Yes, were a bunch of Bananas in a sea of Orange. People wanted a new constitution but they were not going to be manipulated by the new 'eaters'. It was a profound statement: that people wanted to be Kenyan but not according to the designs of the state.

A new Kenya had to be found elsewhere. It has begun to emerge in different ways. My generation is sometimes called the *Reddykulass* Generation, after a group of eponymously-named comedians who made a career out of satirising Moi. We glance at the state and its boots and *rungus*, its seedy representatives and their just-add-water sycophancy, their promises of jobs and opportunities – we look at all that and laugh.

The Reddykulass Generation's central experience is survival: the informalisation of Kenyan life as the rickety idea of ethnic patronage began to wobble underneath its half-truths and lusts. The life that had developed at the margins gradually invaded the bankrupt centre. In place of the English and Kiswahili constituted as the main currencies in which life was transacted across the ethnic divides, we now speak and embrace *Sheng'*. A bastard mixture of the two and long condemned by officialdom, more and more Kenyans find themselves living within its fluid borders.

A new Kenya is developing from the margins. It is chaotic and unstructured but it has a distinct voice. In 2002, a Kenyan writer, Binyavanga Wainaina, won the Caine Prize for African Writing. He returned home from London and the Caine Prize, and along with other budding writers, established a journal, *Kwani?* and sparked off a literary renaissance. The idea behind *Kwani?* was to showcase emergent literary talent. But there was a larger idea and that was to explore the different ways of being Kenyan.

This project of renewal is being replicated elsewhere: in the urban sound of new music, in the media where young journalists are continuously exposing corruption and robbing the state of its formerly unchallenged legitimacy. This emergent democracy has come in spite of the betrayals and backroom deals of a cynical leadership. It is brash and noisy, but it understands fundamentally that the silence and secrets of the past are no longer an option.

Project Kenya may be dead as an idea but *we are*. We continue to be. We cannot run away from what was developed inside us. *Kwani?* is now four years old. Around it has grown a stable of young writers who are redefining the Kenyan space for a new generation. By providing a forum where a multiplicity of experiences of Kenyan-ness are presented, discussed and celebrated, it has broken with the old mould. What we lacked before was this diversity. Being Kenyan was to accept and to arrange oneself inside the mould of the official story of the Firsts. Through *this* assertion of cultural and political diversity, a new reality is taking shape.

Coming home 50 years after Nkrumah

Marianna B. A. Ofosu

Marianna B. A. Ofosu was educated at Howard University and holds an MPhil in International Development from Oxford University, where she studied as an American Rhodes Scholar. She has worked at the Leon H. Sullivan Foundation as its director for government relations and publications, organising the Leon H. Sullivan Summit VII task force that produced two declarations on African–diaspora relations and on corporate social responsibility, which were endorsed by ten African heads of state. Also during her time at the Foundation, she founded Leverage, *an African diaspora think tank magazine which continues to be published by the Foundation.*

She has recently moved to Ghana as managing director of GWI Ventures Ghana, a local subsidiary of GoodWorks International, a consulting firm set up to connect international investors with business opportunities in Africa. Here she reflects on moving home to Ghana at a crucial point in the nation's history.

Dignitaries and well-wishers who arrive in Ghana this year to join in the celebrations of the country's 50th anniversary of independence will find a focus on two very different figures: Kwame Nkrumah, Ghana's radical independence-era leader, and John Agyekum Kufuor, Ghana's current democratic president. The two men are historical markers, representing watershed moments in the country's story: the first transition from colonial rule to independence and the second a political handover from one democratically elected administration to another. Yet, the setting side-by-side of these two leaders suggests that Ghana at 50 should be a different country from what it was at independence, not least because Nkrumah and

Kufuor represent opposing political traditions, which continue to shape Ghana's political development.

Nkrumah's Ghana was a place of endless possibility, radical leadership and pan-African zeal. Yet it was also a place where repression stifled domestic criticism and opposition, and where pan-African overtures and overzealous economic reforms undermined Ghana's opportunity to become an economically prosperous and politically stable nation. Kufuor's Ghana is a hallmark of political stability, judged by the World Bank to be one of the best-governed and most rapidly reforming African nations. Today's Ghana sparkles in very different ways from the way it did at the time of independence and it captures international attention for somewhat different reasons. Those who come to Ghana because of sentiment and ideology will come because of Nkrumah; those who come here to invest their money, resources and time will do so because of Kufuor.

My case is no different. Despite their ideological differences, the respective legacies of Nkrumah and Kufuor made possible my relationship with Africa and with Ghana more specifically. While Nkrumah's nationalist leadership and intellectual and practical contributions to pan-Africanism nurtured my own sense of identity as an African in the diaspora, the economic growth and political stability cultivated by Kufuor's two democratic administrations created the conditions for me to work and live in Ghana, my father's birthplace. As I think about leadership in Africa, I cannot help but think about the impact that these two leaders have had on my own commitment to take responsibility for what goes on in Ghana and in Africa, in other words, to become one of its leaders.

Going home

When I went 'home' to Ghana for the first time as a graduate student at Oxford University, I felt a mixed sense of ownership and alienation. Although my father is Ghanaian, I was raised in Poland by my Polish mother and then educated in high school and college on the East Coast of the United States. At Oxford, I was reading Development Studies, a multidisciplinary subject, focused on exploring the challenges of developing countries from multiple academic angles. I went to Ghana to observe the run-up to the 2004 elections in a small rural district as part of my fieldwork research on the impacts of ethnicity on the democratic process.

Despite a score of multicultural experiences – teenage years on America's East Coast, undergraduate studies at Howard University, 'a black school' in the United States, graduate work in the bubble of Oxford University in the United Kingdom, studies and work in places as diverse as Santorini, San Juan, and Geneva – I knew that my research trip to Ghana would be more challenging than all of the others. This would be my first trip to sub-Saharan Africa, a part of the world I strongly identified with politically and intellectually, which I engaged regularly in my thinking and championed in the US and Europe, but which I was still struggling to understand practically.

In fact, before that first trip to Ghana, what I knew of Africa I learned academically through the prism of pan-Africanism and within the discipline of international development. Within that landscape, Nkrumah has been judged as a leader tragically ahead of his time on both the counts of African unity and economic development. But during my undergraduate studies, I thought that his contributions to the people of African descent were timeless. At one point, he was a young man who translated his passions for freedom and justice and a love for his ancestral land into practical action and led a revolution. For those of us abroad, the way Nkrumah led Ghana to independence through mass mobilisation represented courage and commitment and made us proud to be African.

Educated at Lincoln, a historically black university in America, Nkrumah was an architect of global pan-Africanism and an advocate of civil rights in the United States. He once told Martin Luther King Jr, the leader of the civil rights movement in America, that 'we will make it clear through the United Nations and other diplomatic channels that beautiful works and extensive handouts cannot be substitutes for the simple responsibilities of treating our coloured brothers in America as first-class human beings'. An African was offering a helping hand to Americans – a rarity most of us, who are subjected to MTV specials depicting American entertainers traipsing through African landscapes to raise awareness about humanitarian issues X, Y or Z, might never see again. Nkrumah's Ghana, the first black African colony to become a nation, provided practical reinforcement for the spiritual strivings of Africans in the diaspora: an ancestral homeland no longer blighted by the embarrassing realities of colonisation and an ally in the struggle for racial equality.

Though I was intellectually mesmerised and personally fortified by the project of pan-Africanism and Ghana's and Nkrumah's place within it, I chose to do my graduate research in Ghana for other reasons. The first and less significant reason was a desire to get to know my father's, and my own, homeland, and to connect to Africa more tangibly. That was as much an intellectual project as a spiritual one. 'Africa' – and by connection its diaspora – was to me a symbol of our most impressive weaknesses and most remarkable strengths as social beings. In my mind, the cruelty and degradation of the Middle Passage and violence of the colonial and post-colonial periods was set against the technical accomplishments of African civilisations and the humbling dignity with which many Africans survived the continent's multiple maladies. In my heart, there was the issue of knowing my origins – of reconciling my mother's Polish village with my father's Ghanaian one – to address the sense of disjointed identity that knowing only one side of my heritage created.

The second reason that I chose to travel to Ghana in 2004 was because it is a country often celebrated as a beacon of political stability and economic progress in a region and on a continent more often defined by violent crisis and underdevelopment. Ghana's 2000 elections ushered in a new era of democracy in Africa, when John Agyekum Kufuor and his New Patriotic Party (NPP) won the general elections and ended a 20-year period of first military and then elected rule, by J. J. Rawlings and the National Democratic Congress (NDC). The 2004 elections, which I was going to observe, would test the depths of the democratic transformation and would produce a verdict on the NPP's performance. The NPP triumphed, and for those of us watching, that triumph symbolically coincided with the defeat of the Nkrumahist tradition. The NPP's victory changed the political verdict which had been passed half a century earlier during a time just before independence, when Nkrumah was building his 'political kingdom'.

The nationalist period in Ghana was defined by the opposing struggles of J.B. Danquah and Kwame Nkrumah. These respective struggles produced two political traditions which continue to shape Ghana's current political landscape. As a leader of the United Gold Coast Convention (UGCC), a nationalist movement formed in 1947, Danquah promoted gradual transition to independence and a respect for chieftaincy as a formidable political and cultural institution. He was influenced not only by his powerful brother, Sir Ofori Atta I, the first West African king to be knighted by the British Crown, but also by a score of like-minded royals-cum-professionals-cum-politicos who filled the ranks of the UGCC. The party was known as a conservative organisation with strong sympathies for the British and little grassroots support. So it suffered a major loss in the legislative assembly elections of 1951. When many of the elements of the UGCC re-emerged as the United Party under the leadership of Oxford sociologist Kofi Busia in 1969, a name was assigned to the political movement – the 'Danquah–Busia tradition'.

The other parallel tradition was begun in 1949 with Nkrumah's creation of the Convention People's Party (CPP) as a populist off-shoot from the UGCC. Discarding gradualism, Nkrumah, the parvenu of the nationalist cohort, and his 'veranda-boys', poor youth who slept on the verandahs of rich men, demanded 'self-government now', won the leadership of the country in 1951 and led it to independence in 1957. The CPP was remarkable because it attacked two oppressive forces within what was then known as the Gold Coast: the British colonisers and the wealthy middle class who aspired to lead the Gold Coast to independence, but who were almost completely disconnected from the mass of the people. Ghana's first republic under Nkrumah's rule attacked the powers of the chiefs and prosecuted many who formed the elite professional class, promoted a revolutionary pan-African ideology and challenged Western political and economic orthodoxy with communist/socialist alternatives. Socialist ideologies would inform the basis of a score of 'Nkrumahist' parties that developed in the four decades after Nkrumah's overthrow in 1966.

By the time I arrived in Ghana in 2004, the manifesto of the ruling NDC offered a 'social democracy' that 'seeks to marry the efficiency of the market and private initiative with the compassion of state intervention to protect the disadvantaged and the marginalised and to ensure optimum production and distributive justice'. It was a self-styled party of the oppressed and the poor and its leaders played decisively on class distinctions. J. J. Rawlings, the charismatic and boisterous founder of the NDC, who was perhaps very much like Nkrumah in his populism, set the party in the Nkrumahist tradition of communalism and activism, despite his subjection of the Ghana to the hallmark experience of neo-liberal economics – IMF's stabilisation and the World Bank's structural adjustment.

In 2000, the NPP began its manifesto with the quote from J. B. Danquah, the gradual nationalist of the pre-independence era who was displaced as Ghana's nationalist leader by Nkrumah, the young man he recruited to return to the Gold Coast. The NPP was teeming with intellectuals, teachers and those who would be construed as the vanguard of the middle class. Its economic policy was rooted in promoting the growth of the private sector, advancing the 'golden age for business.' As it turned out, Kufuor's electoral victory in 2004, and the final triumph of the Danquah–Busia tradition, coincided with the near annihilation of the party Nkrumah founded more than 50 years earlier – the Convention People's Party won only one per cent of votes in 2004.

Ghana transformed

The Ghana that I held in my imagination while living in the diaspora was Nkrumah's Ghana, but the country I arrived to in 2004 was being transformed by Kufuor. My homecoming was not unlike that of Ekow Eshun, the writer and art critic who documented his odyssey from the UK to his ancestral home in Ghana in *Black Gold of the Sun*. We both expected Ghana, Africa, to bring some closure to the nagging questions of multicultural, multinational, multilingual and – in my case – multiracial identity that defined our young lives in the 'West'. And for both of us, Ghana answered in mixed and unexpected ways.

In my case, the welcoming generosity and openness of Ghanaians, the tempo of daily life, the verve of its academics, made for an amazing learning experience. But, schoolchildren from the rural areas where I did my research chased me yelling '*obruni*' or 'foreigner' or 'white woman'. I was called white not only by children but also by educated adults. I was disappointed, maybe even hurt, because Ghana, which produced Kwame Nkrumah and which buried W. E. B. Dubois, the famed African American sociologist, was reputed to be a pan-African hub. Perhaps this is a misleading shortcoming of Nkrumah's legacy – the rhetoric of pan-Africanism did not seep deeply into the soil of Ghana or the remainder of Africa. Since Nkrumah's overthrow no administration has been as active in leading the cause of pan-African co-operation across the continent and in the diaspora.

Many of us who come back to Ghana have to settle into the practical realities of everyday life in a developing country. It is impossible to ignore the power outages, the length of time it takes to get anything done, the unpaved roads, and wide-stretching communal rubbish dumps. In his book, Eshun tries to reason through his own reaction to some of these difficulties: 'Europe looked down on Africa. Maybe I'm doing the same thing? Does living in a white country make you, in some way, white?' Eshun's probing question is a familiar conundrum – both pervasive and dissonant – to me and those young Africans who have been raised, educated, or employed for parts or all of their lives in the West, but who have a passionate commitment to the future of their countries of origin in Africa.

During that first trip to Ghana, my own passions for Africa were challenged by the practical experiences of being treated as a stranger in a country that failed to measure up to its historical legacy. I left Ghana after my research was completed with no immediate plan to return. Perhaps I was afraid to commit to a life as different and, therefore, as challenging as Ghana offered. Perhaps if I was older and less idealistic, I would have focused my expectations less on the Ghana Nkrumah represented and more on the country that Kufuor was building. So I wrote my dissertation, finished my studies at Oxford and returned to the United States, to a comfortable life and to familiar pan-African rhetoric.

An interesting time

Now, three years later, by chance or fate, I am back in Ghana, a very different Ghana from what I remember or perhaps it's a Ghana I am viewing with different eyes. After graduate school and a year-long stint at a non-profit organisation, working between Washington DC and Nigeria, I have returned to Ghana to set up the local arm of a global advisory firm. A significant part of our mandate is to serve as a credible broker between American firms and African and Caribbean markets – it seemed like the perfect place for someone like me, a person so 'in between'. Ghana's stability and economic prospects convinced the firm's partners that it would be a sound addition to their African portfolio. Having completed the World Bank's highly indebted poor countries programme, which helped to set off a significant portion of its debt, having qualified for a United States Millennium Challenge Account offered to top performers on economic reform and governance issues, having weaned itself off of the International Monetary Fund's lending, Ghana is becoming as economically attractive as it is politically stable. For me, the job offered an opportunity to work in Ghana and to give our relationship another shot.

I could not have come at a more interesting time. Ghana seems to be on the verge of being a grand country again. Maybe it's all of the corporate buildings springing up around the airport, in an area now fashionably known as Airport City. Maybe it's the influx of Nigerian banks heralding a new era in financial services or the relocation of companies such as Nestlé from a deteriorating Ivory Coast. Maybe it's the 6.5 per cent annual growth of the Ghanaian economy, a number the country has not seen in a long time. Perhaps it's the growing middle class – more and more Ghanaians can eat in and patronise places that were previously the reserve of foreigners and expatriates living in Accra. Even the government is increasingly efficient at taking on Western best practices in the management of state business. There's even a spark of an organising African diaspora in Ghana: the Diaspora Africa Forum, an organisation given a mandate from the African Union to mobilise Africans in the diaspora, is based in Accra with diplomatic status. The media sector has a wide spread and is delivering a critically engaged analysis of politics, society and the economy. President Kufuor has just been unanimously elected to the leadership of the African Union. In many ways, as Kufuor declared in his state of the nation speech in 2007, 'Ghana, the Black Star of Africa, is on the rise again'.

There is a sense in Ghana that Ghanaians can do things on their own without external intervention, but some of that enthusiasm has to be tempered. The reality of it is that Ghana needs international help to accomplish all of the priorities that its leadership has articulated in its 2007 budget statement. Although Ghana has made a conscious move to wean itself off international aid, it is enthusiastically taking on additional loans from the Chinese government, mostly in energy projects, such as the construction of the $600 million Bui Damn. Though Kufuor's administration had planned a 'golden age for business' a power crisis which ensued in August 2006 is crippling the private sector. Nonetheless, macroeconomic indicators and the testimonials of middle-class consumption and political freedom suggest that Ghana is on a sustainable trajectory towards socio-political and economic progress.

As Ghana continues to rise, it will attract more and more of its young people who would otherwise work and live in the diaspora. But, as I know well from my own experience, coming home to Ghana is not without its obstacles. These obstacles are mostly socio-cultural and they confront me every day as a young person trying to bring to bear my own academic and professional experiences in Ghana and abroad. By far the most daunting challenge is the paternalism with which young people are treated. Coming from academic and professional institutions in the United States and Europe, in which the intelligence of youth is a prized commodity, where young people are sought after to bring not only fast minds and technical skills, but also new ways of looking for solutions, this reality in Ghana is a culture shock. A bright peer of mine who was educated at Oxford and who worked for Lehman Brothers in London, but who has since returned to Ghana to start a financial engineering firm, once put it quite cogently: in a country where the youth leader of the ruling party is in his 40s, what leadership roles can there be for us while we're in our 20s? I often feel as if I am struggling against ageism in Ghana, as if I am trapped by the circumscribed expectation of 'elders', who believe that there is a sense of intellectual or technical superiority inherent in their age.

That superiority complex can be an Achilles' heel for Ghana and Africa more broadly because it elevates 'elders' above human error. Expectations of unquestioning obedience lead to sycophancy and conformity, not innovative and strong leadership. In Ghana, people in decision-making positions could be more aware of their own fallibility. I have the opportunity to work with Andrew Young, the civil rights hero, former Mayor of Atlanta and US Ambassador to the United Nations. Those who know him publicly admire his oratorical skills and well-seasoned abilities to build consensus around contentious issues. Those qualities are tremendously admirable to me as well, but what most impresses me about Ambassador Young, a man well advanced in his age and a man of great experience, is a quality that most people will probably never notice. He's not afraid to say 'I don't know'. This is not only in private conversations, but also in public. That fearlessness conveys real substance and a commitment to enlisting the help of others to find answers. That quality – of preferring the truth of the matter to one's own sense of security in a conversation – is not age-sensitive. It has been my experience that many young people, who are still yet to be corrupted by greed and power, pursue answers more effectively because they are conscious of the possibility of making a mistake.

The other socio-cultural challenge that Ghana faces in attracting young people from the diaspora back home has to do with the system of patrimonialism. One of the first books that I read about Ghana's politics was Paul Nugent's *Big Men, Small Boys and Politics in Ghana*. The book's arguments about the social structure of patrimonial networks and the social conformity and stunted progress that they promote have been reinforced every time I come to Ghana. Together with ageism they stifle the potential that Ghana has to do away with inefficiencies in its socio-economic and political systems. Do I have to like you in order to do business with you? No, I have to be resolved that what we're doing is the best thing we can do for the country, weighing the short- and long-term consequences. Do you have to be my brother to receive my help? Or should you simply be a person in need or someone honourable, intelligent and innovative, pursuing a path of action that I support? If people worked together out of mutuality and win/win scenarios, Ghana would become about ideas and efficiency rather then about tribalism or communal brotherhood, both of which can be tremendously divisive. This very sense of communalism and familiarity-based associations may undermine the return of many of us from the diaspora, even those of us who have ancestral villages to refer to as proof of our right to belong in and even lead Ghana.

All of this begs two questions about the future of Ghana and Africa more broadly. Are Africa's leaders and people ready for an influx of new citizens reared in Western democracies who may demand speedier economic and political reforms than are on offer? Are diaspora Africans ready to engage a demystified Africa, a real Africa, which is as challenging as it is full of opportunity, and in which they may sometimes be treated as outsiders? Are we, the bright young things, privileged with elite education in the United States and Europe, where youth and intelligence are often associated, able to integrate into countries which we love, but in which we may be under-appreciated because our youth is seen as a handicap?

Whatever the answers may be, we must try to come back to our countries, despite the sense of alienation and occasional disappointment we may feel. Our challenge is to bend and be bent by our ancestral homes, in order to understand and improve them, from both the inside and outside. As I celebrate Ghana's 50th birthday and my first year as a resident of the country, I am comforted by the pairing of unlikely compatriots Kwame Nkrumah and John Agyekum Kufuor, who together represent the legacy of Ghana as a nation that has led an international movement of pan-Africanism and whose leaders have capably focused on its own challenges and opportunities. What we as young people have in our hands is a tremendous legacy. That legacy applies to us all, whether we live inside or outside of the country. And we should nurture the legacy so that in 50 years' time our successors can congratulate us on our own accomplishments, but also feel free and empowered to criticise our strategies and to stand at the decision-making table, offering their own plans for the future. That will be a true measure of progress.

African leadership: from the outside looking in

Do not long for your home when you are working

Onchsheshonqy (Ptolemaic period)

African leadership for a transnational age
Chukwu-Emeka Chikezie

Chukwu-Emeka Chikezie grew up in Freetown, where he attended university. He completed his studies in the UK and since then has lectured and worked in the private sector. Twelve years ago he co-founded the charity African Foundation for Development (AFFORD), which works to expand and enhance the contributions Africans in the diaspora make to Africa's development, particularly through the support of entrepreneurs and small and medium-sized enterprises.

Introduction

One reasonable starting point for a discussion about future challenges for African leadership is to assume that one of its primary roles is to change decisively and positively the conditions under which the vast majority of Africans on the continent toil. However, an assertion I wish to defend here is that this 'African leadership' is no longer entirely geographically or territorially bound or indeed entirely Africa-based. In fact, some of this African leadership with such onerous responsibilities may not have even been born in Africa. Depending upon your point of view, such an African leadership is either neither here nor there or both here and there.

My purpose here is to set the context for this leadership challenge and to offer a way forward to meet that challenge. I make four points. First, outbound migration from African countries, combined with cheaper communications and travel is creating a transnational existence for many African societies. What some have called globalisation from the bottom up – the movement of people from, say, Africa to Europe and North America – is blurring distinctions between 'here' and 'there'; between domestic and international.

Second, for many African countries, migration-related resource flows – skills outbound and inbound remittances – are creating constraints and opportunities for development. True, nurses and doctors do leave, just when their patients need them most. But when they leave home, does home leave them? Do they or can they put back what they have taken away?

Third, harnessing Africa's considerable resources – human, mineral, and other – regardless of where such resources are in the world, to transform the condition of millions of people is the critical leadership and management challenge facing the continent.

Fourth, given that so much of Africa's resources now lie outside the direct control of leaders in Africa, a new capability of leadership for a transnational age is required to enable Africa to realise her full potential. And, as I have already suggested, this leadership lies both in Africa and in the diaspora.

The political is at times personal. Because of migration I have strong family connections with three African countries as well as the UK and this has long piqued my interest in origins and belongings. A look back just three generations in parts of my own family illustrates this. My great-grandfather migrated from Sierra Leone to settle in what was then Fernando Po (now Malabo, capital of Equatorial Guinea). There he had several children, some with a Bubi woman, my great-grandmother. While some stayed in Fernando Po, many of my grandmother's siblings migrated to different countries – Sierra Leone, Nigeria, and Spain. During her own sojourns from Sierra Leone to Nigeria, my grandmother gave birth to my mother, who was educated in Sierra Leone and migrated to London, where she met my father, a Nigerian (born and bred), and had me. My mother subsequently returned to Sierra Leone and my father to Nigeria. They both live in their respective countries. I, in turn, spent an early childhood in Sierra Leone and have since migrated (back) to the UK, but still consider future migration a possibility. If, according to traditional understandings of identity and belonging, I am to bear allegiance to one 'place', which should it be?

Physical departure, virtual return

Today, according the 2001 UK Census, so-called 'Black Africans' constitute London's fastest-growing and second-largest minority ethnic group. They have overtaken the 'Black Caribbean' group and are now chasing the Indians. As the *New York Times*[1] reported, more black people have been arriving in the United States since 1990 – some 50,000 annually – than did during the slave period before the US government outlawed international slave trafficking in 1807.

Significantly, not only have many African migrants congregated in specific cities – nearly 80 per cent of Africans in the UK live in London – they have often also formed ethnic enclaves. Thus, the London Borough of Southwark is home to the highest concentration of Africans of any borough in the land and more Sierra Leoneans are concentrated in Southwark than anywhere else.

Visible and colourful on Peckham High Street in south-east London is the shop Kumasi Market. Step inside and you can buy yams, plantains, shitto, and a range of products and brands familiar to West African shoppers. Delve deeper into the dense web of shops and stalls in Peckham and you can find the latest CDs from popular Africa-based artists, young and old. Every other tiny kiosk in Peckham and other areas occupied by immigrants does a roaring trade in international calling cards and Africans in these enclaves are usually no more than a few minutes away from a money transfer operator able to get that lifeline cash injection to the relative who called at 4 a.m. that morning (coincidentally pay-day for the call's recipient) to make a request. Many of these businesses are owned by transnational entrepreneurs and the enterprises they establish help other Africans to live their transnational existence with ease and at minimal cost.

Leave the buzz of the high street, as the weekend winds up and it is time for the numerous hometown associations, alumni 'old school' clubs, ethnic associations, and countless other volunteer-led African diaspora organisations, that combine social affairs with poverty alleviation back home. Perhaps they have also gathered to hear their home president or minister passing through London, Washington or Paris. Even more lively are the meetings of ruling and opposition parties alike among the diaspora: the heated debates, the jockeying for position, the elections, the ambitions of a high-profile appointment back home... .

This, then, in a nutshell is the look and feel of the transnational existence that characterises many African migrants' daily lives. In this transnational field, there is a constant flow of people, information, ideas across borders. Networks play hugely important parts in influencing the sorts of migratory choices people make and then subsequently how people interact and with whom. To varying degrees, people also opt in and out of this transnationalism. At particular moments, say when an incident of concern occurs at home, the interest is strong. Then it may drop back for all but the most ardently involved.

All in all, though, transnationalism does amount to a novel phenomenon that has impact both 'here' and 'there'.

What, then, is the impact of this transnational existence created by contemporary migration?

Transnational transformations

The increasing pervasiveness and declining cost of information and communications technology – mobile phones, the internet – and fierce competition over many travel routes plus, of course, people's desires, help to facilitate this growing transnationalism. Modern migration is largely a response by people to the narrowing options for a decent living in their home regions – insufficient well-paid jobs or opportunities to establish businesses, political instability or outright civil conflict and breakdown in law and order – are just some of the supply-side factors. Migrants also make choices in response to real or perceived demands for their labour or opportunities to make a living in other countries, often in the developed world. Similarly, transnationalism is part of migrants' integration strategies. People rely upon their networks and those ethnic enclaves to secure the products and services they need, the information about home, job openings, housing options, or other things they need to adapt to their new life.

However, in this section we shall focus more on the impact of migration generally and transnationalism more specifically on development prospects in Africa. To illustrate both the development opportunities and constraints posed by migration, I shall consider two highly significant areas: remittances and the 'brain drain'.

Remittances (or the monies that migrants and diasporas send to families, friends, and communities in their regions of origin) are perhaps the most potent evidence of the growing significance of the link between migration and development. Many African governments have come to realise that the flows of money from their diasporas into their countries, through both formal and informal channels, exceed flows from export earnings, aid, and sometimes foreign direct investment. President Museveni of Uganda, only half-joking, once claimed that Ugandans themselves are Uganda's biggest export, earning the country more than its coffee.

In the UK, according to a survey of black and minority ethnic (BME) households,[2] 'Black Africans' have the highest propensity to remit. A third of all remittances from within the UK's BME community emanate from black Africans, although they constitute only ten per cent of the BME population as a whole. In fact, to be more specific, black African women are likely to be more responsible for remitting money home than are black African men.

For the countries receiving them, remittances have proved to be a stable source of finance. In fact, they are counter-cyclical in that when an economy is in trouble, remittance inflows actually increase, as those outside send more to desperate relatives. If current trends continue (and there are few reasons to expect otherwise), remittances will rise significantly in the long term. Perhaps most significant of all and if handled strategically, remittances could even be a source of development finance that provides Africans and their governments with the opportunity to pursue alternative paths to development, with a different, more acceptable set of strings attached.

Currently, there is the anomalous situation in which many aid-dependent African governments are more accountable to their donor country partners for how they allocate budgetary resources than they are to their own citizens directly affected by those decisions. Tax-payers in donor countries, through their governments, effectively have a huge say in directing decisions in recipient countries. Given that African migrant and diaspora communities typically have little to do with conventional development structures via which international non-governmental organisations (NGOs) lobby, say, the UK or US governments, we really do have a situation of taxation without representation for those diaspora groups.

Alongside this, many of these migrants and diasporas also use their own taxed income to send even more resources to their countries of origin, to support families and other relatives. This represents a double whammy of tax. (This is why the African Foundation for Development (AFFORD) has mounted a campaign in the UK for tax relief on remittances that are used for developmental purposes.)

Remittances, of course, are not all good news. There are significant downsides. First, there is a risk that they create and perpetuate a sense of dependency and helplessness among Africans in Africa.

Second, remittances often help people deal with day-to-day survival, without aiding 'development' in any way. Some 39 per cent of the black African remitters surveyed in the UK responded that relatives use the money they send to purchase food, suggesting that remittances really are a lifeline for some very destitute people in Africa. Other significant uses include education, medical needs, accommodation, and durable goods.

We can expect that households in Africa that have better access to nutritious food, education, and healthcare via remittances will, in time, be better placed to navigate their way out of poverty. However, in the meantime, they remain vulnerable to countless shocks that can easily set them back in this quest. This can trap people in a vicious cycle of poverty and dependency.

Third, the pressure upon Africans in the diaspora to remit monies home may actually distract them from investing in their own career development that will pay dividends in the future. We would expect remittance amounts to correlate strongly with amount of disposable income. However, the UK remittance survey found that the gross monthly incomes of some 42 per cent of BME remitters are in a low band, between £430 and £1,299 per month. Another 39 per cent are in a medium income band. Given that black Africans' mean and median incomes rank quite low compared with other BME groups, we can assume that many of the remitters among this group are sending home significant proportions of their disposable income to support relatives.

In response to these sorts of challenges, increasingly, Africans in the diaspora are forming associations that enable them to tackle – collectively – the sorts of problems for which remittances are less suited. Interestingly enough, many of these associations are also tackling issues such as education and healthcare that reflect priorities for remittances and indeed the Millennium Development Goals.

Obviously, remittances and the efforts of hometown associations and other diaspora-led groups are not a panacea for all Africa's ills. But a growing body of evidence demonstrates that they can help tackle poverty, not just among the benefiting households or communities – but through the multiplier effect, these benefits do spread.[3] Moreover, some examples among, say, Latin American immigrants in the United States point some ways forward for Africans. For instance, Mexican hometown associations in the US work with federal, regional, and local state authorities in a '3 + 1' scheme which sees the authorities match hometown associations' contributions to support development initiatives in their regions of origin.

The point here is that large numbers of Africans in the diaspora have shown, beyond any doubt, that they are willing – individually and collectively – to devote considerable proportions of their hard-earned money, their time, and their organisational efforts, to effecting change positively in Africa. There is a great deal more they could do and improvements in performance will come, in part at least, through better co-ordination with key institutions and players on the ground in Africa, including governments. This is where the leadership challenge comes in.

But money is only part of the resource constraint holding Africa back. Arguably, skills and organisational capacity to do the right things and do them right are far more important. The skills outflow from Africa is part of the picture. After all, the International Organization for Migration[4] claims that at least 35 per cent of university graduates from 21 African countries reside abroad. Furthermore, more than 80,000 skilled professional Africans leave the continent each year, including 23,000 university graduates and 50,000 at the executive and professional levels.

These skilled people are voting with their feet, seeking greener pastures where they can use their talents more productively and receive decent reward for their efforts. A form of 'common hypocrisy'[5] characterises debates around international migration. Receiving governments depend upon the unskilled migrants who are willing to do work that natives will not, and the skilled migrants to fill gaps in the labour market that others are ill-equipped to take up. Yet the media in these countries frequently vilify migrants with xenophobic, racist, and generally hostile attacks. Opportunistic and often cowardly politicians fan these flames of mistrust and hate with inflammatory speeches or with pointed silences. Sending governments, for their part, also demonstrate this common hypocrisy. They are content to portray emigrants as little more than traitors for abandoning ship. Meanwhile, through policy failures, misallocation of resources, and mismanagement, they fail to create the enabling environments in which people can flourish. They omit to mention that their countries depend heavily on the remittances these migrants send home. They do not admit that they are in fact relieved that at least some among the ranks of unemployed and underemployed are not hanging around to demand profound social and political changes.

Governments in Africa are beginning to accept that they need a '3Rs' strategy to manage their migration challenges. The three Rs stand for retention, return, and retrieval. Retention underpins the entire strategy. It entails improving conditions of service, by valuing the work of nurses, doctors, teachers, and other vital workers, and by giving workers the tools they need to do a proper job. Without retention, governments and employers simply create the conditions for a revolving door – more people would be leaving even as others were returning. Under the right conditions, migrants do return home – usually, where there is political stability, good economic prospects, and opportunities to deploy resources acquired abroad. However, for most African countries, the prospects of attracting home a large number of their citizens from abroad are slim at best. In the short to medium term, retrieval offers the most realistic prospect for African countries to tap into the skills and knowledge networks of the African diaspora without requiring or expecting permanent return.

Retrieval is the skills transfer mechanism for the transnational age in which we live. Such schemes are in the early, experimental phase. For instance, AFFORD has initiated SEEDA (Supporting Entrepreneurs and Enterprise Development in Africa), a project to build a virtual resource pool of African diaspora talent to help support micro, small and medium-sized enterprises and entrepreneurs in Africa to plan for growth, improve performance, exploit market opportunities, and create some of the much-needed jobs for young people in target African countries. The African diaspora resource persons combine short-term visits of intensive face-to-face contacts with virtual, long-distance mentoring using phone and internet.

Simply put, some – but by no means all – of the resources that Africa needs to harness to develop lie outside the continent, within the control of the African diaspora. Harnessing and utilising these resources is a leadership challenge both for the African diaspora and for counterparts on the continent. How, then, are these two sets of actors to develop their working relationships to achieve shared objectives?

Africa's leadership challenge

There are probably almost as many definitions of leadership as there are people wishing to define leadership[6]. One useful definition that will serve us here is:

> Leadership is the process of influencing others to understand and agree about what needs to be done and how it can be done effectively, and the process of facilitating individual and collective efforts to accomplish the shared objectives.[7]

Similarly, the Leadership Trust refers to 'using personal power to win hearts and minds to achieve a common purpose'. For the most part, leaders in Africa have no coercive power over the African diaspora[8] and vice versa. Thus, influencing and winning hearts and minds are the operative phrases here.

In 1961, Sierra Leone was wealthier (or at least less poor) than Singapore and seemingly enjoyed brighter prospects. We could make a similar unfavourable (though slightly less unflattering) comparison between Ghana and Malaysia, which both won their independence from Britain in 1957. While some countries in Asia have seen dramatic economic growth leading to impressive reductions in poverty over the last few decades, too many African countries have moved in the opposite direction, with disastrous effects for many millions of increasingly poor Africans.

According to the Economic Commission for Africa (ECA), average unemployment rates in sub-Saharan Africa have remained at around ten per cent since 1995, the second highest in the world after the Middle East[9] (but this does not take account of the fact that many people working in the informal sector actually earn very little and are effectively the working poor). The most visible consequence of such high unemployment is growing poverty in Africa. At least 61 million more Africans go hungry today than in 1990, according to the ECA. Between 1994 and 2004, the number of workers living on less than a dollar a day increased by 28 million in sub-Saharan Africa.

What accounts for the markedly different trajectories of Africa and parts of Asia? As Matthew Lockwood[10] has convincingly argued, while Asia had its 'capitalist developmental states', Africa has had largely weak states that have been anything but developmental. One notable exception, as the British government in its third White Paper[11] on international development acknowledges, is Botswana, in which a strong developmental state did emerge after independence.

While we can recognise that governance is the critical challenge that Africans must grapple with if development is to be within our grasp, we certainly cannot rely upon the international donor community with its limited understanding of governance to solve the problem. As Lockwood points out, critics note that for donors, governance is 'government minus politics'. It is up to Africans, in Africa and the diaspora, to put the politics into governance and to build – brick by brick – the developmental states that will deliver the goods.

This is not, however, a suggestion to make a fetish out of politics or to seek the political kingdom to the total exclusion of all else. The American management guru Peter Drucker once argued that there are no underdeveloped countries, only undermanaged ones. In his view, management creates economic and social development:

> Management is the prime mover and that development is a consequence. All our experience in economic development proves this. Wherever we have only capital, we have not achieved development. In the few cases where we have been able to generate management energies, we have generated rapid development. Development, in other words, is a matter of human energies rather than of economic wealth. And the generation and direction of human energies is the task of management.[12]

So, we have seen how Africa's human resource base has migrated across continents but remains somehow connected and we have a sense of some of the challenges ahead. But how likely is it that Africans in the diaspora and in Africa will rise to the challenge?

Leadership for a transnational age?

Where do the allegiances of the vast majority of African diaspora groups lie vis-à-vis the developmental states we need to build in Africa? Similarly, how does the African state view its diaspora? For now, a disconnect between the two exists. Some of the most active and vibrant African diaspora associations are the hometown, ethnic, or alumni associations. In other words, it appears that Africans organise around manageable aspects of their identity that they can touch and feel.[13] It probably has something to do with operating on a scale at which they can hold themselves and their counterparts accountable and deliver tangible results within a reasonable timeframe. This does not, however, mean that Africans in the diaspora totally reject their national identities. Simply observing Ghanaians at home and abroad celebrating their World Cup 2006 win over the United States confirms this. When it comes to the more serious business of 'doing development', however, the Ashanti king may generate more resonance than the president of the republic.

To their credit, African governments have been proactive in recent years in reaching out to their diaspora communities. Both Ghana and Sierra Leone have organised homecoming summits. Mali, Senegal, and Ghana are just three examples of countries with ministers with portfolios that include diaspora affairs. The Nigerian government, under President Obasanjo, established a Special Presidential Advisor for diaspora affairs. Indeed,

President Obasanjo went one step further to encourage the formation of the Nigerians in Diaspora Organization (NIDO). Ruling and opposition parties actively fundraise in the diaspora, and few transnational politicians lack ambitions or reticence in claiming that they could do a better job of running their home countries. In the run-up to the 2007 Nigerian presidential elections, presidential hopeful Pat Utomi launched a 'Contract with the diaspora' tour of the United States and the UK.

In spite of these encouraging developments, at least two outstanding issues remain. First, African governments have largely failed to integrate their diaspora-mobilisation efforts into their overall development strategies. Thus the donor-driven poverty reduction strategy policies seem not to incorporate diaspora engagement. This approach might have some merit if African governments were seeking to leverage diaspora resources to reduce their aid dependency, to pursue more autonomous policies, or if they were seeking to wrest concessions from their international bilateral and multilateral aid partners. However, there is no evidence that that is what they are seeking to do. Instead, given the weak state capacity that afflicts most African countries, this two-pronged approach is often a stretch too far and meaningful delivery suffers.

Even where poverty reduction strategies do incorporate a diaspora element, as Ghana's does, they do not take account of the local, decentralised focus of most diaspora efforts. Rather, it operates on the premise that most Ghanaians will rally to the nation-state-building cause. In fact, action-research AFFORD undertook to connect the Ghanaian diaspora to development efforts in Ghana highlighted some unfinished business of the decolonisation era:

> Ghana's venerated chieftaincy institutions enjoy something of a comparative advantage in the diaspora mobilization business, given the appeal and hold of cultural identity, especially for a diasporic community. And yet, diaspora resource mobilization for development via the chieftaincy raises intriguing challenges around accountability, participation and civic rights. These are not necessarily new themes in modern day Africa but both migration and decentralization throw them into sharp relief. How can the expectations of citizenship be reconciled with the constraints of subject-hood? What are the lines of demarcation between the roles and responsibilities of Chiefs and District Assemblies? These are broad constitutional questions of which diaspora is but one part.[14]

One size does not fit all when it comes to harnessing the African diaspora's resources for development.

The second outstanding issue is the question of dual nationality. While some African states have begun to recognise the non-resident status of some of their citizens, progress is slow, even grudgingly so. Yet migration will create more complex identities and allegiances.

Citizenship implies a complex balance of rights and responsibilities. The UK BME remittance survey found that a quarter of remitters were actually born in the UK. Thus citizenship demands of Africa (and elsewhere) are not predicated on wanting to get something for nothing.

It is tempting, but misguided, to present this new transnational era and the leadership demands it imposes as a brave new world with no antecedents. After all, freed and self-educated slave Olaudah Equiano and other members of the Sons of Africa were leading campaigners for the abolition of slavery in 18th-century London. Indeed, Equiano also played a pivotal role in organising the resettlement of a number of destitute Africans from London to Freetown, Sierra Leone. Similarly, Kwame Nkrumah, Jomo Kenyatta, and others converged in post-war Britain and campaigned successfully for an end to colonial rule. There is continuity and change in this narrative. The struggle for the rights of Africans to determine their own future and to live in dignity with equal opportunity to make their own way in life is as pressing today as it was back in the 18th century. However, the context and means to achieve these ends are different today. Yesterday's approaches, and certainly yesterday's rhetoric, will not make the changes we need to see.

Conclusion

Albert Einstein reportedly once said, 'we can't solve problems by using the same kind of thinking we used when we created them'. The first job of African leadership in this transnational era is to take responsibility for the challenge we face. Our second task is to better equip ourselves for the journey ahead. We must dispense with the myth that leaders are born not made and develop our competencies to lead and manage ourselves in this age.

Africans will continue to migrate from Africa in search of opportunities, better conditions or just some excitement for the foreseeable future. Some will return, but the net flow will be outbound. The EU estimates that the number of working-age people in the Union will fall by 20 million between 2010 and 2030 and that migration is part of the answer to a looming labour shortage.[15] Many corporate leaders believe that their future success depends upon their ability to secure the right human resource talent. The victors will either move the talent to where they need it or move to where the talent is located. That battle has only just begun. According to a World Bank commissioned study, a further three per cent increase in migration to developed countries could yield a $356 billion increase in global income, dwarfing aid or foreign direct investment.[16]

The African diaspora's role in supporting Africa's development will grow. But how prepared for that responsibility are they? At times, there is evidence of arrogance. At one public meeting in the US at which Nigerian Vice-President Atiku Abubakar spoke, six US-based Nigerians stood up and boasted that between them they could run the whole country. The diaspora has an image problem among counterparts in Africa. One Ghanaian MP, a former US resident, arrested on drug-trafficking charges in the US has been enough to convince public opinion in Ghana that all well-living Africans in the diaspora must be drug smugglers. Yet none of this will or should deter Africans in Africa and the diaspora from working together for the common good.

The challenge, though, is to initiate leadership development programmes that take into account the goals, the context, and the people involved. We need a transnational leadership development programme – that encompasses Africans in the diaspora and Africans in Africa, building the right organisational capacities, the right working relationships, and individual competencies that will enable them to translate their shared aspirations into tangible outcomes.

To date, Africa as a whole has little to show for decades of development effort. Today we need a new compact between African peoples at home and abroad, but not one based on more of the same.

The first leadership task is to agree some clear goals to achieve, underpinned by adherence to some broad principles. These cannot and should not be overly prescriptive but they should be detailed enough to guide action. For the most part, the frameworks already exist. For instance, job-creation is already an agreed top priority for Africa, endorsed by heads of state, the African Union, and other important bodies. Countless surveys of Africans' attitudes and opinions have highlighted how much importance they attach to having a decent job that enables them to take responsibility for their own lives. Health and education, which, apart from being at the core of the Millennium Development Goals, represent vital investments in human capital formation that will pay dividends for years to come.

The good news is that the African diaspora already puts considerable effort in these areas. Nonetheless, clarifying what we intend to achieve is an important part of the mutual accountability that needs to be in place. It also sets up clear performance criteria by which we can judge results.

Important ideas to underpin leadership action principles might include the following:

- A recognition that the benefits of migration must spread far and wide throughout African societies, and not accrue just to migrant sending households, regions, or countries. We can achieve this via a number of mechanisms and policies. For instance, proactive policies to maximise the multiplier effects from remittances directed at households with migrants abroad will spread benefits beyond migrant-sending families. Ensuring remittances flow through formal channels will assist the flow of capital throughout the system. At the national level, we can create resource pools of talented Africans to work in countries other than their own to share skills. We can also pool the tax relief on remittances and apply these to development initiatives.

- Another important principle is commitment to institutional development in Africa, including that of developmental states.

- We should also consider the principle of demand pull rather than supply push. No one should be pushing resources from the diaspora into Africa without assurances that someone with the right calibre, credentials, and authority is in place to champion the process and that systems exist to make adequate use of those resources and to account for them. This has wider implications for the sequencing of activities and the need to rely upon a demonstration effect to bring about systemic change over time.

- Another principle is that of reciprocity and mutual gain. No longer should we perpetuate the myth that Africa constantly takes and gives nothing in return. The African diaspora gains greatly from engaging in African affairs, it has a stake in a resurgent Africa and the relationship is very much a two-way give and take one, based on a symbiosis between Africa and her peoples in the diaspora.

- A further principle is the commitment to building organisational structures as spaces where a diversity of African peoples, particularly of different generations – male and female – can realise their aspirations to be the best Africans they dream of being. No longer can we afford to have African diaspora organisations that are places where only male African elders and elites realise their aspirations. Ordinary members of organisations shall have to do more to hold their leaders to account and shape their organisations in ways that meet their needs and aspirations.

- A major principle is to build upon what we already have that works, while committing to continuous improvement and not holding ourselves hostage to sacred cows no longer fit for purpose.

- Perhaps a most fundamental principle is to learn from past mistakes. Liberia and the Americo-Liberians who returned from the diaspora to dominate all aspects of life in that country for centuries until the 1980s is a case in point.

■ Finally, an important principle is to be mindful of power dynamics and to ensure that the balance of power remains with or shifts to people in Africa on the frontline of the struggles for their own self-determination. People in Africa will need to be vigilant to ensure that they retain a determination to shape their own destiny and not allow the diaspora (or anyone else) to drive that agenda.

Although this process starts with dialogue and although dialogue needs to be an ongoing element of the process, what counts are results. Results will build confidence, generate momentum, and create a virtuous cycle. What this transnational age calls for is not an inspirational, charismatic leadership but a focused, hardworking and pragmatic leadership at all levels of society focused on delivering results and bringing about lasting change.

We may be at a time of unique historical opportunity given the international community's focus on migration and development but also because more African countries today have important decision-makers and people in senior positions in society who have returned from the diaspora to take up leadership positions. These range from Ghana's Asantahene (King of the Ashantis) to the President of Liberia, heads of corporations, chancellors of universities, members of clergy, and so on. These people understand the potential of the diaspora to make a useful contribution in all African societies in the 21st century. They understand the need to bridge whatever divides exist.

None of this is pie in the sky or wishful thinking. To some extent, it is already happening but we need to step up the pace, scale and scope of efforts under way.

Our best way to predict Africa's future is to invent it. And, as Peter Drucker once said, 'plans are only good intentions unless they immediately degenerate into hard work,' so let the hard work begin.

Notes

1   Sam Roberts, 'More Africans Enter U.S. Than in Days of Slavery', *New York Times*, February 2005.

2   Martin Boon, *BME Remittance Survey: Research Report* London: Department for International Development, 2006.

3   For example, see Çaglar Özden & Maurice Schiff (eds.). *International Migration, Remittances & the Brain Drain*, Washington DC: The International Bank for Reconstruction and Development/ The World Bank, 2006.

4   International Organisation for Migration, 'Managing Migration: Challenges and Responses for the people on the move', *IOM World Migration Report Series, Vol. 2*, Geneva: IOM, 2003.

5   Dr Mamphela Ramphele, then co-chair, Global Commission used this phrase at the COMPAS Public Lecture on 1 February 2005, entitled 'Disparities, development and international Migration' (see *www.compas.ox.ac.uk/events/Reports per cent20Presentations/Dr per cent20Ramphele per cent20speech per cent20010205.pdf*).

6   Gary Yukl, *Leadership in Organizations*, 5th edition, New Jersey: Prentice-Hall, 2002.

7   Ibid: 7.

8   A notable exception is the Eritrean government that has managed over the years to develop a number of means by which to coerce the Eritrean diaspora to pay taxes and support the government, whether they wish to or not.

9   Economic Commission for Africa, Economic Report on Africa 2005: *Meeting the Challenges of Unemployment and Poverty in Africa*, Addis Ababa: ECA, 2005.

10 Matthew Lockwood, 'States of development', *Prospect Magazine*, Issue 16, November 2005.

11 Department for International Development, *Eliminating World Poverty: Making governance work for the poor*, London: TSO (The Stationery Office), 2006, p. 59.

12 Peter F. Drucker & Joseph A. Maciariello, *The Daily Drucker*, Elsevier, 2005, p. 56.

13 Chukwu-Emeka Chikezie, *Supporting Africa's regional Integration: The African Diaspora-prototype pan-Africanists or parochial village-aiders?* Paper presented at the African Development Forum (ADF) III 'Defining Priorities for Regional Integration in Africa', Addis Ababa, Ethiopia, 3–8 March 2002.

14 Samuel Zan, *One nation, one people, one destiny'? The Ghanaian diaspora's contribution to national development using diverse channels,* London: AFFORD, 2004 (see *www.afford-uk.org/resources/ download/one_nation.pdf*).

15 *Financial Times*, 21 December 2005.

16 The Development Research Centre on Migration, Globalisation and Poverty 'New Directions for International Migration: implications for Britain' press release, 9 December 2005.

Journeying to excellence: knowledge, diaspora and leadership

Paul Tiyambe Zeleza

Paul Tiyambe Zeleza *is a Malawian historian and novelist, who left his homeland during the dictatorship of Hastings Banda. Since then he has studied and lectured in the UK, Jamaica, Kenya, Canada and the United States. He is currently Professor and Head of the Department of African and American Studies at the University of Illinois. He has held a long interest in the history of African institutions of higher learning, the history of knowledge produced on Africa and the challenges facing African intellectuals as they seek to provide understanding and solutions to Africa's many problems.*

His essay traces his own intellectual journey over the last 30 years, and like many other African intellectuals, it has unfolded as 'a season of migrations to the north' and the diaspora. At the same time he meditates on the issue of knowledge production in Africa, and the reasons Africa's political leaders appear unable to trust their own intelligentsia or support the financing of world-class research and learning institutions that generate home-grown solutions.

My intellectual journey is fairly typical of African scholars of my generation notwithstanding the obvious differences of detail. It is a complex story that raises critical questions about the troubled relationship between the post-colonial state and academia, between African political leaders and scholars, as well as the perils and promises of intellectual exile. I was educated and have worked both within and outside the continent, and I am a product of both the triumphs and tragedies of post-colonial Africa. I have witnessed the twists and turns of knowledge production on Africa, the shifts in analytical paradigms and attitudes, from Afro-optimism to Afro-pessimism, the growing marginality of African universities in the production not only of Africanist knowledge but global knowledge at the same time as the African academic diasporic presence has risen and is increasingly repositioning, for the better, the terms of intellectual engagement between Africa and the rest of the world.

Early days

I went to university in my home country, Malawi, in 1972 and graduated four years later with a major in History and English, then spent a year as a teaching assistant before proceeding for a Master's in African History and International Relations in England from 1977 to 1978, and I finally ended up in Canada for my PhD in Economic History between 1978 and 1982. Since then I have taught in four countries on both sides of the Atlantic, first for two years in Jamaica, then nearly six years in Kenya, five years in Canada, and since 1995 I have been based in the United States. It has been a fascinating journey from Southern Africa to the global North and the diaspora, a trajectory that captures the complex formation of Africa's post-colonial intelligentsia, the ebbs and flows of its troubled relations with both Africa and the global North, with the enduring seductions of African nationalism and the sanctions of Euro-American hegemony, its problematic engagements, politically, with the post-colonial state and, paradigmatically, with the Western epistemological order.

In the 34 years since I first went to university, Africa has undergone profound changes in its political and cultural economies as well as in the intellectual, ideological, and institutional configurations of its universities and academic communities. Politically, we witnessed the transition from the euphoria of independence to the agony of one-party and military dictatorships and most recently the tantalising promises of democracy. Economically, the developmentalism and relatively high rates of growth of the 1960s and early 1970s gave way to neo-liberalism and the crises of structural adjustment in the 1980s and 1990s, followed by the intermittent recoveries of recent years. Socially, Africa's population exploded and is now lurching towards a billion amidst the ravages of old and new epidemics especially HIV/AIDS; urbanisation accelerated notwithstanding rising unemployment and overstretched services; class differentiation deepened as the elite and middle classes expanded, becoming richer while the working and peasant classes became more impoverished; national identities became consolidated at the expense of sub-regional and pan-African loyalties in the face of persistent sectarian ethnic and religious affiliations that periodically erupted into conflict and warfare.

Many students in my generation did their Bachelor's degrees in Africa's newly established post-independence universities – the University of Malawi was merely seven years old when I enrolled. We found ourselves trekking to Western Europe or North America for our graduate studies, where we were trained in newly established African studies programmes by newly minted Africanist scholars, who belonged to the same cohort as the relatively young and eager lecturers who taught us back home. We differed from the generations immediately before and after us: the former were pioneers in the establishment of African studies as respectable academic fields and they did most of their training in the 1950s and 1960s in overseas institutions because higher education was still in its infancy during these turbulent years of decolonisation, while those who came after us in the 1980s and 1990s could receive their entire education on the continent, confronting universities undergoing the crises of structural adjustment. This suggests that students of my generation were educated during the golden years of African universities when African institutions were the legitimating centres for the study of Africa in the disciplines and various interdisciplinary fields.

I can vouch for all of this from my own experiences. In my days as a student and young lecturer, Africanist historians from Western Europe and North America were not taken seriously until they had cut their academic teeth teaching in African universities. And I recall the days when publishing in African historical journals was mandatory for Africanists. For example, no one studying Kenya, to use the country on which I did my PhD research, was taken seriously unless they published in the *Kenyan Historical Review*. The last issue of the journal appeared in 1978 and today there are Kenyanists who hardly go to Kenya, let alone interact with Kenyan historians. On the other hand, in the 1960s and 1970s African graduate students eagerly returned home to take up positions in the expanding universities, assured not only of middle-class comforts and respectability but also eager to write their beloved ethnic groups, nations, and continent into the empirical and theoretical corpus of the disciplines, and to strip the disciplines, including history, of their Eurocentric blinkers and conceits. When I finished my doctorate in 1982 the idea of working in North America appeared absurd, and so I went to teach in Jamaica, then Kenya.

Knowledge production and the state

Thus in the early post-independent years it seemed, for a while at least, that the organic relationship between the state and intellectuals evident in Africa's ancient universities, the Islamic universities of Ez-Zitouna (founded in Tunis in 732), al-Qarawiyyin (founded in Fez in 859), al-Azhar (founded in Cairo in 969), and Sankore (founded in Timbuktu in the 12th century), which were generously endowed by the state, was set to be reproduced. The ancient African universities were not only among the first institutions of higher learning to be established anywhere in the world, but also among the very best in their time, the pacesetters in the development of the intellectual and institutional architecture of knowledge production.

In the post-independence golden years before the recessions of development and democracy set in, there was lively conversation between academics and politicians, regular traffic between the academy and the cabinet, and many of Africa's political leaders such as Kwame Nkrumah (1909–72), Julius Nyerere (1922–99), Léopold Sédar Senghor (1906–2001), and Jomo Kenyatta (1893–1978) were intellectuals in their own right, philosopher kings in the mould of Imhotep, the Egyptian administrator, physician, poet, philosopher and architect, and Uthman dan Fodio (1754–1817) a prolific scholar and the founder of the Sokoto Caliphate, West Africa's largest state in the 19th century. The euphoria of independence and the struggle to reclaim Africa's historical and humanistic agency led to the emergence of towering intellectuals such as Cheikh Anta Diop (1923–86), the Senegalese historian, archaeologist and scientist, who recalled Ahmed Baba (1564–1627), a distinguished historian who wrote more than 60 books on various subjects including medicine, law, philosophy, mathematics, and astronomy. African academics sought, and were expected, to address the pressing challenges of development and nation building facing their newly independent countries, and the African universities strived for international excellence.

Before long, the golden years began to dim as African universities fell on hard times and many failed to cast aside either their colonial origins or neo-colonial dependencies. Also, relations between intellectuals and the political class soured, and the centrality of African universities in knowledge production on Africa declined as they became less attractive to Northern Africanists worried about the tightening job markets at home as the old protections of white male employment privilege were eroded by affirmative action that increasingly brought white women and racial minorities to American campuses. At the same time, growing numbers of Africans educated in the global North opted to stay there. One of the few empirical studies on the rates of return of African PhDs trained in North America between 1986 and 1996 conducted by Pires et al. shows that variations were engendered by different patterns of economic growth and the state of political stability in specific African countries, the relative size of immigrant populations in the host countries, nature of sponsorship, discipline, and age of the graduate students.[1] The likelihood of return was higher for those in the older age cohorts, for those in the life sciences as compared to those in the humanities and social sciences.

Diaspora and brain mobility

The reasons for Africa's 'brain drain' to the global North are not hard to find. Deteriorating economic conditions, political tyranny and conflicts in our countries that threatened our professional and personal security, robbing us of middle-class comforts, pushed many of us into the trails of international migration. This is an issue that has been of great curiosity for me, having tried to understand it in a series of papers on African international migrations in general and academic migrants in particular.[2] It is quite clear that a process as complex as international migration is the result of equally complex forces operating at various levels in space and time. International migration flows are determined by conditions in both the sending and receiving countries, including the state of the economy, political stability and freedoms, and immigration law, all of which are affected by broader forces in the global political economy. Whatever might initiate immigration, the factors and forces that perpetuate it can be quite different. It stands to reason that migration involves both social networks and enabling institutions and is a cumulative process.

The interplay between these factors obviously varies in specific contexts. Africa's challenge is to turn this 'brain drain' into 'brain gain' through 'brain circulation' or 'brain mobility'.[3] It is an old question in a new age: how can Africa most productively engage its diasporas both the historic and new diasporas? There can be little question that the historic costs of the drainage of Africa's human resources from the time of the Atlantic slave trade, both brain and brawn, have been extremely high. Nevertheless, it is important to remember the enormous contributions African diasporas have made to Africa. The diaspora has been a critical site of knowledge production on Africa for a long time. As both a place and a project, a cultural and cognitive community, the diaspora has provided an unusually fertile space for imagining and writing Africa. For example, pan-Africanism, the progenitor of the numerous territorial nationalisms in Africa and the Caribbean emerged out of the diasporic condition experienced by the diasporas of enslavement and exposure to the diasporic experience for the diasporas of colonialism. During the late 19th and early 20th centuries, as colonialism reconfigured the global civilisational presence of Africans and reconnected Africa to its diasporas, the latter became crucial to the (re)constructions of Africa as an idea, Africa as an object of study, Africans as academics, and pan-Africanism as a project. I believe, therefore, that African diasporas, both the historic and contemporary diasporas and their intelligentsia in particular, have the potential, which they have exercised during some key moments of modern African history, for a productive and progressive engagement with Africa. The challenge is to decipher the tendencies and instances among the academic diasporas in contemporary times – a conjuncture characterised by the vast and complex processes and projects of capitalist globalisation, technological change, and new economies of knowledge production and the production of knowledge economies – that can be mobilised for African intellectual development at multiple spatial and social scales, from the local to the global and from generation to gender.

When I left Malawi in 1977 I had no idea that I would become part of Africa's new intellectual diaspora, let alone did I reflect on the perils and possibilities of the diaspora condition. I left at the height of Dr Banda's dictatorship when political disappearances and detentions were quite common, especially for the intelligentsia. I recall several of my lecturers and fellow students were detained and sent to 'high school', as the detention centres were euphemistically, if a little cynically, called between 1974 and 1976. The special branch, the infamous 'SB' – there was never a more frightening acronym in those days – whom we used to call the 'soul brothers' to assuage our fears, would come to the campus to pick up new recruits for 'high school' on Fridays, always on Fridays, and so many of us would try to escape campus on Fridays, even Thursdays, and return the next Sunday or Monday. I later wrote about this harrowing period in a short story, 'Suspended Dreams', published in my second collection of short stories, *The Joys of Exile*.

I had been writing short stories since 1972 when I went to college and one of my English professors encouraged me to pursue writing after he read a story I had written for his class assignment. For the next four years I wrote many stories, some of which were broadcast on the national radio and others published in magazines. I was particularly thrilled when one was published in a Zimbabwean magazine and I was paid some $20! My parents were then living in Zimbabwe, having escaped political and religious persecution in Malawi. What an irony: they felt safer in settler Rhodesia which was then under Ian Smith's white minority rule and besieged by an escalating war of national liberation.

Like all my colleagues gathered around the Writers' Group at Chancellor College, I was acutely aware of the dangers of writing under such a capricious regime: one wrong word could land you in detention.[4] The dangers came home to me in 1975 when I was invited to meet the Chairman of the Censorship Board to go over some of the stories included in my forthcoming collection of short stories, *Night of Darkness and Other Stories* – the choice of title and the lead story were a deliberate commentary and mockery of the prevailing political order. The Chairman chastised me in no uncertain terms about six of the stories, which he warned should not be published anywhere for their potentially subversive implications. All publications at the time had to be vetted by the Censorship Board. I almost suspended publication of the book, but I was persuaded otherwise by my English professors and the publisher. The book came out a few weeks after my graduation, but its amputation left sour memories that have lasted to this day.[5]

Not surprisingly, I was immensely relieved the moment I got out of the country to study abroad, thrilled at the opportunity to rewrite my experiences of the Malawi of the 1970s. In a 1995 presentation on censorship in Malawi at the 1995 Zimbabwe International Book Fair,[6] I characterised Banda's Malawi as the land of pervasive fear where words were constantly monitored, manipulated and mutilated, a country stalked by silence and suspicion, a nation where only the monotonous story of the Ngwazi's achievements could be told and retold, a state of dull uniformity that criminalised difference, ambiguity, and creativity, an omniscient regime with a divine right to nationalise time and thought, history and the popular will. And so it censored memories, stories, and words that contested and mocked its singular authority, banishing and imprisoning numerous opponents, real and imaginary, hunting and murdering exiled 'rebels,' and appropriated and dissolved the boundaries between private and public spaces, personal and political spheres, individual and collective lives, so that no one was sure of anyone, not of friends or colleagues, nor relatives, not even of partners and spouses, and even one's careless dreams could be dangerous. All was contaminated by this naked, arbitrary power. The result of my freed, but enraged, imagination was my first novel, *Smouldering Charcoal*, a bitter indictment of the deformities of Africa's post-colonies. The book came out as Malawi was emerging out of the fog of terror and the winds of democratisation were beginning to blow across the continent.

New winds of change

In May 1994 Banda's dictatorship was dumped into the dustbin of history. I recall the electric impact during the elections and sense of rebirth and renewal that filled this beautiful land of undulating hills and towering mountains, meandering rivers and the shimmering waters of Lake Malawi. I returned to witness and partake in this historic moment, my first extended return in 17 years. While in opposition, the party that proceeded to win the elections, had appointed me to its 'shadow cabinet', but I declined appointment to a ministerial position after the elections to the chagrin of relatives and amusement of my friends: I was unsure of the commitment of the new ruling party composed mostly of recycled politicians who had fallen out with Dr Banda, and obviously hungry and ambitious businessmen – to the ideals of building a democratic developmental state. Unfortunately, my misgivings turned out to be correct: President Bakili Muluzi's administration was unrestrained in its venality and corruption.

Democratisation was exhilarating in its political and intellectual possibilities. I remember attending a conference at York University in 1993 in the midst of Malawi's transition from dictatorship that brought together academics, writers, politicians and religious leaders, both Malawian and non-Malawian, where we examined the contemporary archival records and interrogated the memories of the participants and observers of Malawi's first independence in the mid-1960s. It was a serious, open, and sometimes, painful enquiry, aimed at re-examining and correcting the historical record, pondering the present, and divining the future. Lurking beneath the celebratory reflections there were also concerns about our role as writers in the unfolding drama, in the emerging new dispensation. Tyranny had created us, imprisoned and exiled many of us, enraged our consciences and nourished our imaginations. It had given us the moral inspiration to write and the themes to write about, and had often determined the languages, forms and styles of our writing as well as our audiences and production outlets. Now we were about to be orphaned from this tyranny. We were being challenged to recreate messages, our imaginations, practices, and ourselves.[7] That is when I decided to recast my literary imagination by writing my next collection of short stories, *The Joys of Exile*, in which the stories are set in the different locations of my diasporic journeys and deal with various types of exile as a metaphor of human alienation.

If my creative writing represented a deeply charged emotional and existential engagement with the politics of my post-colonial upbringing, my academic work reflected an epistemic and experiential attempt to comprehend the African condition and the way it has been analysed. As with many academic journeys, it began with my MA, which was then followed by the often-tortuous PhD dissertation. I had always been fascinated by both history as the study of the African past, and international relations as the study of Africa's global engagements, so for my Master's degree I took courses in both fields in 1977–78 at the School of Oriental and African Studies and the London School of Economics, both constituent colleges of the University of London. My first year overseas and in the legendary city of London, the old imperial capital we had been raised to imagine as the centre of cosmopolitan glory, was truly intriguing: the taste of new freedoms, the fascination of new experiences, the joys of making new friends, the challenges of new studies, the unsettling confrontations with the politics of race and my baptism into blackness. I was 22 then. A year later I enrolled for my PhD at Dalhousie University in Nova Scotia, Canada.

New approaches

By then I had grown weary of Britain, of being a post-colonial in the unforgiving and unforgetting imperial metropolis, but I had no intention of trekking into the belly of the contemporary imperial beast, the United States. So I opted for middling Canada, a country that straddled the settler and multiracial energies of North America and the familiarities of the Commonwealth, and espoused a form of state capitalism, a kind of social democracy, more amenable to my socialist inclinations than the unbridled free market capitalism across the border. The fact that I did not feel safe to return to Malawi did affect the choice of my topic of study for research. I chose to work on Kenya, which was close enough to Malawi, and where I hoped I would be able to meet exiled Malawians or Malawians in transit since Nairobi was the region's major transportation hub; Johannesburg was then isolated in its apartheid *laager*. It would also give me the opportunity to learn Kiswahili, the language none other than Wole Soyinka had decreed should be elevated into the continent's lingua franca. And Kenya was the quintessential neo-colonial state, on which I could test Marxist and dependency theories that were then the rage in our intellectual circles.

Before the rise of the 'radical' approaches in African studies, the nationalist school held sway in African historiography. Independence and the establishment of national universities and the need for new charters of Africa's historical and humanistic agency facilitated the production of nationalist history. Nationalist historiography overthrew imperialist history that had valorised colonialism and vilified Africa, celebrated the policies of colonial governments and the activities of colonial auxiliaries from European merchants to missionaries to the settlers. When Africans appeared in the Eurocentric narratives, it was to condemn their societies and cultures, or to record their Westernisation or modernisation. Nationalist historians focused primarily on African activities, choices, and adaptations, and chronicled the rise and fall of Africa's ancient states and empires, long-distance trade, migrations, the spread of religions, and critiqued colonial policies, commemorated the growth of nationalism, and reincorporated Egypt and North Africa into the mainstream of African history from which they had been severed by Hegel and his descendants. They gave the fragile new states historical identity and a legitimising ideology.

The nationalist historians who had taught me in Malawi and England had done their job well: we never doubted that Africa had its own history, but we were troubled by the continued dehumanisation of Africans. By the time I entered graduate school criticisms of nationalist historiography had become common: that it focused largely on the 'voices' of the ruling classes, rather than the 'masses;' it was too preoccupied with showing that Africa had produced organised politics, monarchies, and cities, just like Europe, so that it wrote African history by analogy and subsumed it to the teleological logics of European history, and failed to probe deeper into the historical realities of African material and social life before colonial rule; and as for the colonial period, nationalism was made so 'overdetermining' that only feeble efforts were made to provide systematic analyses of imperialism, its changing forms, and their impact, not to mention the processes of local class formation and class struggle.

Clearly, these critiques were in part inspired by creeping disillusionment with *uhuru* and the rise of more radical ideologies. In particular, Marxism became increasingly popular as a paradigm of social science research. I wrote my dissertation on 'Dependent Capitalism and the Making of the Kenyan Working Class During the Colonial Period', a title that wears its theoretical and ideological influences loudly. Marxist influence grew with the triumph of radical liberation movements in southern Africa in the early 1970s, and the adoption of Marxism as a developmentalist ideology by several African political parties and states, and by Western intellectuals who were dissatisfied with bourgeois liberalism and Western imperialism in the Third World. The Marxist historians examined the processes of production, social formation, and class struggle, as well as the complex mediations and contradictory effects of imperialism in modern Africa. There were of course many Marxisms and Marxists, some of the labels worn by choice others by association, either in self-congratulation or derision. Some of the Marxist-inspired work was schematic, doctrinaire, and pretentious. But some of it was rich and enlightening. Particularly impressive were the studies on labour and workers, agriculture and peasants, and the changing structures of Africa's incorporation into the world economy.

Despite some of the fine work the various approaches inspired there was one glaring omission: their coverage of gender and women's history was poor. The under-representation of women could be found virtually in all the major historical texts written up to the 1980s as I chronicled in a survey of dozens of continental, regional, national, and thematic histories.[8] From the turn of the 1970s feminist historians began to challenge women's marginalisation in African historiography, a challenge buoyed by the growth of the women's movement. Some African feminists relentlessly attacked the epistemological hegemony of Western feminism, criticising the very foundational categories of Western feminist scholarship such as 'gender', 'woman' and the 'body', arguing that these categories must be subjected to critical analysis and the need to privilege the categories and interpretations of African societies. From the 1980s there was an explosion of feminist-inspired histories, many of which simply sought to restore women to history, to record women's activities and experiences in the conventional themes of African historiography, and some to engender African historiography as a whole. I jumped on the bandwagon with a book on women in the Kenyan labour movement, recasting my neo-Marxist work. This was my first published academic book. I never published my dissertation, although I cannibalised one section into a short monograph and other bits and pieces into journal articles or book chapters.[9]

Africa in the world

When I completed my dissertation, I felt stranded: I could not go back to Malawi and I did not want to stay in Canada. I had three job offers, one in

Nigeria, another in Zambia, and another in Jamaica at the University of the West Indies. The latter proved more seductive: I reasoned I could always go back and work in Africa, but this might be a rare opportunity to work in the Caribbean. And so begun my long intellectual engagements with the African diaspora. Teaching in Jamaica proved decisive in the development of my intellectual interests. While I gave seminar papers on Kenya, I was given two courses to teach on the history of West Africa and Southern Africa, respectively, and when I gave public lectures to various communities, including schools, my audiences were interested in Africa in general, in broad African history, struggles, and achievements. This underscores the power of the diaspora space to imagine and write Africa in more holistic ways, the incredible potential of the diaspora imagination to conceive and critique Africa, an Africa for itself and an Africa of the world, to construct both a continental and a global Africa.

I recall vividly one day I was invited to address high school students in Kingston and to my consternation their questions focused predominantly on the nature of African economies before the coming of Europeans: what did Africans produce, eat, wear, trade, what kinds of houses did they live in, what was the nature of gender and inter-generational relations, the dynamics and structures of power, why did they sell their people into slavery? In my own work I had focused predominantly on colonial capitalism to give satisfactory answers. I decided to study pre-colonial African economic history, a decision that was reinforced when I went to Kenyatta University in Nairobi and I was asked to teach a course on the subject when the person who had been hired to teach it was late in coming. This resulted in my book, *A Modern Economic History of Africa. Vol. 1: The Nineteenth Century*, which won the Noma Award for Publishing in Africa in 1994. It is arguably the most comprehensive history of African economies before colonial rule. Since then I have been working on and off on *Volume 2*, covering the 20th century.

The five and half years I spent in Kenya constituted a period of enormous personal and intellectual growth for me. I met many people who have since become lifelong friends, most importantly Professor Bethwell Alan Ogot, one of the founders of nationalist historiography and editors of the *UNESCO General History of Africa*,[10] the supreme compendium of historical knowledge produced by his generation, who became my mentor and from whom I learned much about the development of African history, the need to vigorously challenge Western hegemony over African studies, and the power and perils of public intellectualism. And I had the opportunity to translate academic history into history textbooks for schools.[11] But I also experienced the agonies and challenges of being an exiled academic in a foreign African country and the limits of pan-African intellectual solidarities, which I commemorated in an essay on 'The Lightness of Being an African Expatriate Scholar', delivered a few months after I left Kenya at a conference on Academic Freedom organised by the Council for the Development of Social Science Research in Africa (CODESRIA).[12]

That marked the first time I attended a CODESRIA Conference. It was an indescribable experience meeting the luminaries of African social science and social thought, whose publications I had devoured with such relish. I had already been a beneficiary of CODESRIA's research network and largesse when I received, in late 1989, a fellowship that allowed me to leave my job at Kenyatta and focus, for six months, on research for my economic history book, which I undertook at the United Nations Economic Commission for Africa in Addis Ababa and at my old alma mater, Dalhousie, the latter largely dictated by reasons of familiarity and family. That was the beginning of my lifelong commitment to CODESRIA, one of the academic NGOs that emerged in the 1970s and were to flourish in the 1980s and 1990s, which has done so much to keep the fires of African research and publishing burning as African universities went into the crises of structural adjustment engendered by the inane policies of the international financial institutions that Africa did not need universities and the short-sighted connivance of African governments.

I have deliberately published many of my most important books with CODESRIA, including *A Modern Economic History of Africa, Manufacturing African Studies and Crises*, which received the Special Commendation of the Noma Award in 1998, the co-edited two-volume collection, *African Universities in the Twenty-First Century*, and the recently published *The Study of Africa*, also in two volumes, as part of a strategy to strengthen scholarly production on the continent. I believe this shows that African scholars can make significant contributions to African intellectual production even if they are located outside the continent. This represents, in a sense, the repatriation of academic capital, a form of intellectual remittances. Publishing is the lifeblood of the academic enterprise, the medium through which scholarly ideas and collective identities are created, codified, circulated, and consumed, through which informed conversations between civilisations, cultures, countries, and communities are conducted across generations.

It was this growing preoccupation with the role of African intellectuals and institutions of higher education in African socio-economic development and transformation that sparked my interest in the state of African universities, an interest that was also inspired, in part, by my experiences in Kenya, where I witnessed conditions in the public universities deteriorate and where I was forced to survive by teaching at a private Catholic university and undertaking consultancies. *African Universities in the Twenty-First Century* covers the history and contemporary trends in African higher education.

Specifically, *Volume 1*, subtitled 'Liberalization and Internationalization,' examines the impact and implications of globalisation and the neo-liberal agenda on African universities as well as the challenges of incorporating information technology and promoting academic exchanges and transnational linkages. The second volume is subtitled 'Knowledge and Society' and it analyses, in the first part, the dynamics of knowledge production including debates about endogenisation, the disciplinary architecture of knowledge, and the state of scholarly publishing and research libraries. In the second part, the book looks at relations between African universities and the state, industry, the labour market, civil society, and secondary and primary education, as well as the changing nature of student and staff politics and women's participation. The book concludes with an exhaustive list of research topics that my co-editor, Adebayo Olukoshi, the current Executive Secretary of CODESRIA, and I believe are crucial for the emerging field of African higher education research.

Structural adjustment

There is little doubt in my mind that universities are not a developmental luxury, but fundamental to Africa's regeneration in a world increasingly characterised by knowledge-intensive economic and social activities. Even a cursory glance at the currently rapid development of China and India, which if it continues at the present pace will enable Asia to overtake Euro-America economically in the next few decades, shows the crucial role played by massive investments in education including higher education, the mobilisation of economic and intellectual capital from the diaspora, and the close collaboration between the political class and the intelligentsia, which has facilitated the integration of knowledge produced by the latter in national planning. China and India have grown rapidly not by following Euro-American advice and prescriptions, but by spurning them, by ignoring if not actively resisting the Washington Consensus of structural adjustment programmes that have wrecked so much havoc on African economies since the 1980s. In contrast, African governments remain more enamoured with Euro-American expatriates than the expertise of their own intelligentsia, and African middle classes are more willing to copy Western consumption tastes than to invest and master modern technologies of production.

We live in a very complex world with complex problems, pressures and possibilities in which the importance of informed policy dialogue is more important than ever. For Africa, this raises the question of relations between the academy and the intelligentsia more broadly, and the state and civil society. During the brief, exhilarating moment of decolonisation, African intellectuals and political leaders shared faith in the emancipatory potential of independence. But the honeymoon between them did not last. By the

1980s, many of Africa's repressive and strapped structural adjustment states were suspicious and dismissive of their own intellectuals, which left little room for the latter to occupy public space or to engage in critical discourse openly. Yet the same governments became increasingly subservient to foreign policy advice and conditionalities. Indeed, the growing reliance on foreign expatriates for development models and research, bankrolled by the donor agencies, enabled African governments to ignore their own intellectuals and to lower the short-term costs of intellectual repression. This led to the ironical situation whereby these governments could only access their own intellectuals through donor-contracted reports as the latter sought pecuniary and political salvation in consultancies. The transformation of African intellectuals into 'paid native informants' for foreign donors and researchers was a tragic testimony to the collapse of the nationalist project.

In my view, then, the problem in many African countries is not whether intellectuals and research inform public policy, but whose research informs which policies. By and large, researchers in African universities and research networks have played second fiddle to researchers from Euro-American institutions and think tanks whose ideas and fantasies often inform the policies of bilateral and multilateral donor agencies. The real challenge is to increase the relevance and receptivity of African research for African policy makers without the mediation of donor driven research and policy priorities. Progress is of course being made, not least because of democratisation and the growth of activist academic NGOs, but the road ahead will remain a difficult one. As African intellectuals, we really have no choice but to continue striving to articulate clear agendas for African societies and peoples, especially as the continent encounters new processes of capitalist globalisation and imperial racism and barbarism. In my view, these agendas must be rooted in the unfinished tasks of progressive African nationalism – development, democratisation, and self-determination – revised to reflect current contexts and changing circumstances.

If African intellectuals are to play a more decisive role in Africa, the revitalisation of the institutions that produce and reproduce them, namely, the universities, is imperative. I dream of truly decolonised, democratised, and decentralised universities; universities that are autonomous yet accountable, committed to the pursuit of intellectual excellence yet rooted in their communities, effectively managed internally yet working closely with all stakeholders; universities that are Africanised in their staffing, values, pedagogy, epistemologies, and instructional languages yet are capable of competing globally, contributing to the global pool of knowledge, and responding quickly and effectively to global changes and emerging local needs; universities that attract students and faculty from across the continent and the diaspora, and that participate in extensive academic exchanges with universities in other parts of the world; universities that provide inclusive education, where access is open regardless of physical or class disabilities or various cultural and social affiliations; universities with ample and up-to-date learning facilities, instructional technologies, and well-equipped libraries and laboratories, manageable student–teacher ratios, that provide multiple entry and exit points as well as individual and group enrolments for lifelong and flexible learning; universities with vibrant communities of scholars, where public debates flourish, research and publishing are valued but not subjected to the mindless 'publish and perish' syndrome, and where African scholars can engage in 'idle contemplation' as well as provide solutions to practical problems; universities where gender is mainstreamed, curricula are creative, and which produce students who are literate in the major fields of knowledge, innovative and entrepreneurial, as well as critical thinkers and citizens; universities where the professors are highly trained and motivated and productive; universities, in short, that are the spearhead of the African renaissance.

Writing Africa

Over the years my interest in the history of African institutions of higher learning has been complemented by a growing interest in the history of knowledges produced on Africa. This dual analytical agenda, the history of knowledge producing institutions and the history of ideas, was reinforced when I became director of the Center for African Studies at the University of Illinois at Urbana-Champaign in 1995, one of America's leading African studies programmes. My first encounter with the Africanist community at its annual meeting in November that year, at which there was heated confrontation over Philip Curtin's controversial remarks, published in an op-ed piece in *The Chronicle of Higher Education*,[13] that the increased hiring of black scholars was leading to declining standards in the teaching of African history in American universities brought home to me the incendiary racial politics of African studies in the American academy that inspired the book *Manufacturing African Studies and Crises* and an abiding interest in excavating the intellectual constitution and social composition of African studies in the United States and the global North more generally.

I eventually introduced a graduate seminar at Illinois on the 'Development of African Studies', which examined the intellectual, institutional, and ideological dynamics in the construction of Africanist knowledges in different disciplinary, interdisciplinary, and international contexts. One year I decided to bring scholars from around the world for intensive and stimulating discussions highlighting new developments and the theoretical, methodological, and pedagogical challenges in African studies within their respective fields and locations. This culminated in the edited book, *The Study of Africa (Vol. 1: Disciplinary and Interdisciplinary Encounters, Vol. 2: Global and Transnational Engagements)*. This book was motivated, in part, by the need to capture and demonstrate the diverse and complex configurations of African studies in different world regions, in addition to encompassing and examining African studies on a much wider disciplinary and interdisciplinary canvas than had been attempted to date. The disciplines covered include anthropology, sociology, literature, linguistics, history, political science, economics, geography, and psychology, while the interdisciplines and interdisciplinary fields include women's and gender studies, art studies, religious studies, public health studies, communications studies, cultural studies, post-colonial studies, and globalisation and transnational studies. The regions covered include Asia (China, India, Japan, and Australia), Europe (Britain, France, Germany, Sweden, and Russia), and the Americas (the United States, Caribbean, and Brazil). It is probably not an exaggeration to say that this collection is perhaps the most comprehensive overview of African studies ever undertaken.

The eight years I spent as director of the Center for African Studies at Illinois was one of the most productive periods in my intellectual career. I was able to organise numerous conferences and bring hundreds of scholars from around the world, including from across Africa, to discuss and debate issues of theoretical and great policy relevance. I strongly believe that research is fundamental to policy formulation, or should be. We live in a very complex world with complex problems, pressures and prospects in which the importance of informed policy dialogue is more important than ever.

Some of the results from the sumptuous intellectual feasts of my time as Director at Illinois can be seen in the various books I edited from some of the conferences such as, *Sacred Spaces and Public Quarrels: African Cultural and Economic Landscapes, In Search of Modernity: Science and Technology in Africa, Leisure in Urban Africa*, and *Human Rights, the Rule of Law and Development in Africa*. I also became involved in large encyclopaedic projects out of the conviction that it is crucial to inscribe our scholarly voices in this popular medium of intellectual consumption: as the chief editor for the Routledge *Encyclopedia of Twentieth Century African History* and an associate editor for the six-volume *New Dictionary of the History of Ideas* (Horowitz 2005). I maintained my old interest in gender studies with the publication of *Women in African Studies Scholarly Publishing*. More recently, I veered into one of the afflictions of modern Africa and co-edited a large study, *Managing and Resolving African Conflicts. (Vol.1: The Causes and Costs of Conflicts; Vol. 2: Conflict Resolution and Post-Conflict Reconstruction)*. And thanks to the communication possibilities opened by the internet I set up a personal website where I maintain a list of online resources on Africa and African studies and post regular blogs or commentaries on current events taking place on the continent and the world more generally (*www.zeleza.com*).

I have always tried to respond as critically and creatively as possible to emerging intellectual and ideological trends. By the 1990s, globalisation and the 'posts' – post-modernism and post-coloniality – had become a discursive craze. The former extolled the inevitability and irreversibility of globalisation as the grand narrative of our age, the latter eschewed all metanarratives including those of class, nation, and even gender and the positivism and dichotomies of modernist history, and insisted on the hybridity, contingency, decenteredness, and ambivalence of reality and experience. I tried to understand these new paradigms by writing a series of papers and a book, *Rethinking Africa's Globalization. Vol.1: The Intellectual Challenges*, in which I sought to examine Africa's troubled encounter with the ever-changing conceptual registers of Western scholarship. Let me hasten to point out that I have tempered my old antagonism to the 'posts' as I have come to appreciate how congenial they have proved to feminist and ethnic studies, encouraged the study of historically despised or marginalised groups, the examination of how identities are constructed and constituted, explorations of how situations and events are understood and represented, and their emphasis on the importance of language and literary sensibility for historical writing. But I remain wary of the imperiousness with which their advocates seek to export them to Africa, to impose them on Africa's complex realities that demand empowering knowledges not the navel-gazing angst of much 'post-something' theorising.

Living as long as I have in the global North, the question of Africa's diasporas increasingly looms large. Africa's recent immigrants in the cities and institutions of the global North, especially in North America, find themselves and especially their offspring identified with Africa's historic diasporas in their new communities and countries of residence. I have not escaped the pull of the diaspora as a condition and a concept, an experiential reality and an epistemic concern. My main area of present research focuses on the African diaspora, both the historic and contemporary diasporas, of which I have become part. I am currently undertaking a large project on the subject entitled, 'Africa and Its Diasporas: Linkages and Dispersals.' I embarked on this project partly out of a growing conviction that African history needs to be broadened in its spatial scale to advance beyond the confines of nationalist historiography, not to mention the idiocies of Eurocentric historiography that tends to excise Africa from world history and worldly historical significance.

Diaspora studies are crucial, in my view, to inscribing Africa's global historical presence; such a rewriting of history helps to provincialise

Europe that has monopolised universality and to universalise Africa beyond its Eurocentric provincialisation. The project seeks to map out the dispersal of African peoples in all the major world regions – Asia, Europe, and the Americas, compare the processes of diaspora formation within and among these regions, and examine the ebbs and flows of linkages – demographic, cultural including religion and music, economic, political and ideological, intellectual and educational, artistic and iconographic – between these diasporas and Africa over time. The sheer volume of literature on the subject has been a source of inestimable intellectual pleasure and some trepidation for me. I spent six weeks recently on my first field visits to Venezuela and Brazil of what will be three years of visits to all the major African diaspora centres across the globe.

A project such as this has immense intellectual and policy relevance: it can help deepen our understanding of the complex histories and constructions of African diasporas and their equally complex and sometimes contradictory and always changing engagements with Africa, which is especially critical at this juncture as the African Union and other continental agencies as well as national governments seek to build more productive relationships between themselves and their diasporas. Already, Africa's contemporary diasporas, many of them reluctant refugees from structural adjustment programmes and Africa's vicious post-colonial conflicts, currently remit more than $25 billion and in some countries account for larger inflows of foreign exchange and investment than foreign 'aid'. Also, as global African migrations increase the challenges of integrating new African diasporas in the host countries increase as has been seen across Europe (most recently in the uprising in France), and so do the challenges of integrating them into the communities with long-established historic African diasporas as is evident in the Americas (especially the United States). Thus, diaspora studies enable us to insert Africa into global history and rewrite the histories of the various regions to which Africans were dispersed whether voluntarily or by force. The Africans who went to Portugal and Spain and ruled for eight centuries during the Andalusian period did so voluntarily, while those who were shipped to the Americas during the era of the Atlantic slave trade were coerced. Both left an indelible mark on the history of Europe, Africa and the Americas, whose effects are still with us and are central to understanding the history of Euro-America – the whitened West.

The possible intellectual benefits of the work of African academic diasporas in terms of their teaching, research, and service functions and activities – the triple mission of the modern university – are often not fully appreciated, as more emphasis tends to be placed, often rightly, on the costs of the 'brain drain'. It cannot be overemphasised that the academic diasporas constitute important, but under-utilised links in trans-Atlantic communication and exchange, in the mediation of relations between Africa and the global North including the transfer of technology and intellectual capital from the latter to the continent. African diaspora scholars have a responsibility to be Africa's intellectual eyes and ears. As we all know, Africa is routinely defamed and denigrated in the popular media and in scholarly publications in the global North. Given their very location there, the African diaspora intellectuals are in much better positions than scholars based on the continent, and ought to continuously challenge Afrophobia and Afropessimism, and to raise the intellectual costs of maligning and misrepresenting Africa. Thus they are indispensable to the intellectual and ideological defence of Africa, to the redefinition of African identity, modernity, and transnationalism, to challenging Euroamerican myths of autogenesis and conceits of civilisational superiority; in short, to the globalisation of Africa and the Africanisation of globalisation. Obviously, diasporic location is not the only, let alone even the most important, space from which to critically and productively engage Africa. The most decisive space of African enunciation and intellection will always be within Africa itself, but I would like to believe that my contributions to African scholarship, whatever they may judged to be, have been shaped because, not in spite, of my diasporic journeys and locations.

Thus far, my personal and professional journey, intellectual and individual voyages from Malawi in Southern Africa to the global North and the diaspora have been truly fascinating and enriching. To be sure, there are moments of nostalgia, of wonder what might have been had I stayed in one place, in my native homeland, but I also realise the immense possibilities a life of rooted cosmopolitanism, guided by the abiding principles of a global pan-Africanism, has afforded me as an African intellectual who came of age in the late 20th century.

Notes

1   Mark Pires, Ron Kassimir, and M. Brhane (1999), *Investing in Return: Rates of Return of African PhD's Trained in North America*. New York, Social Science Research Council.

2   For example, 'The African Academic Diaspora in the United States and Africa: The Challenges of Productive Engagement,' in *Comparative Studies of South Asia, Africa, and the Middle East*, 24, 1, 2004, pp. 265–278; 'African Migrations in a Global Context,' *African Issues*, XXX, 1, 2002, pp. 9–14.

3   See the special issue I co-edited on the 'brain drain', P.T. Zeleza and C.R. Veney, eds. (2002), *African Issues* xxx, 1. Special issue on 'The African Brain Drain to the North: Pitfalls and Possibilities'.

4   For a history of the Writers' Group by one of the participants, see Lupenga Mphande (1996), 'Dr. Hastings Kamuzu Banda and the Malawi Writers Group: The (un)Making of a Cultural Tradition,' *Research in African Literatures* 27, 1, pp. 80–101.

5   I discussed this incident at greater length with Don Selby, 'Interview with Paul Tiyambe Zeleza.' *Peterborough Review* 2, 1, 1995, pp. 32–41.

6   Published later in the years as, 'Banishing Words and Stories in Banda's Malawi,' *Codesria Bulletin* 3, 1995, pp. 1–4.

7   I discuss this conference and the challenges of democratisation as a condition and concept in African literature in, 'The Democratic Transition in Africa and the Anglophone Writer,' *Canadian Journal of African Studies* 28, 3, 1994, pp. 472–97.

8   'Gender Biases in African Historiography,' in Ayesha M. Imam, Amina Mama and Fatou Sow, eds. (1997), *Engendering the Social Sciences in Africa*. Dakar: Codesria Book Series, pp. 81–115.

9   The book chapters include, 'The Colonial Labour System in Kenya,' in W.R. Ochieng' and Robert Maxon, eds. (1992), *An Economic History of Kenya*. Nairobi: Heinemann Kenya/East African Education Publishers, pp. 171–199; 'Labour Coercion and Migration in Early Colonial Kenya,' in A. Zegeye, ed. (1989), *Forced Labor and Migration: Patterns of Movement Within Africa*. London: Hans Zell, pp. 159–179; 'Kenya and the Second World War Years, 1939–1952,' in W.R. Ochieng', ed. (1989), *A Modern History of Kenya: 1895–1980. Essays in Honour of B. A. Ogot*. London and Nairobi: Evans Brothers, pp. 144–172; 'The Establishment of Colonial Rule in Kenya: 1905–1920,' in W.R. Ochieng', ed. (1989), *A Modern History of Kenya: 1895–1980. Essays in Honour of B.A. Ogot*. London and Nairobi: Evans Brothers, pp. 35–70, 'Kenya's Road to Independence and After.' In P. Gifford and W.R. Louis, eds. (1988), *Decolonization and African Independence: The Transfers of Power, 1960–1980*. New Haven: Yale University Press, pp. 40–426 (with B.A. Ogot). The journal articles include, 'The Moral Economy of Working Class Struggle: Strikers, the Community and the State in the 1947 Mombasa General Strike,' *Africa Development* 20, 3, 1995, pp. 51–87; 'The Strike Movement in Colonial Kenya,' *Transafrican Journal of History* 22, 1993, pp. 1–23; 'Trade Union Imperialism: American Labour, the ICFTU and the Kenyan Labour Movement,' *Social and Economic Studies* 36, 2, 1987, pp. 145–170; 'Pan-African Trade Unionism: Unity and Discord,' *Transafrican Journal of History* 15, 1986, pp. 164–190; 'The Political Economy of British Colonial Development and Welfare in Africa.' *Transafrican Journal of History*, 14, 1985, pp. 139–161; 'Colonialism and Internationalism: The Case of the British and Kenyan Labour Movements,' *Ufahamu* 14, 1, 1984, pp. 9–28; and 'African History: The Rise and Decline of Academic Tourism,' *Ufahamu* 13, 1, 1983, pp. 9–42.

10   *UNESCO General History of Africa*. Vols. 1–8. 1981–1993. London: Heinemann.

11   I worked with a team of other academics and staff from the Kenyan National Examinations Council setting exams for the secondary school history syllabus, and published *Revising for History and Government for K.C.S.E*, London and Nairobi: Evans Brothers, 1989 (with A. Williams and M. Sharman). Unfortunately, the four-volume textbook I wrote, *Themes in Kenyan and World History* which was supposed to be published by Evans Brothers, was shelved when the Kenyan shilling was devalued and the costs of the books in local currency became too high; it was a harsh lesson in the economics of multinational publishing! Years later, I published three texts on three Kenyan ethnic groups, the *Maasai, Akamba*, and *Mijikenda* (New York: Rosen Publishing Group, 1994) out of my conviction that academic researchers need to write for schools as well as for popular audiences.

12   It is published in *Manufacturing African Studies and Crises*.

13   Philip D. Curtin, 'Ghettoizing African History,' *The Chronicle of Higher Education 3*, 3 March 1995, pp. A44.

Global pan-African leadership in the new millennium

Ali A. Mazrui

Ali A. Mazrui *is one of Africa's leading political scientists. In his second essay in this collection, he outlines the issues, themes and tensions facing global pan-African leadership in the 21st century.*

Pan-Africanism, development and democracy in global Africa for the new millennium demand exceptional leadership. In this essay, I trace the challenges for future leadership in global Africa. The emergence of a new style of leadership is critical not only for global Africans, but also for a world confronting globalisation and complexity on an unparallelled scale.[1]

Pan-Africanism

We know that Africa has been served well by leaders of liberation. We are, however, concerned that we have not produced enough leaders of development or democracy. What about leaders of pan-Africanism and wider transnational solidarity? Clearly this is a fourth goal together with liberation, development and democracy.

In the new millennium all those four goals (liberation, development, democracy and pan-Africanism) may have to be examined in the context of globalisation. Let us now turn to these dimensions.

What, for example, is the impact of globalisation on relations between Africans and African Americans? Is globalisation bringing them closer together or pulling them farther apart?

Let us first define 'globalisation' itself. Some analysts have seen it mainly through the expanding world markets and deepening interdependence within the world economy. Other analysts have seen 'globalisation' through the information superhighway and the internet revolution. But it is possible to take an even more comprehensive view of globalisation – regarding it as consisting of all the forces which are leading the world towards a global village. Globalisation is thus the villagisation of the world.[2]

But for people of African ancestry is there a globalisation within the globalisation? Is there a globalisation of the black race within the globalisation of the world? I first coined the term 'Global Africa' for the final episode in my television series *The Africans: A Triple Heritage* (BBC/PBS, 1986).[3] By it I meant the experience of people of African descent worldwide. Until the middle of the 20th century 'global Africa' meant the people of Africa itself combined with the African diaspora in the Americas, the Caribbean, Europe, and the Middle East. What has been happening in the 20th century is a more extensive globalisation of global Africa – making the African factor on earth more truly omnipresent and omnidirectional. Let us explore those forces which have been further globalising the phenomenon of global Africa.

Globalising the dual diaspora

A major factor has been the dualisation of the African diaspora. There has been the new migration of Africans to the Middle East, Europe, the Americas, Australia and elsewhere – the new bantu migration on a global scale. In a sense this process has been creating two African diasporas – the new Diaspora of Colonialism alongside the older Diaspora of Enslavement.

The Diaspora of Enslavement consists of survivors of the Middle Passage and their descendants. The Diaspora of Colonialism are the survivors of the partition of Africa in exile and their descendants. The Diaspora of Colonialism are casualties of the displacement caused either directly by colonialism or by the aftermath of colonial and post-colonial disruptions.[4]

As part of the Afro-Atlantic paradigm, the Diaspora of Enslavement has played a major role in shaping the culture and lifestyle of the Western hemisphere. Perhaps never in history has a people in bondage exerted a greater influence on the culture of their masters.

It is arguable that whatever is uniquely American in the culture and lifestyle of the United States has been due to two very different forces — the impact of the frontier and the impact of the black presence in the American experience. As Isidore Okpewho has said:

> European influences were a 'given'. Thomas Jefferson and the founding father looked to such European thinkers as John Locke . . . Euro-Americans liked to think of themselves as heirs to Greece and Rome. But where was the American personality?[5]

Frederick Jackson Turner (1861–1932) provided one answer – the significance of the frontier in American history. He argued that the American character was decisively shaped by conditions of the frontier, which evoked such qualities as 'coarseness and strength... acuteness and inquisitiveness, that practical turn of mind ... restless, nervous energy ... that buoyancy and exuberance which comes with freedom ...'.[6] He argued that what was uniquely American in her institutions was not the *Mayflower*, but boundless land, and the spirit of taming the rugged frontier. But Frederick Jackson Turner forgot one thing — what was uniquely American was also the black presence alongside the frontier. This is the presence which nurtured American capitalism in its infancy and nurtured American democracy in its maturation.

In its infancy, American capitalism needed black labour. This is the link between America and the imperative of labour. In its maturation in the 20th century American democracy needed the civil rights movement and deracialisation to realise its original concept that 'all men are created equal.' It was black people who held American democracy accountable to its own ultimate ideals. The echoes were heard all over Africa in the new Afro World Wide Web. The African presence in America has also deeply influenced music, literature, food culture, sports and the performing arts.

The distinction between the Diaspora of Enslavement and the Diaspora of Colonialism gets more complicated with the distinction between (a) *African Americans* (Americans is the noun and African the adjective) and (b) *American Africans* (Africans is the noun). The great majority of African Americans are a product of the Diaspora of Enslavement. The term 'African Americans' can be either hemispheric (meaning all descendants of enslavement in the Americas) or national (meaning all descendants of enslavement in the United States).

American Africans (or Americo-Africans) on the other hand, are products of the Diaspora of Colonialism. They are usually first or second generation immigrants from Africa to the Americas. They may be citizens or permanent residents of Western hemisphere countries.[7]

What is distinctive about American Africans is that their mother tongue is still an African language. (In the case of Americo-Liberians, they could still speak Liberian English.) Secondly, American Africans usually still have immediate blood relatives in Africa. Thirdly, they are likely to be still attached to the food culture of their African ancestry. Fourthly, American Africans are still likely to bear African family names, although this is by no means universal, especially among Lusophone Africans, Liberians and Sierra Leoneans.

On the whole African Americans tend to be more race-conscious in their political orientation than American Africans. On the other hand, American Africans might still be more fundamentally 'tribal' when the chips are down.

When does an American African family evolve into an African American family? When it loses its ancestral language. The umbilical cord is language. The children of Professor Nkiru Nzegwu of Binghamton University are still American Africans (hemispherically) because the children still speak fluent Igbo. On the other hand, my children are now more African Americans — their linguistic umbilical cord has been cut.

But when American Africans become African Americans, it does not mean other ties with Africa are cut. Relatives in Africa still abound. Concern for Africa is often still intact. And the internet is now providing a new network of Afro-Atlanticism, a new language.

Let me repeat that in the case of African Americans the noun is 'Americans'. What kind of Americans? *African* Americans. In the case of American Africans, the noun is 'Africans', the adjective is American. What kind of Africans? *American* Africans!

Between African Americans and American Africans

We must focus not just on relations between African Americans and Africans but also between African Americans and Africa as a continent. Do African Americans empathise with Africa? If so, how much? Indeed it is worth examining relations within the United States between American Africans and African Americans. There are areas of solidarity in those relations; and there are areas of tension.

When Amadou Diallo was killed in New York City by four white policemen pouring 41 bullets into him, it sent shock waves in the Big City, not just among immigrant Africans but also among African Americans, Latinos and other disadvantaged groups. Being fellow victims of white racism and police brutality is an area of solidarity.

And yet many African Americans feel that Africans generally are not concerned with race enough because of vastly different historical experiences. Among African Americans many give race 60 per cent relevance in their lives while Africans give it only 35 per cent relevance. This difference in racial preoccupation can be a cause of stress.

The majority of Africans (or American Africans) and African Americans are in support of affirmative action. This is an area of solidarity. But who precisely gets the jobs or the educational opportunities?

In reality the greatest beneficiaries are probably white women, but there is sometimes rivalry between African Americans and American Africans over jobs, business opportunities, and other scarce resources. This area of professional and occupational competition can be a source of stress.

Until recently the great majority of Africans in the United States were college graduates or in the process of acquiring college degrees. Many Africans who came to the USA came for educational purposes or got their visas and green cards on the basis of special qualifications. The majority of African Americans, on the other hand, did not have college degrees. This introduced a partial class factor between the two groups.

This class factor is now eroding for two reasons. There are more Africans in the United States who do not have a college degree and are not seeking one. Secondly, there are more and more African Americans who are exceptionally well trained and educated.[8] So this difference is evening out between African Americans and American Africans.

Many African American heroes are also African heroes. This includes the late Martin Luther King Jr, the boxer Muhammad Ali, the basketball player Michael Jordan, the novelist Toni Morrison, and many African-American singers. This is an area of solidarity. Even controversial Louis Farrakhan has millions of African admirers. On the other hand, African heroes are seldom well known in black America – apart from Nelson Mandela. Only the staunchest pan-Africanists among African Americans have ever heard of Kwame Nkrumah, Sékou Touré, Julius Nyerere or Wole Soyinka.

African-American lack of familiarity with African heroes is not really a cause of stress. It just represents a missed opportunity for further solidarity.

Expanding globalisation may restore the balance. In any case African-American heroes get much more global publicity because they are citizens of a super-power. It has therefore been easier for Africans in Africa to know about them than for African Americans in the United States to hear of Julius Nyerere or Olusegun Obasanjo.

Globalisation has also witnessed the rise of Africans to positions of leadership in global organisations. But here it may be worth distinguishing between *Africans of the soil* and *Africans of the blood*. Boutros Boutros-Ghali, the first African Secretary-General of the United Nations, was an African of the soil. Kofi Annan, the second African Secretary-General is an African of the blood. North Africans like Boutros-Ghali belong to the African continent (the soil) but not to the black race (the blood). On the other hand, African Americans are Africans of the blood (the black race) but not of the soil (the African continent). Sub-Saharan Africans like Kofi Annan are in reality both Africans of the soil (the continent) and of the blood (the race). Globalisation has given Africans of the soil and of the blood new opportunities for leadership at the global level itself.

Even before the two African Secretaries-General of the United Nations, Africa had already produced a Director-General for UNESCO in Paris (the United Nations Educational, Scientific and Cultural Organization). He was Amadou Mahtar M'Bow, an African of the blood from Senegal. His openly pro-Third World policies infuriated the United States, which finally withdrew from UNESCO in 1985 followed by its compliant ally, the United

Kingdom. The United Kingdom returned to UNESCO after the sweeping victory of the Labour Party in the 1997 election.

With regard to the United Nations itself, Africa is the only region of the world apart from Europe to have produced more than one Secretary-General for the world body in the 20th century. Europe has produced three Secretaries-General, Africa two, and the other regions of the world have produced either one each or none so far.

The International Court of Justice at the Hague elected in 1994 an African of the soil for its President – Mohammed Bedjauni of Algeria. The World Bank since the 1990s has had two African Vice-Presidents – Callisto Madivo, an African of the blood from Zimbabwe, and Ismail Serageldin, an African of the soil from Egypt. In 1999, Serageldin was also a serious candidate to become the first UNESCO Director-General of the new millennium.

The Commonwealth (what used to be called the British Commonwealth) has 54 members. Its Secretariat is at Marlborough House in London. Throughout the 1990s the Commonwealth had Chief Eleazar Emeka Anyouku as its Secretary-General. The Chief is an African of the blood from Nigeria. The largest member of the Commonwealth in population is India; the most industrialised include Canada, the United Kingdom and Australia; and the largest black member of the Commonwealth is of course Nigeria.

Globalisation has also permitted the emergence of black and African moral leadership on a world scale. It began with the Nobel Prize-winners for peace. Over the years these have included Ralph Bunche (1950), Albert Luthuli (1960), Martin Luther King Jr (1964), Anwar Sadat (1978), Desmond Tutu (1984), Nelson Mandela (1994), and F.W. de Klerk (1994).

Ralph Bunche and Martin Luther King Jr were of course African Americans and therefore Africans of the blood in our sense, but not of the soil. Anwar Sadat and F.W. de Klerk were Africans of the soil but not of the blood. Albert Luthuli, Desmond Tutu and Nelson Mandela were Africans of both the soil and the blood. All three were South Africans, as was F.W. de Klerk. But we should note that F.W. de Klerk is an African of the soil by migration rather than by indigenous roots to the continent. Most North Africans, on the other hand, are indigenous to the continent, although there has been considerable racial mixture with immigrants over the centuries.

As the 20th century was coming to a close Nelson Mandela achieved a unique status. He became the first truly universal black moral leader in the world in his own lifetime. Martin Luther King Jr achieved universal status after his death. When Dr King was alive half of mainstream America rejected him and regarded him as a troublemaker. Mandela was fortunate to have achieved universal moral admiration without having to undergo an assassination beforehand. No other black man in history has pulled off such a 'pre-humous' accomplishment (as distinct from a posthumous elegy). In the recognition of Mandela the human race may have taken one more step forward in the search for universalised ethical sensibilities.

As for Abdulsalami Abubakar, he played the role of midwife to the rebirth of Nigeria's democracy. He is a Nigerian of distinction and an African of historical dimensions. But he is also a Muslim. Let us now turn to Islam in the African and black experience.

Between the global *Ummah* and global Africa

Globalisation has also forged new links between Islam and global Africa, and provided opportunities for African Muslims to play a bigger role in both the global *Ummah* and among countries in global Africa.

When Mahtar M'Bow was the Director-General of UNESCO he was the highest-ranking Muslim of any race in the United Nations system. Professor M'Bow was an African of the blood from Senegal, as indicated.

Ismail Serageldin, as one of the Vice-Presidents of the World Bank in the 1990s, has been one of the highest-ranking Muslims in this International Bank for Reconstruction and Development. Serageldin is, as indicated, an African of the soil from Egypt.

Another African Muslim of the soil became head of the World Court at The Hague when Justice Mohammed Bejaouni of Algeria was elected President of the International Court of Justice in 1994.

The Organization of Petroleum Exporting Countries (OPEC) – with its headquarters in Vienna, Austria – has four African members. These are Nigeria and Gabon (Africans of the blood) and Algeria and Libya (Africans of the soil). From time to time these African countries have provided Secretaries-General and other OPEC leaders, often Muslim.

And of course the Organization of African Unity, the most important continent-wide organisation in Africa, had a Muslim Secretary-General throughout the 1990s into the new millennium. Salim Ahmed Salim is an African of the blood from Tanzania.

There are 1.2 billion Muslims in the world – but the only continent which has a Muslim majority is Africa. The total population of Africa is over 700 million of whom over half are now Muslim.

Nigeria has more Muslims than any Arab country. When Nigeria is combined with Ethiopia, Egypt and Congo (Kinshasa) – the four most populous African countries – the Muslim population is over 180 million.

There is now a significant number of Muslims in the United States. The population of Muslims in the United States has begun to outstrip the population of Jews. Of the 6 to 7 million Muslims in the USA 42 per cent are black.[10] The Nation of Islam under Louis Farrakhan is part of that 42 per cent but only a fraction of it. However, a highly visible fraction.

Between Lugardisation and globalisation

The coming of the Nobel Prize to Nigeria in 1986 was a symptom of yet another major force – the force of cultural globalisation, which has recently coincided with the digital revolution. We said that globalisation consists of the forces which are leading the human race towards a global village. But since the 1990s globalisation has also carried the seeds of cultural revivalism – ranging from ethnic resurgence to religious revival. In Northern Nigeria globalisation has converged with the legacy of Lord Lugard, the British unifier of Northern and Southern Nigeria in 1914, and the author of the colonial policy of Indirect Rule.[11]

Nigeria has the largest concentration of Muslims on the African continent. It has more Muslims than any Arab country, including Egypt. Since Olusegun Obasanjo became President in May 1999, some predominantly Muslim states in the Nigerian federation have taken steps towards implementing the Sharia in their own states, although the country as a whole is supposed to be a secular republic. This has caused consternation among non-Muslim Nigerians. Indeed, in Lord Lugard's own Kaduna state, this Christian consternation exploded into inter-communal riots which cost hundreds of lives early in the year 2000. But the momentum for Shariacracy still continues. Is Shariacracy an inevitable part of the legacy of Lord Lugard's Indirect Rule in the North?[12]

Many different reasons have been advanced for the rise of Sharia advocacy and Sharia implementation in Northern Nigeria. One explanation is that the Nigerian federation is getting more decentralised, and part of the decentralisation is taking the form of cultural self-determination. In Yorubaland this cultural self-determination is taking the form of Yoruba nationalism. In Igboland it is taking the form of new demands for confederation. In the Muslim North cultural self-determination is taking the form of Shariacracy.

Another explanation for the rise of Sharia militancy is to regard it as a political bargaining chip. As the North is losing political influence in the Nigerian federation, it is asserting new forms of autonomy in preparation for a new national compact among the contending forces which Indirect Rule helped to demarcate.[13]

What has not been discussed is whether the rise of Sharia militancy is itself a consequence of globalisation. One of the repercussions of globalisation worldwide has been to arouse cultural insecurity and uncertainty about identities. Indeed, the paradox of globalisation is that it both promotes enlargement of economic scale and stimulates fragmentation of ethnic and cultural scale. The enlargement of economic scale is illustrated by the rise of the European Union, and by the North American Free Trade Agreement (NAFTA). The fragmentation of cultural and ethnic scale is illustrated by the disintegration of the Soviet Union, the collapse of Czechoslovakia into two countries, the rise of Hindu fundamentalism in India and Islamic fundamentalism in Afghanistan, the collapse of Somalia as a state after penetration by the Soviet Union and the United States, and the reactivation of genocidal behaviour among the Hutu and Tutsi in Rwanda and Burundi.

Because globalisation is a special scale of Westernisation, it has triggered off identity crises from Uzbekistan to Somalia, from Afghanistan to Northern Nigeria. Fragile ethnic identities and endangered cultures are forced into new forms of resistance. Resisting Westernisation becomes indistinguishable from resisting globalisation.[14] In Nigeria the South is part of the vanguard of Westernisation and therefore the first to respond to globalisation. When, in addition, the South appears to be politically triumphant within Nigeria under Obasanjo's presidency, alarm bells are sounded in parts of the North. This may not necessarily be northern distrust of Yoruba or Igbo cultures. It may be northern distrust of Westernisation. Is Southern Nigeria a Trojan horse for globalisation? And is globalisation in turn a Trojan horse for Westernisation? Paradoxically a Westerner – Lord Lugard – had helped to nurse northern distrust of cultural Westernisation.

The Sharia under this paradigm becomes a form of northern resistance – not to Southern Nigeria, but to the forces of globalisation and to their Westernising consequences. Even the policy of privatisation of public enterprises is probably an aspect of the new globalising ideology. Privatisation in Nigeria may either lead to new transnational corporations establishing their roots or to private southern entrepreneurs outsmarting northerners and deepening the economic divide between North and South. Again the Sharia may be a northern gut response to these looming clouds of globalisation.

In Nigeria the Sharia is caught between the forces of domestic democratisation and the forces of wider globalisation. On the one hand, Lord Lugard had helped to protect Islam in Northern Nigeria – and Islam had been an earlier form of cultural globalisation within a worldwide community of believers. On the other hand, the legacy of Lord Lugard had helped to heighten Hausa-Fulani identity, and was therefore a particularising force. Both globalisation and Lugardisation in Northern Nigeria had therefore contributed to the rise of Shariacracy.

Islam and global Africa: in search of partnership

Beyond Nigeria and even Africa, why has there been a black fascination with Islam? Why is the Muslim population in global Africa still expanding?

Among African Americans there have been push-out factors in the mainstream culture, and pull-in factors in the cultural and ethical attraction of Islam. The push-out factors in the wider American society have made African Americans feel excluded or rejected at some levels. The pull-in factors in Islam and Islamic culture have made some African Americans feel welcome and intrigued. The push-out factors in the wider American society are rooted in centuries of racial experience and the sociology of racial exclusion.

The pull-in factors in Islamic culture offer a paradoxical alternative – both cultural autonomy and religious universalism for African Americans. Sobriety and prohibition of alcohol in the Islamic ethos have also fascinated sections of the black diaspora that have been decimated by drug abuse and alcoholism.[15]

Africa is not only the first continent to have a majority of Muslims; it is also witness to the largest continuing expansion of Islam. Conversions to Islam are faster in the black world than elsewhere.

Natural population growth among Muslims in Africa and in the world is faster than among most non-Muslims. Indeed, the Muslim world as a whole is expected to become 25 per cent of the human race in the course of the 21st century.

The largest country in population in Africa is Nigeria – which as a country probably has a majority of Muslims. The second largest country in population on the African continent is Egypt – which is of course an Islamic leader.

The largest African country in territory is Sudan – which is about two-thirds Muslim. Almost half the members of the Organization of the Islamic Conference (a worldwide, 53-member, inter-governmental, Islamic fraternity) are African. Its Secretaries-General have ranged from the African of the blood Hamid Algabid (Niger) to the African of the soil Azzedine Larak (Morocco).

Should African Muslims establish links with global Africa as a whole? African Americans are of course a large, African-descended population lodged in the most powerful nation on earth. Perhaps Muslims of all races in the United States should join forces with African Americans of all faiths in a joint struggle for both racial justice and cultural dignity. The American Muslim Council in 2001 held its first joint consultations with the NAACP in Washington DC. The Nation of Islam and other Muslim groups in the country have also sometimes adopted that coalition principle as a cornerstone of their national agenda.

Though as already indicated there are now at least as many Muslims as Jews in the USA the Muslims are more subdued and far less powerful than the Jews.[16] And yet, numerically there are more African Americans than there are Jews in the whole world. What black and Muslim people can learn from the Jews include the following:

- solidarity in a common cause

- organisation and mobilisation

- purposeful manipulation of the political process

- creative tapping of the guilt complexes of former oppressors

- turning martyrdom into a political resource.

This is where the crusade for black reparations looms into relevance. Jews have received partial compensation for the horrors of the Holocaust under the Nazis in Europe (1933–45). From the 1990s Swiss banks have been held accountable for illegitimate gains they might have made from Jewish victims of genocide during the Second World War. Also, from the 1990s German manufacturing corporations were being forced to set aside billions of dollars to compensate those who had worked under slave-labour conditions during the Third Reich. Relatively few Jewish activist organisations have been able to hold powerful economic giants in Europe liable for compensation for exploited and victimised Jews. What about compensation for hundreds of years of black enslavement? Or is that a cruel joke?

In search of historic reparations

Globalisation has reawakened the crusade for Jewish reparations. Also getting globalised is the reparations movement to compensate black people for hundreds of years of enslavement and exploitation. The fighters for the abolition of slavery became known as 'abolitionists'; the new crusaders for black compensation are the reparationists.[17]

In 1992, I and eleven others were sworn in before the Presidents of Africa. We were to constitute the group of eminent persons to pursue and to explore the modalities and logistics of campaigning for such reparations. The 'swearing in' occurred in Dakar, Senegal. Reverend Jesse Jackson came to meet our committee to give us moral support. So did Nelson Mandela, who was at the time newly liberated, but not yet elected President of South Africa.

We elected Chief Moshood Abiola as Chairman of our group of 12 eminent persons. Abiola was a Nigerian philanthropist and publisher. He ran for the Presidency of Nigeria – and won in June 1993. However, he was not allowed to take office. The army in Nigeria aborted the final election announcement. When he called a rally and declared himself President of Nigeria, he was arrested and charged with treason.

In 1996 I saw General Sani Abacha, the Military Head of State of Nigeria at the time. I asked him to continue Nigeria's support for the reparations movement and to release our Chairman of the Reparations Group, Chief Abiola. President Abacha was gracious to me, but unbending on the issue of Abiola.

Chief Abiola was still in prison when General Abacha died suddenly in June 1998. Prospects for Abiola's release improved. Unfortunately Abiola too was suddenly taken ill and died unexpectedly on the eve of his being released from prison. The reparations movement received a severe blow because Abiola had been a man of means committed to the cause. Nigeria lost a gifted leader.

There is a distinct reparations movement in the United States – including a brave attempt in Congress by Representative John Conyers Jr to get a bill passed to appoint a commission to go into the feasibility of reparations.[18] Other figures in the United States include TransAfrica's former head, Randall Robinson, who wrote a book on the topic in 2000.[19] There is also a reparations movement in the United Kingdom. It had one champion in the House of Commons (the late Bernie Grant). Reparations has also been a topic on talk-shows in the Caribbean. Globalisation has given reparations a new momentum, but just as the abolitionist movement took generations, so will the reparationist crusade.

Also relevant was President Bill Clinton's tour of Africa in 1998 – the first US president to go to so many African countries, meet so many African leaders in Africa, and come so near to apologising for the wrongs that America had done to the Africans across the centuries.[20] Of course Clinton did not offer compensation – nor was he asked for it. But the next best thing to compensation is an apology for the sins of one's forebears. Clinton in Africa came near to expressing deep regret, though not a formal apology.

Under the administration of George W. Bush can the appointment of an African American be counted as a form of reparation if the social mobility is high enough? Is a Secretary of State of African descent (Colin Powell and Condoleezza Rice) a form of reparation? If Rice one day became the first American President of African descent could that be counted as a form of reparation? Reparation needs to be multifaceted. When a descendant of a former slave governs descendants of former slave-owners, is that a particularly poetic form of reparation? What of Barack Obama, a descendant of an American African?

Conclusion

The National Summit on Africa, a movement led by distinguished African Americans like Leonard Robinson, Herschelle Challenor, C. Payne Lucas, and Andrew Young seeks to draw greater attention to African problems in the United States, help to find solutions to those problems, and strengthen the economic, trade and cultural ties between the peoples of Africa and those of the United States.

A literal national summit of leaders of opinion took place in Washington DC in February of 2000. Meanwhile, members of the movement are in support of the African Growth and Opportunity Act which went before Congress in 1998 and 1999 – seeking new linkages between American investors and African opportunities, and a new equilibrium between where aid ends and trade begins. Congressman John Conyers Jr of Michigan has an even more progressive concept, which aspires to have the African debt cancelled. Congressman Jesse Jackson Jr has been even more radical in his sympathies for Africa.

Meanwhile, the physical African presence in the world is expanding demographically. But the leadership of Africa's crusade is beginning to come from sons and daughters of the continent and Africa's descendants in the diaspora. In 1996, I was in Australia as a guest of Australian organisations. My last two days were reserved for the African community of Melbourne. I addressed them in their hundreds about their ancestral continent. When I first visited Australia more than a quarter of a century earlier, such a thing would not have happened. There would not have been much of an African presence in Melbourne.

In 1997, I was in Sweden as a guest of the Nobel Foundation. My official hosts were therefore Swedes. But on my first night in Stockholm guess who entertained me to dinner? Afro-Swedes! Africans who are now Swedish citizens. Also in 1997, I was in Malaysia. At the International Islamic University in Kuala Lumpur there were male and female African students from different parts of the continent. The students asked the University for a special African session with Ali Mazrui, and they got it. I was also stopped once or twice in the streets of Kuala Lumpur by other Africans (complete strangers) who recognised me from my television series. In the 1950s there would not have been much of an African presence in Kuala Lumpur.

What does all this experience tell us? It tells us that the demographic African presence in the world is expanding. There are more countries with black people in their populations today than there have ever been in history. The black skin is becoming less and less exotic as a sight in the streets of the major cities of the world. The globalisation of Africanity is at hand.

Sir Seretse Khama, after falling foul of the colonial regime because of his inter-racial marriage did live to become President of Botswana with Ruth as the white First Lady after independence. Africa has had other heads of state with white First Ladies — such as Léopold Senghor of Senegal. And Jerry Rawlings, President of Ghana for two decades, had a Scottish father. Africa leads the way in racial tolerance. It leads the way in religious ecumenicalism. Africa has had leaders of liberation. It now needs leaders of development and democracy.

The African diaspora continues to expand with or without conspiracy theories. The globalisation of the African peoples is struggling to come home. People of African descent continue to multiply in the most unexpected parts of the world. Pan-Africanism has yet to catch up with them. To paraphrase the words of 'Global Africa', the final episode of *The Africans: A Triple Heritage* (BBC/PBS, 1986):

We are a people of the day before yesterday and a people of the day after tomorrow.

Long before slave days we lived in one huge village called Africa. And then strangers came and took some of us away, scattering us in all directions of the globe.

Before the strangers came our village was the world; we knew no other.

But now we are scattered so widely that the sun never sets on the descendants of Africa.

The world is our village, and we plan to make it more human between now and the day after tomorrow.

Notes

1   The many issues that will demand outstanding and ingenious leadership are detailed in Thomas F. Homer-Dixon (2000), *The Ingenuity Gap*, New York: Knopf.

2   One of the more scintillating accounts of the forces of globalisation and its implications is *The Lexus and the Olive Tree*, New York: Farrar, Strauss, Giroux, 1999, by the foreign affairs columnist of *The New York Times*, Thomas L. Friedman. More academic treatments of globalisation may be found in Bruno Amoroso (1998), *On Globalization: Capitalism in the 21st Century*, Houndsmills, Basingstoke: MacMillan, and New York: St. Martin's Press, and Robert K. Schaeffer (1997), *Understanding Globalization: The Social Consequences of Political, Economic, and Environmental Change*, Lanham, MD: Rowman and Littlefield Publishers.

3   The companion volume is Ali A. Mazrui (1986), *The Africans: A Triple Heritage*, London: BBC Publications.

4   There is a plethora of writing on the African diasporas. See, for instance, Darlene Clark Hine and Jacqueline McLeod, eds. (1999), *Crossing Boundaries: Comparative History of Black People in Diaspora*, Bloomington, IN: Indiana University Press; E. L. Bute (1997), *The Black Handbook: The People, History and Politics of African and the African Diaspora*, London and Washington: Cassell; Joseph E. Harris (1996), *The African Diaspora*, College Station, TX: Texas A & M University Press; and Michael L. Coniff (1994), *Africans in the Americas: A History of the Black Diaspora*, New York: St. Martin's Press.

5   Isidore Okpewho (1999), 'Introduction' in Isidore Okpewho, Carol B. Davies and Ali A. Mazrui, eds., *The African Diaspora: African Origins and New Identities*, Bloomington, IN: Indiana University Press, p.xiii.

6   Frederick Turner, *The Frontier in American History*, New York, Chicago, San Francisco, Toronto, London: Holt, Rinehart, and Winston, p.37.

7   On recent African immigrants to the United States, see Kofi A. Apraku (1991), *African Emigres in the United State: A Missing Link in Africa's Social and Political Development*, New York, Westport, CT, and London: Praeger, and April Gordon, 'The New Diaspora: African Immigration to the United States,' in *Journal of Third World Studies* 15, Spring 1998, pp.79–103.

8   According to Census Bureau statistics, the number of blacks with associates, bachelors, masters and doctoral degrees has been steadily rising since the 1980s; see Table No. 308, *Statistical Abstract of the United States*, 1997, Washington, DC: Bureau of the Census, p.194.

9   See Mary H. Cooper, 'Muslims in America,' in *Congressional Quarterly Researcher 16*, 3, 30 April 1993, p.364.

10 On this important figure in British colonial history in Nigeria, see Dame Margery F. Perham, *Lugard* (two volumes), London: Collins, 1956–60.

11 See Michael Crowder, 'Lugard and Colonial Nigeria: Towards an Identity,' *History Today* 36, February 1986, pp.23–29.

12 An overview of the North-South and other cleavages bedeviling Nigeria may be found in *The Economist*, 15 January 2000, pp.14–5.

13 One of the influential books in this area is Benjamin R. Barber's *Jihad vs. McWorld: How the World Is Both Falling Apart and Coming Together – And What This Means for Democracy*, New York: Times Books, 1996.

14 For one treatment of Islam's interactions with African Americans see Richard Brent Turner (1997), *Islam in the African-American Experience*, Bloomington, IN: Indiana University Press.

15 On the limited political influence exerted by an estimated 6 million US Muslims and the hindrances to their full participation, see *The New York Times*, 27 October 2000, p.1.

16 Consult Ali A. Mazrui, 'Global Africa: From Abolitionists to Reparationists,' in *African Studies Review* 37, 3 December 1994, pp.1–18.

17 A report on this effort is in *The New York Times*, 21 July 1994, Section B, p.10. Not surprisingly, the bill stalled in the Republican-dominated House Judiciary Committee; see *The Tri-State Defender* 45, 48, 4 December 1996, p.7A.

18 Randall Robinson, *The Debt: What America Owes to Blacks*, New York: Dutton, 2000.

19 For an overview of the Clinton visit, see *The Economist*, 4 April 1998, p.53.

6

African leadership: from the inside looking out

He who hides behind his master shall get five hundred masters.

Onchsheshonqy (Ptolemaic period)

Riding the Dragon: African leadership and China's rise

Onyekachi Wambu

China is destined to be the next economic superpower. It is already the second largest investor in Africa. Onyekachi Wambu *considers the meaning of China's rise for Africans.*

Seeing the future?

In the middle of the 1990s, when I was writing a weekly newspaper column for the UK's leading black newspaper, I would be invited to speak at special events. The majority of the invitations would come from college and university societies of young Africans in the diaspora. I always found it a pleasure to address potential future leaders of the next generation. As the invitations increased in number, I eventually developed a set piece presentation, which aimed to challenge the students as much as inspire them. The challenge was reminding them that having got so far, on paper, at least, they were the brightest and the most successful potential lawyers, historians, you name it, of their generation. They had to make that count once they left university. If not them, then who? If not now, then when?

The inspiration part was a story drawn from my own life and the importance of not 'believing the hype' to paraphrase a hip hop poet. The hype was about one's own self-importance and the self-importance of received wisdom. The story was a simple one, really. In the early 1980s I was doing a postgraduate degree in international relations at Selwyn College, Cambridge, trying to assess the interventions of the superpowers which had turned Africa into the hot battlefield of the Cold War. The focused case study of my research project was the Angolan civil war in 1975 and the attempts by the USA (and their South African proxies) and the Soviets (and their Cuban proxies) to protect their spheres of influence.

At Cambridge I had access to some of the best scholars in the world who understood the closed world of the Soviets both at home and abroad; access to a well-stocked library that contained the distilled knowledge on both Soviet domestic and foreign policy, and also access to the highest level personnel from various think tanks to those who had personally negotiated with the Soviets or had the privilege of classified intelligence material from the spy agencies. (On one occasion, Bill D. Rogers, the US Under Secretary of State for Economic Affairs and an assistant to Secretary of State, Henry Kissinger, spoke to our small group.) So I felt pretty well informed and was intoxicated with my own awareness of issues.

Towards the end of my course I returned home for a weekend and ran into an old Rasta man, the late Jah Bones, who was a venerable institution in the area of north London where I spent some of my teens. For my younger brother, who had recently become a Rasta, Bones was a man of great wisdom, an important leader and elder. Deep down, I must admit I had not taken Jah Bones or his creed too seriously, but I was always polite, and enjoyed listening to him.

During our conversation, he asked what I was doing, and I explained I was trying to understand Soviet behaviour in Africa. Immediately, he laughed cynically, told me I was wasting my time and then gently explained things to me. First, he denounced Soviet support for the godless Marxist regime then running Ethiopia and responsible for the death of his divine, Emperor Haile Selassie. Then he denounced the Americans and the other imperialists that he claimed were destroying Africa. It was, however, the final statement he made, just as we were about to part, that has stuck most vividly in my mind. He repeated, in reference to the Soviets, that I was wasting my time, because by the end of the decade the Soviet empire would be finished.

I tried to convince him otherwise, but he wouldn't budge. Eventually I walked away, wondering what planet he was on, which think tank he was plugged into, and what access to real information he had, to be able to throw out what I thought were pretty wild statements. I was almost annoyed with myself for having wasted time and energy trying to convince him of the veracity of my own information and the durability of the Soviet regime.

I soon forgot about him, returned to Cambridge and immersed myself once again in the world of experts, especially the Kremlinologists, who could tell at a glance from the positioning of members of the Soviet leadership in May Day Parade photographs, who was in, who was out. Soaking up this sort of specialist 'divination', while working on my own, interpreting the volumes of Soviet English-language publications, and doing some 'informed' speculating of my own, eventually earned me my MPhil.

Of course, the old Rasta man was to come back to haunt me. With the fall of the Berlin Wall in October 1989, Jah Bones, with uncanny precision, had singularly predicted the beginning of the end of the Soviet empire, an event that had taken all, and I mean all, the Kremlinologists by surprise. He might have been just lucky in his prediction, or he might have been one of that band of special old African seers that in our moments of weakness, we sometimes romantically believe understand the secrets of the world. However, I was to find out later that he and his group of Rastas had implemented the habit of avidly reading, processing and discussing, the contents of the three to four daily newspapers that they subscribed to.

The lessons from that story that I passed on to to the various students I spoke to were:

Don't believe the hype. The truth sometimes emerges from the strangest places. Never be surprised by developments. Listen to different voices. Expect the unexpected. Small things, which we are unaware of, have huge consequences. A flap of a butterfly's wing today can create a tsunami in months, oceans away.

China rising

Even Jah Bones, as he predicted the collapse of the Soviet Union, did not at the time foresee the extraordinary rise of China. At the time in the early 1980s China was in retreat in Africa, which is why she hardly featured in my MPhil study. Yet now, 25 years later, the world is about to turn again. And if the Chinese Dragon is rising on the horizon, what has she got in store for Africa? And how should Africans manage their relations with her?

Well, in responding to those questions we could start by taking a much longer perspective of China, understanding what we think the Chinese want from Africa and why, and then make a judgement against our own clearly laid down priorities and interests, given that as Africans, the only thing we truly control in any of this is the ability to formulate our own priorities and interests.

So first, what do we think the Chinese want from us?

Myths

According to Kwok Man-Ho, the dragon is the symbol of the Emperor, the son of Heaven. It is blessed with magical powers, which can see it turn invisible at a stroke, shrink to the size of a silkworm or expand to fill the gap between Heaven and Earth. Four dragons rule the four oceans of the earth.

One day, the wife of one of the sea dragons was ill and told her husband that the only thing that would save her was to eat the heart of a monkey. The dragon went in search of a monkey. He swam to an island and saw a monkey up a tree, harvesting fruit. He told the monkey that he could take him on his back, across to the trees on another island, which were believed to contain an abundance of fruits. The monkey agreed and climbed on his back. On the way across, the dragon dived into the water, and sank deeper and deeper. Eventually he revealed to the monkey the truth about his wife's need for a monkey's heart. 'That's a pity,' the monkey replied, 'because I left my heart in the tree where you found me. Let us go back so I can get it,' he whispered to the dragon. The dragon swam back to the top of the water, and deposited the monkey on the beach. The monkey ran up the tree, looked down and started laughing.[1]

Realities

In the 15th century, China's great explorer Admiral Zheng He, whose fleet was, at the time, the biggest and the most technologically advanced in the world, visited Africa. He traded with the Mwene Mutapa Empire (Great Zimbabwe), taking back giraffes, hides, gold and other goods to China. He went on further to other parts of the world. On his return to China and following a difficult internal policy review, the ocean-going fleet was broken up, and the country turned inwards, deciding that there wasn't very much of durable interest in the outside world. The Ming Dynasty, which ruled the 'Middle Kingdom', raised most of its revenue from land tax,[2] had all that it needed and was not particularly interested in trade taxes. Despite being potentially better placed than most of the other rising mercantile powers, China decided against a long-distance, overseas imperial enterprise. In the short term this decision didn't seem to matter, for even as the other mercantile powers increased their profits and economies from exploiting gold and enslaved Africans in the New World, in 1820, China and that other giant, India, were still the two biggest economies in the world, having between them nearly 50 per cent of the world economy.[3]

However, in the long run, its own internal preoccupation and lack of curiosity in the outside world was to cost China dearly, as it lost its technological superiority, its markets, parts of its territories and eventually its independence, to more curious, aggressive and better-armed powers intent on building imperial holdings that they could exploit and dominate. After suffering occupation at the hands of these powers (principally from the West, but also Japan) and the chaos of squabbling warlords, the victory of the Communist Party in 1949 began the process of Chinese modernisation and renaissance.

Behind the cover of a huge internal market, an independent nuclear shield and a seat on the Security Council, the Communist Party elites have made clear their intention to recover China's former pre-eminence, and erase the years of living under the 'maps of shame', where important Chinese territory (the coastal cities, the islands of Macau and Hong Kong) were under foreign control, and where the so-called 'rebellious province' of

Taiwan needed to be reincorporated back into China.

The renaissance has been championed by a highly disciplined, centrally controlled vanguard (albeit one with millions of members) and underpinned by an army of more than two million. In a highly controlled society the structure of delivery has been top-down, with little room to manoeuvre or freethinking allowed for those at the bottom. The price has frequently been high in terms of the millions killed in politically induced famines, cultural revolutions, politically charged executions, one-child policies; and where millions of others have suffered political and other human rights abuses, and environmental degradation and damage.

But undoubtedly a renaissance is under way, especially, since 1979, a rapidly expanding economy (nine per cent a year) has lifted, according to DFID, over 200 million people out of poverty since 1985. Within 20–30 years this economy is predicted to become the largest in the world.[4]

For Africans, it is important to recognise that China is never again going to make the mistake of isolationism and unpreparedness, which had cost her so dear during the last 500 years. In any case Western-led globalisation efforts have made sure of that. So by implication, China's renaissance will have a global dimension and impact.

China's post-1949 foreign policy has to be understood within this 'interest' framework. A key plank, especially in relation to Africa, has been about minimising recognition of the 'rebellious' province of Taiwan and to reassert the 'one China' policy. The post-1949 foreign policy can perhaps also be understood and characterised by two phases, the ideologically driven phase, before 1979, and the pragmatic phase following the 'open door' policy. We may also usefully talk of a transition phase between 1973 and 1979.

During the ideologically driven phase, and particularly during China's rivalry with the Soviet Union over leadership of the world communist system, African liberation movements were funded and armed (with the Chinese frequently supporting groups that had fallen out with the Soviets), and aid given to other countries (e.g. the offer of 'barefoot doctors'; building the TanZam railway between Tanzania and Zambia). Two broad objectives were expected in return – de-recognition of Taiwan and recognition of the 'one China' policy; and a general endorsement of Maoist ideas, which implicitly held out, at the time of the bi-polar Cold War, the existence of a multi-polar world.

Since 1979 and the 'open door' policy, engagement with Africa and the world has been more pragmatic – around responding to the market-driven demands of the new economy, increasingly seen in terms of securing energy resources, raw materials, markets and spheres of influence. To paraphrase: 'It doesn't matter what colour the cat is, as long as it catches mice.'

In the absence of political legitimacy, the regime has also been under tremendous pressure to sustain economic growth and spread wealth. An increasingly wealthy population which trusts the regime to bring more prosperity is less likely to rock the boat politically.

Underpinning all this has been a fairly consistent guiding philosophy, or perhaps rhetoric, of 'non-interference' or what Premier Wen Jiabao called 'a new type of strategic partnership' founded on 'political equality and mutual trust, economic win-win co-operation and cultural exchanges'.[5] From all this one can see how with some consistency China can operate both in Sudan and in South Africa, Nigeria and Zimbabwe, and Sierra Leone and Angola.

Africa and China

As the world faces this renascent Dragon in its pragmatic phase, what should Africans do?

Africans should welcome an engagement with China but the engagement should be qualified. Anyway, the idea of not engaging with what will become in 30 years the world's biggest economy, is simply absurd. If you don't engage with it, it will engage anyhow, and increasingly on its own terms. So China represents an enormous opportunity, especially if we remember that in written Chinese there are similarities in the characters for 'problem' and 'opportunity'. The challenge is how you manage the Dragon, how you play to your strengths, minimise your weaknesses, discover areas of synergy and opportunity with the Dragon, and exploit its vulnerable spots.

As we move forward with China, we should also look at the engagement through a particular historic prism. China depended on African votes to join the UN and remains grateful for that. Further back, Admiral He came, traded peacefully with Africa and went home. China does not have the slavery or colonial baggage of the West.

However, as Africans we must also recognise that slavery and colonialism were partially a two-way process – Western aggression succeeded because of African naïvety, complicity, weakness and disorganisation. As it confronts the new Dragon breathing fire on the horizon, a naïve, weak and disorganised Africa will only end up repeating the mistakes of the past, with all the fatal consequences experienced by the continent.

Strengths

We have a lot of things that China needs – energy, raw materials, markets, vast and under-utilised arable land to feed its billions, UN General Assembly votes. The Chinese sourcing of some of these things has already benefited us tremendously in the last five years. According to Stephen Marks, 'China alone was responsible for 40 per cent of the global increase in the price of oil demand between 2000 and 2004.' China's (and India's) demands have driven the prices of commodities and other raw materials upwards after years of flat prices or stagnation. As a result, 'Sub-Saharan Africa's real GDP increased by an average of 4.4 per cent in 2001–04, compared with 2.6 in the previous three years. Africa's economy grew by 5.5 per cent in 2005 and is expected to do even better this year [2006] and next.⁶ At the November 2006 Beijing Africa–China Summit, Premier Wen Jiabao anticipated Africa's trade with China rising from its current US $40.6 billion to US $100 billion by 2010. This cannot be anything but good news, given that the balance of trade is still overall in favour of Africa, with China buying more than it sells to us, and a more diversified client base is better than the old overwhelming reliance on Western markets, for which we were frequently punished.

How then to maximise our strengths? We need the prices for the goods we sell to continue to increase in value, and with the kinds of goods we have (raw and unprocessed goods) this usually only happens in a tight market. But that market shouldn't be so tight that customers begin to explore and invest in possible alternatives. However, we should be wary also of selling out our non-renewable raw materials too cheaply, and too quickly even if the price is right. One day we will need those self-same materials to drive our own industrialisation when it comes. So African countries need to come together to effectively manage their raw materials, perhaps along the lines of OPEC, which has been an interesting producer model, attempting to provide the sort of price stability which enables medium to long-term planning for both producers and consumers.

Weaknesses

Part of our current strength is also part of our weakness. Our states are weak, and economies are mostly basic, either extractive or agriculturally based, with very little value added before export. There is a very weak manufacturing base, weak energy, transport and communications infrastructure, weak health sector, and weak managerial and skilled capacity, and exceptionally poor and sometimes venal leadership. For these reasons, we have suffered for years in our trade relations with the wider world. Beyond our commodities we simply do not produce, at the right price, anything that the world wants.

Minimising these weaknesses means that we need to be using the windfall money from high commodity prices to invest in infrastructure works, alongside health and education – particularly skills, management, entrepreneurial and leadership training. If tomorrow, Africa got all it desired by way of investment, it would not have the capacity to manage the huge funds.

Africans have recognised this. The African Union and the New Economic Partnership for Africa's Development (NEPAD) are, after all, structures to deal with some of these issues on a national, regional and pan-African level. For instance, the NEPAD leadership peer review mechanism was intended to deal with the issue of venal leadership. However, these structures are not moving along quickly enough, or indeed dealing with the threats and opportunities on the horizon. It is surely time for Africa to negotiate on a pan-African basis with China on the main outcomes we seek. Even President Hu recognised this at the November summit when he pledged to build a conference centre for the AU 'to support African countries in their efforts to strengthen themselves through unity and support the process of African integration'.

Perhaps one thing such a centre could do is look for Chinese investment in strategic regional infrastructure, which will ease travel, power and communications, flows, increasing both the internal market and making export cheaper and easier. Another is that Africans might prioritise the issues of jobs and enterprise, bringing this much more to the fore in pan-African, regional and bilateral negotiations and agreements. A recent study for the UN Economic Commission for Africa estimated that Africa south of the Sahara must create eight million new jobs just to absorb those coming onto the job market. It has also estimated that the creation of low paid jobs was the single most effective way of dealing with poverty.[7] Meanwhile, opinion polls show that most Africans have identified employment as the biggest issue they face. In part, in Africa's dealings with China (and others) we could make this a cornerstone of our engagement: i.e. the degree to which the engagement creates new businesses and new jobs and reduces unemployment could be an important criterion for judging effectiveness. Current Chinese actions in various countries where cheap manufactured Chinese goods (particularly textiles) are being dumped, destroying an already fragile manufacturing base, or where Chinese build major infrastructural projects by importing workers from China, would thus be reviewed critically within this framework.

Africans cannot afford to repeat the pattern of merely being the sellers of cheap raw materials, which is then value-added elsewhere and sold back as a finished product at exorbitant rates.

For the time being individual African leaders (not the AU or African people) are still in the driving seat, striking deals and encouraging investment from the Chinese, which in some cases enrich them and their cliques, without adding to a broader agenda of reducing unemployment, poverty or dealing with the human and other structural problems of African economies and states. Darfur is an example, but much more off the radar, according to Anabela Lemos and Daniel Ribeiro, are the Chinese investments that are taking place in the Mozambique power sector, where finance is readily forwarded for the Mphanda Nkuwa dam, ignoring the need for environmental impact studies on the local communities, in a vulnerable earthquake prone region, or in the logging which is leading to deforestation in the Zambezia region.[8]

As they ponder not having the leverage to negotiate effectively with China, and the importance of working together in pan-African structures, African leaders should remember a joke by Ugandan President Yoweri Museveni about a Martian, landing at the UN General Assembly, and immediately thinking that Africans ran the world because of the 55 African diplomats he saw, representing the continent's sovereign nations. It wasn't until a few hours later that it dawned on the Martian that on earth less is more, and that the proliferation of African countries at the UN actually reflected their weakness. The Martian came to this realisation after watching a single man, sitting under the Chinese sign, who represented the interests of a billion and half people.

Synergy and opportunity

It is a matter of record that as a developing country China has pulled over 400 million people out of poverty since 1950, so as fellow developing countries, there is much more that we can learn from their developmental model, not least interrogating the six key principles in that model noted by China insider Wei-Wei Zhang:

- people matter – so focus on pressing needs and 'seek truth from facts' not dogma
- constant experimentation – trial and error on a small scale, then roll out
- gradual reform not big bang'
- a developmental state that shapes national consensus, ensues political and macro-economic stability
- selective learning – learn from others but preserve your own policy space on when and how to adopt foreign ideas
- correct sequencing and priorities – easy reforms first, difficult second, rural first, urban second, coastal areas first, inland second, economic reforms first, political second, etc.[9]

The main attitude Africans can benefit from here is that of autonomy of thought and action, particularly the idea of letting our own reality as much as possible determine our solutions, as opposed to theories dreamed up as part of a 'consensus' somewhere else. Again Wei-Wei Zhang: 'I well remember Deng telling the visiting president of Ghana, Jerry Rawlings, in September 1985: "Please don't copy our model. If there is any experience on our part, it is to formulate policies in light of one's own national conditions".'[10]

You can be sure that some African leaders already heartily welcome the Chinese model because it has shown that the top down approach can work and you can achieve development without 'good governance' or democracy (despite what the 'Washington Consensus' asserts).

But, unlike their leaders, who are so easily tempted, African people must also never forget the huge price paid by the people of China for this impressive economic turnaround. It may just be that other models might be better, such as the Indian one, which has achieved equally impressive growth rates, but within a democratic framework.

Meanwhile, there are also synergies between Africa and China in deepening genuine South–South co-operation and trade, working to reform the increasingly unstable international relations, trade and monetary architecture established after the Second World War, which still heavily benefit the West. Even as we have seen, with the so-called 'War on Terror' , those Western powers increasingly lose their ability to control or shape events.

Finally, China has also achieved a green revolution, and as it seeks new sources for feeding its huge population, it offers African governments a new option for sharing agricultural expertise, particularly those that might benefit the kind of small farm holdings that predominate over the continent.

Vulnerability

China is becoming a more powerful and entrenched global player, and the more established it becomes, the more it will begin to play by the same rules as everybody else or be punished. Its state-owned multinational corporations are beginning to behave like Western multinational corporations. Chris Alden and Martyn Davis believe that though they will remain highly politicised (not necessarily unique to China, think Elf in Africa), they are also becoming Chinese 'corporate champions'. According to Alden and Davis, Fu Chengyu, chief executive of China's oil giant CNOOC, which was blocked by the US Congress from taking over Unocal, has said, 'We aim to be a participant in the global industry, like all the international majors, supplying the global marketplace as well'.[11]

In which case, increasingly, like many global corporations, China's 'corporate champions' will be open to boycotts and consumer pressure. Nigerian human rights activist Ndubisi Obiorah, sees this as way through which African civil society, working in partnership with the broader human rights community, can exert pressure on new global Chinese 'brands'.[12]

Hopefully, the Chinese, with talk of 'a new type of strategic partnership' will not want to make the mistakes of the old imperialists. Enduring relationships are with the people of a country, not governments or regimes, which come and go. As we saw in Iran, when foreign powers are associated with supporting despotic regimes and those regimes are overthrown, the foreign powers will frequently be chased out with the departing despotic regime. Countries dealing with Africa have to begin to understand that fairness, integrity and a mutual beneficial relationship for all, will secure the kind of stability that might in the long run make Africa a good trading partner. The days of the greedy, unprincipled, short-term smash and grab strategy should be put behind us.

An initial conclusion

Ultimately, like all powers on the rise, the Chinese have their interests and, given their own internal pressures and contradictions, will pursue those interests aggressively. As outlined above, Africa can take advantage of the opportunities that China brings and tap into the synergies. In order to do this it means planning and setting up structures, and a degree of unity and working together that the continent has not hitherto shown.

However, there is also likely to be a downside, and the possibility of minimising that downside depends on how African people begin to carry out their politics. As with the experience of the West over the last 100 years, if an Africa leader invites the Chinese in and encourages them to help him (it is usually a him) exploit and abuse segments of his own people, the Chinese may well privately consider him a barbarian, but it is likely they will continue to engage with him in order to advance their interests. In the absence of a powerful and active home-grown civil society, which has not effectively mobilised against human rights violations in China, let alone abroad, there is likely, for the next few years at least, to be very little internal Chinese constraint or pressure on external Chinese behaviour.

External pressure on any potential Chinese misbehaviour will come from the Western, and increasingly global, human rights movement, and from within Africa itself. African people and their civil societies, I still believe, are the most effective factor in all of this. There is a real and pressing urgency for us in our African diversity to define our core interests and then to control our governments and make them accountable in carrying out those interests.

A deeper conclusion

Remembering the moral of the story with which I started this essay, it could also be that rise of China is yet another illusion, and we shouldn't all be getting carried away with the hype. As Jah Bones might have said, were he alive, 'You are getting it mixed up again and wasting time on the wrong country', like he saw me do over 20 years ago when I focused on the Soviet Union instead of China. It could be that in 20 years' time the country I really should have focused on in this essay is India – the tortoise to China's hare. Especially, given the huge cultural and political commonalities between Africa and India: the historic trade links between India and East Africa via the Indian Ocean; the shared colonial history; the role Africa played, through Gandhi, in triggering the successful phase of India's anti-colonial struggle; the shared membership of the Commonwealth; the large numbers of Africans of Indian origin (in Kenya, Tanzania and South Africa) who can facilitate effective trade links (Durban in South Africa, is the biggest city of people of Indian origin outside India); and the importance of India's democratic credentials. All this could mean that I really should have focused on India.

Or perhaps it isn't even about India. Perhaps it is even more profound than that and that the environmentally minded Jah Bones and the Rasta movement were raising altogether different kinds of questions. I can see Jah Bones laughing cynically again – you just don't get it! The real issue might just be whether this fragile blue planet can cope with 7.5 billion Chinese, Indians and Africans in 30 years' time having the same standard of living as Americans and Europeans? The real questions about China's rise may be about our perpetual growth models and whether we will have to change them to prevent the anticipated global environmental collapse. Will we need to wait until the resource wars, current and future, really heat up as globalisation retreats because of scarce oil? Then there is the problem of water, already disappearing in vast areas of the world.

It could be that for Africans the really important meaning of the rise of China (and India) is environmental. And the most independent and radical thing we should be doing at this time is looking at sustainable environmental models, local small-scale production, and learning again serious lessons from those communities on our continent that we have long derided and looked down on, who have nevertheless managed to live sustainable lives without damaging the environment. Perhaps the answers really do lie closer to home, and we should grasp this moment, look out with confidence, and bring the world back to its senses.

The lessons I passed on to the young leaders from my initial story about Jah Bones are still relevant: Don't believe the hype. The truth sometimes comes from the strangest places. Never be surprised by developments. Listen to different voices. Expect the unexpected. Small things, which we are unaware of, have huge consequences. A flap of a butterfly's wing today can create a tsunami in months, oceans away.

Indeed, some of Africa's deepest experiences support this questioning. The Great Zimbabwe empire visited in the 15th century by the Chinese Admiral, Zheng He, collapsed soon after because of an environmental catastrophe. Unable to sustain the energy and water needed for a great medieval city, its people drifted away, abandoning the fortifications and returning once more to small communities and subsistence farming. Years later, European travellers coming upon the abandoned ruins of the city believed that it had been built by an unknown white tribe, aliens, anybody in fact but the local African farmers who lived in the surrounding communities.

I got it wrong once, predicting the fall of the Soviet empire – so I am not predicting which future it will be any more. But I still believe in looking at all eventualities and planning for the scale of living that will guarantee us security, accountability and sustainability. In other words the future we want to see.

Notes

1   Man-Ho Kwok, *Dragon*, Dorling Kindersley, London, 1995.

2   Alan Hutchison, *China's African Revolution*, Hutchinson, London, 1975.

3   Angus Maddison. *Historical Statistics for the World Economy: 1–2003 AD.* OECD, Paris, 2006.

4   While the USA remains the largest global economy in real terms, China is likely to overtake the USA with respect to purchasing power by 2020. World Trade Organisation, '*Trade and growth in 2005 to slow from record 2004 pace*' press/417, 27 October 2005. www.wto.org/english/news_e/press05_e/pr417_e.htm

5   Quoted from Stephen Marks, 'The Summit in Beijing', *Pambazuka News* (issue 282, 14 December 2006).

6   Ibid.

7   Economic Commission for Africa (2005) *Economic Report on Africa 2005: Meeting the Challenges of Unemployment and Poverty in Africa*, Addis Ababa: ECA.

8   Anabela Lemos and Daniel Ribeiro, 'Taking Ownership or just Changing Owners', *Pambazuka News* (issue 282 of 14 December 2006).

9   Wei-Wei Zhang, 'Allure of the Chinese Model', *International Herald Tribune*, 2 November, 2006. Wei-Wei Zhang is a senior research fellow at the Centre for Asian Studies in Geneva and a visiting professor at Tsinghua and Fudan Universities, China. He worked as a senior English interpreter for Deng Xiaoping and other Chinese leaders in the mid-1980s.

10   Wei-Wei Zhang, ibid.

11   Quoted from Stephen Marks, 'The Summit in Beijing', *Pambazuka News* (issue 282, 14 December 2006).

12   Ndubisi Obiorah, 'From China with Love, Trade and Guns: a human rights perspective on China and Africa', in (ed) Leni Wild and David Mepham, *The New Sinosphere: China and in Africa*, Institute for Public Policy Research, London 2006.

Afterword

A word about how this book came about. When, 18 months ago the British Council invited Onyekachi Wambu to develop a book which became *Under the Tree of Talking*, there were two very urgent reasons. If anything, they are even more urgent reasons today.

The first is the need to recognise that new ideas in cultural relations come from all cultures, but that without a dedicated international effort to communicate, understand and discuss them, new thinking about our common planetary future will be markedly poorer and less effective. Our cultural relations think-tank, Counterpoint, was founded for this purpose. We hope that *Under the Tree of Talking*, which draws on a wide range of views from African thinkers from both inside and beyond the continent and which will reach English-speaking readers in many of the 109 countries where we work, will make an important contribution to this aim.

The second is that the British Council is delivering a very ambitious project called InterAction, a pan-African initiative to identify, network and support the next generation of African leaders across 19 African countries. InterAction is run by Africans for Africans. It is based on the mutually beneficial principle of developing a modern and forward-looking relationship between Africa and the rest of the world based on trust, shared values and mutual interest. Kimani Njogu contributes a chapter informed, among many other things, by the insights from that ongoing project.

In his introduction, John Githongo wants the book to 'further tease out the central contemporary debate about the location of the modern African and the African nation state in a globalised world'. We join him wholeheartedly in this hope and, as an organisation, remain open to the new ideas it will generate to help us plan our work with partners around the world.

Philip Goodwin, Regional Director
British Council East and West Africa, Nairobi
Ali Fisher, Director Counterpoint, London

The contributors

Chinua Achebe is the father of the African novel and one of the continent's leading intellectuals. His novels, including the legendary *Things Fall Apart* (1958), *No Longer at Ease* (1960), *Arrow of God* (1964), *Man of the People* (1966), and *Anthills of the Savannah* (1987), have influenced a generation of African writers. Indeed *Things fall Apart* has sold over 8 million copies globally and been translated into 40 languages. *A Man of the People* was included by Anthony Burgess among the best hundred novels of the 20th century. He is also a formidable literary and social critic – *Morning Yet on Creation Day* (1975)), *The Trouble with Nigeria* (1984), *Hopes and Impediments* (1988, and '*Home and Exile*' (200). He has been a strong supporter and promoter of African writers. He was the founding editor of the Heinemann African Writers series (1962), an important platform for exposing African writers and their visions to the world.

Taddy Blecher, a qualified actuary, is Chief Executive and co-founder of CIDA City Campus, the only virtually free higher education institution in South Africa. He is a former senior project leader with the international strategic management consulting firm Monitor Company, where he was voted consultant of the year three years in a row, and was rated in the top one per cent of consultants in the firm. He has won several awards and scholarships including the Liberty Life Gold Medal for top actuarial science honours student in South Africa.

Dr Blecher was chosen in 2005 as a Young Global Leader by the World Economic Forum. He was chosen by *Glamour* magazine in April 2005 as their favourite business personality in South Africa, and the publication *South Africa's Leading Managers*, 2004, produced by the Corporate Research Foundation, ranked him fifth among business leaders in South Africa. In

2002, he received the Global Leader of Tomorrow Award from the World Economic Forum, convened in New York. He was recognised as one of 100 young leaders under the age of 37 around the world who are making an exceptional contribution to 'making a better world'.

Jean Bosco Butera is the Director of the Africa Programme of the University for Peace (UPEACE), based in Addis Ababa, Ethiopia. He was Vice Rector for Academic Affairs (1995–2003) at the National University of Rwanda where he also taught, before joining UPEACE in April 2005. In 1999, he co-published on the conflict in Rwanda under the UN-sponsored initiative on 'Comprehending and Mastering African Conflicts' and co-founded the Centre for Conflict Management at National University of Rwanda. He was the National Director of the Centre until 2002. He holds a PhD in veterinary parasitology.
E-mail jbbutera@upeace.org

Chukwu-Emeka Chikezie is the Executive Director of the African Foundation for Development (AFFORD). AFFORD's mission is to expand and enhance the contribution that Africans in the diaspora make to Africa's development. He is also a private consultant advising institutions on ways to work effectively with the African diaspora for maximum developmental gain.

Before AFFORD, Chukwu-Emeka worked as a senior industry analyst for a US-based international research and consulting firm helping clients design strategies to harness the benefits of the commercialisation of advanced technologies and understand their social implications. Previously he lectured in media studies at a London university and helped establish an international institute for telecoms regulators at another London university. He served as adviser on the United Nations Economic Commission for Africa's Technical Advisory Committee. Research and active interests revolve around maximising the African diaspora's contributions to Africa's development (see *www.afford-uk.org*); leadership and bottom-up enterprise development; extending access to the internet in Africa; and strategic use of ICTs to link Africa and the diaspora. Another interest is pan-Africanism for the 21st century and the role of the African diaspora. He is a Fellow of the Royal Society for the Encouragement of Arts, Manufacture and Commerce.
E-mail cechikezie@gmail.com

Martha Chinouya is a social scientist who has vast experience in research and practice with and for African families affected by HIV in England and in Africa. She has a particular interest in religions, human rights, disclosures/communications, gender and generations. She is very interested in interrogating human rights discourses or ethics that are informed by

'Africa'-based epistemologies such as the concepts of *ubuntu* (Zulu or Ndebele), *hunhu* (Shona) or *obuuntu* (Luganda). She was awarded a two year post-doctoral fellowship by the Nuffield Foundation to explore the *ubuntu/hunhu/obuuntu* concept in more detail, with regard to tensions experienced by those living with HIV in preserving their rights to confidentiality while promoting the rights of sexual partners to know and share information about HIV.

Dr Chinouya has published widely in journals and book chapters and has presented at local and international conferences. Her publications include: with E. O'Keefe (forthcoming), *Pachedu-Zenzele in the Diaspora: Promoting Sexual Health Amongst Zimbabweans in England*; and, also with E. O'Keefe (forthcoming), 'Zimbabwean Cultural Traditions in England: Ubuntu Hunhu as a Human Rights Tool' in *Journal of Diversity, Health and Social Care 3*.

E-mail mchinouya@londonmet.ac.uk

Chinweizu, an institutionally unaffiliated Afrocentric scholar, has published the following books: *The West and the Rest of Us* (1975); *Energy Crisis and other Poems* (1978); *Invocations and Admonitions* (1986); *Decolonising the African Mind* (1987); *Voices from Twentieth-century Africa* (1988); *Anatomy of Female Power* (1990). He is also a co-author of *Towards the Decolonization of African Literature* (1980). His pamphlets include *The Black World and the Nobel*, (1987); *Recolonization or Reparations?* (1994).

Eva Dadrian is a British-Egyptian independent broadcaster and writer with extensive experience in Africa, the Middle East and Europe. After graduating from Cairo University, she pursued her studies in France and England where she started as a journalist. Specialising in African affairs, she covered the struggle for self-determination of the peoples of the Sahel region, from the Polisario (Western Sahara) and the Tuaregs in Mali and Niger to Sudan People's Liberation Army. She works as a political risk analyst for *Arab Africa Affairs* (London and Cape Town) and writes regularly on African affairs in *Al Ahram Weekly* (Cairo) and has a regular column in *Al Ahram Hebdo* (Cairo). Currently she is a reporter with the BBC World Service.

She is member of the Egypt International Economic Forum (Cairo), and is on the Council of Management of Cairo-based Al Mawred Al Thaqafi (Culture Resources), which promotes South–South cultural dialogue, focusing on Arab–Africa cultural exchange.

E-mail arabafricaffairs@yahoo.co.uk

John Githongo is a prominent Kenyan journalist and columnist, who became an outspoken anti-corruption fighter. His articles in the *East African* were renowned for their broadsides against the corruption that was endemic in Kenyan society. Between 1999 and 2003 he was on the Board of Transparency International in Berlin and the Executive Director of Transparency International Kenya, where he continued his anti-corruption crusade against the regime of President Moi. In 2003 he was became Permanent Secretary in the Office of the President of Kenya in Charge of Governance and Ethics, appointed by President Mwai Kibaki, Kenya's new leader, who vowed to root out corruption. A year later he accused senior government ministers of being involved in the fraudulent awarding of contracts to a fictitious company and, following popular protests, he left the country following threats to his life. He is currently Senior Associate Member, St Anthony's College, Oxford University and Visiting Fellow, IDRC/CRDI, International Development Research Centre/Centre de Recherches pour le Développement International.

Wangui wa Goro is a UK-based Kenyan public intellectual, academic, writer, translator and cultural promoter and has been engaged in promoting literary practice in the Europe, Africa and the USA over the last 20 years. She has been involved in the campaign for human rights in race, gender and democratisation over the last 20 years. She is currently the president of both the African Literary Translators and Subtitlers Association (ALTRAS) and the Translations Caucus of the African Literature Association (TRACLA). She serves on the Translation Advisory Committee of Pen International (UK). She is also a founder editor of *JALA*, the African Literature Association's journal.

She is a pioneer in translation of African literature and its promotion and her translation of Ngugi wa Thiong'o's work from Gikuyu to English brought her global acclaim (*Matigari*). She also translates groundbreaking and award-winning authors from French to English and Gikuyu including Véronique Tadjo's *As the Crow Flies*. She is currently translating Fatou Keita's *Rebelle* from French to English and *The Decameron* from Italian to Gikuyu. Wangui wa Goro is also a poet and writer and her own short stories, published in anthologies *Heaven and Earth* (Macmillan Kenya, 2004), *Half a Day* and *Deep Sea Fishing* (2006) in *African Love Stories* (Ayebia, UK) have been well received by critics as 'groundbreaking'.

She is currently involved in researching 'The black female body in Europe through translation' through the Caribbean and African Studies Association (CAFSRA) at Goldsmiths College (University of London). E-mail wagoro@netscape.net

William M. Gumede is Senior Associate and Oppenheimer Fellow, St. Antony's College, Oxford University. He is course leader of the graduate course: Problems of democracy in the graduate summer institute of the New School for Social Research. He was Deputy Editor of *The Sowetan*, the national daily newspaper in Johannesburg and chairperson of the Media Institute of Southern Africa. Prior to 1994, when South Africa became a democracy, he occupied national leadership positions in the South African student movement, including as national editor of the South African Students' News Agency, as well as in the trade union movement. He is the author of *Thabo Mbeki and the Battle for the Soul of the ANC*, Zebra Press. His forthcoming books are *Africa's Democracy Deficit, The Role of Public Intellectuals in Post Liberation Studies.*

Parselelo Kantai is a Kenyan writer and investigative journalist. Now based in London, he previously lived and worked in Nairobi. He edited *Ecoforum*, an environmental magazine. His features focused on the politics of conservation and the experiences of people living away from mainstream Kenyan life. His fiction has appeared in *Kwani?*, the Kenyan literary journal. In 2004, he was shortlisted for the Caine Prize for his short story 'Comrade Lemma and the Black Jerusalem Boys Band'.

Susan Nalugwa Kiguli is a Ugandan poet and academic. She studied at the University of Makerere, Kampala where she obtained a BA in education and MA in literature. She later joined the University of Strathclyde in Glasgow, Scotland where she acquired a MLitt in Literary Linguistics. She recently completed her PhD in English at the University of Leeds under the prestigious Commonwealth Scholarship Scheme. She is a lecturer in the Department of Literature, Makerere University, Uganda, and is currently the chairperson of FEMRITE, the Uganda Women Writers' Association.

Her first volume of poetry, *The African Saga* (1998), situated her among the most exciting recent poets from Eastern and Southern Africa. The volume won the National Book Trust of Uganda Poetry Award (1999) and made literary history in Uganda by selling out in less than a year. A critic of poetry herself, she has written on Ugandan poetry, oral performance and the position of women writers in African literature. She has served on the panel of judges for the Commonwealth Writers' Prize (African Region, 1999).

Juliet Kiguli is currently a lecturer at the Makerere University Institute of Public Health. She is an anthropologist with experience in gender studies and participatory development research. She has published widely on gender and access to land, agriculture, politics and education.

Ali A. Mazrui is Director of the Institute of Global Cultural Studies and Albert Schweitzer Professor in the Humanities, State University of New York at Binghamton; Senior Scholar in Africana Studies and Andrew D. White Professor-at-Large Emeritus, Cornell University; Chancellor, Jomo Kenyatta University of Agriculture and Technology, Kenya; and Albert Luthuli Professor-at-Large, University of Jos, Nigeria. He is author of more than 30 books and hundreds of scholarly articles published all over the world; author and narrator of television programmes, especially *The Africans: A Triple Heritage* (BBC/PBS, 1986).

He is a former President of the African Studies Association of the United States and recipient of the Association's Award of Distinguished Africanist; Founder-chair of the Center for the Study of Islam and Democracy (Washington DC); member of the Board of Trustees of the Oxford Centre for Islamic Studies, Oxford, England; consultant to the United Nations, the World Bank, the Organization of African Unity, UNESCO and broadcasting media including the BBC, PBS, ABC, NBC, Voice of America.

He was appointed Commander of the Burning Spear (CBS) by the President of Kenya; awarded title of Living Legend by Organization of West African States and African Communications Agency; nominated Icon of the 20th century by Lincoln University, Pennsylvania; nominated by *Foreign Policy* magazine as one of the top 100 public intellectuals in the world and appointed to the Order of Oliver Tambo by the President of the Republic of South Africa.

Kimani Njogu is a linguist, literary critic and researcher on cultural leadership. In 2000 he won the pan-African Noma Award for Publishing in Africa for a book (with Rocha Chimerah) titled *Ufundishaji wa Fasihi: Nadharia na Mbinu*, the first Kiswahili book ever to receive the award. The book provides major parameters for the teaching of literature. In 2006, he was awarded the Head of State Commendation (HSC) by the President of Kenya for his work in indigenous languages.

In 2004 he was appointed a member of the three-person task force to fast-track the formation of the East African Kiswahili Council in the East African Community. As Kenya's representative in the task force he is contributing to ensuring that Kiswahili and other African languages contribute in national and regional development. Since 1998, he has been a Council Member of the International African Institute (University of London). He is also a member of the Global Leadership Network. He also runs Twaweza Communications and Africa Health and Development International (AHADI), a non-governmental organisation. In 2002, he was appointed by the Kenya Constitutional Review Commission to head a team for the translation into Kiswahili of the Draft Constitution and other constitutional documents. His books include *Reading Poetry as Dialogue: An East African Literary Tradition* (Jomo Kenyatta Foundation, 2004); *Zilizala* (a play, Longman, Kenya 2006); *Sudana* (play, Longhorn, 2006); *Sarufi ya Kiswahili: Uchanganuzi na Matumizi.* (a grammar book, Jomo Kenyatta Foundation, 2006), *Kiswahili Kwa Vyuo vya Ualimu* (Jomo Kenyatta Foundation, 2006) and *Isimu Jamii kwa Wanafunzi* (Jomo Kenyatta Foundation, 2006). Currently he is leading a team of East African scholars in the writing of new a Kiswahili dictionary as well as editing a number of books on culture and leadership in Africa.

Ndidi Okonkwo Nwuneli is the founder and CEO of Leadership Effectiveness Accountability and Professionalism (LEAP) Africa, a non-profit organisation which is committed to inspiring, empowering and equipping a new cadre of African leaders. Ndidi is also the founder of NIA (*Ndu* – life, *Ike* – Strength, *Akunuba* – Wealth), a non-profit organisation committed to empowering female university students in south-eastern Nigeria to achieve their highest potential in life. Prior to establishing LEAP and NIA, Ndidi was the pioneer executive director of FATE Foundation Nigeria, a non-profit organisation which promotes entrepreneurship and business development. Ndidi also worked as a management consultant with the Bridgespan Group and with McKinsey & Co.

Ndidi holds an MBA from the Harvard Business School. She was recognised in 2003 and 2005 as a Global Leader of Tomorrow and a Young Global Leader by the World Economic Forum in Davos, Switzerland. In December 2004, she received a National Honour – Member of the Federal Republic from the President of the Federal Republic of Nigeria.

Marianna B.A. Ofosu is the managing director of GWI Ventures Ghana, a local subsidiary of GoodWorks International, a consulting firm set up to connect international investors with business opportunities in Ghana, and to provide strategic advice on international policy and private sector development to the Ghanaian public and private sectors. Prior to joining GoodWorks in 2006 in order to establish and manage its venture in Ghana, Marianna worked at the Leon H. Sullivan Foundation as its director for government relations and publications. While at the Foundation, Marianna organised the Leon H. Sullivan Summit VII task force that produced two declarations on African-Diaspora relations and on corporate social responsibility, which were endorsed by ten African heads of state. Also during her time at the Foundation, Marianna founded *Leverage*, an African diaspora think-tank magazine which continues to be published by the Foundation.

Marianna holds a BA in Classics from Howard University and an MPhil in International Development from Oxford University, where she studied as an American Rhodes Scholar.

Paul Tiyambe Zeleza is Professor and Head of the Department of African American Studies at the University of Illnois, Chicago. He formerly served as Professor of African Studies and History at the Pennsylvania State University, and Professor of History and African Studies and Director of the Center for African Studies at the University of Illinois at Urbana-Champaign. He has also worked at universities in Canada, Kenya, Jamaica, and Malawi. He specialises in African economic, social and intellectual history, as well as development studies, gender studies, and diaspora studies. He is also a short-story writer, novelist, and literary critic.

He has written and edited more than 20 books. These include: *The Study of Africa*, Vol. 1 *Disciplinary and Interdisciplinary Encounters*, Vol. 2 *Global and Transnational Engagements* (2006); *African Universities in the Twenty-First Century*, Vol. 1 Liberalization and Internationalization, Vol. 2 Knowledge and Society (2004); *Human Rights and Development in Africa* (2004); *Rethinking Africa's Globalization* Vol. 1 The Intellectual Challenges (2003); *Leisure in Urban Africa* (2003); *In Search of Modernity: Science and Technology in Africa* (2003); *The Routledge Encyclopedia of Twentieth Century African History* (2003). He served as an associate editor for the six-volume *New Dictionary of the History of Ideas* (2005). His forthcoming books include *Managing and Resolving African Conflicts* Vol.1 The Causes and Costs of Conflicts, Vol. 2 Conflict Resolution and Post-Conflict Reconstruction (2007); and *Africa and Its Diasporas: Linkages and Dispersals*. His creative publications include two collections of short stories among them *The Joys of Exile* (1994) and the novel, *Smouldering Charcoal* (1992).

He is the winner of the 1994 Noma Award for his book *A Modern Economic History of Africa* (1993), which was shortlisted in 2002 as one of Africa's 100 Best Books of the Twentieth Century, and the 1998 Special Commendation of the Noma Award for *Manufacturing African Studies and Crises* (1997).